DEERING'S

CALIFORNIA DESKTOP CODE SERIES

CIVIL—CIVIL PROCEDURE—EVIDENCE—RULES OF COURT

With The

CALIFORNIA RULES OF PROFESSIONAL CONDUCT

RULES & POLICY DECLARATIONS OF THE COMMISSION ON JUDICIAL PERFORMANCE

Selected Provisions of the Government Code

2006 EDITION

As revised by Legislative Enactments
up to and including the
first year of the
2005–2006 Legislative Session
and Rules of Court changes
issued by the Judicial Council
through October 2005

Questions About This Publication	
For assistance with replacement pages, shipments, billing or other customer service matters, please call our Customer Services Department at	1-800-833-9844
Outside the United States and Canada please call	(518) 487-3000
or fax	(518) 462-3788
To place an order, call	1-800-223-1940
or contact your Matthew Bender representative.	
FOR EDITORIAL ASSISTANCE or reprint permission, please call	
Katie Solomon at	1-800-424-0651 EXT. 3251
or	
Kathleen Hoover at	1-800-446-3410 EXT. 5203
or e-mail	CalCodes@lexisnexis.com
FOR 2006 UPDATES TO THE RULES OF COURT, please call	1-800-424-0651 EXT. 3466

Copyright © 2005
By Matthew Bender & Company, Inc., a member of the LexisNexis Group

This publication is designed to provide accurate and authoritative information in regard to the subject matter covered. It is sold with the understanding that the publisher is not engaged in rendering legal, accounting, or other professional services. If legal advice or other expert assistance is required, the services of a competent professional should be sought.

LexisNexis and the Knowledge Burst logo are registered trademarks of Reed Elsevier Properties Inc., used under license. Matthew Bender is a registered trademark of Matthew Bender Properties Inc.

No copyright is claimed in the text of statutes, regulations, and excerpts from court opinions quoted within this work. Permission to copy material exceeding fair use, 17 U.S.C. § 107, may be licensed for a fee of $1 per page per copy from the Copyright Clearance Center, 222 Rosewood Drive, Danvers, MA. 01923, telephone (978) 750-8400.

All Rights Reserved

Printed in United States of America

ISBN 0-820-58287-5 (SB)

ISBN 0-820-58281-6 (HB)

MATTHEW BENDER & CO., INC.
EDITORIAL OFFICES
744 BROAD STREET, NEWARK, NJ 07102 (973) 820-2000
201 MISSION ST., SAN FRANCISCO, CA 94105-1831 (415) 908-3200

PREFACE

This 2006 Edition incorporates all changes required by legislative enactments up to and including the first year of the 2005–2006 Regular Session and the First Extraordinary Session.

This Edition gives the legislative history of each section. Amendments made in 2005 are highlighted by printing in boldface type all matter added to a section and indicating by a figure within brackets, such as [1], each point of deletion. The deleted matter is then shown by footnotes keyed to the corresponding figures. Where changes are extensive, the former section may be reprinted in full.

The following reproduction of Code of Civil Procedure Section 134, as amended by 1992 Chapter 460, clearly illustrates the "stressed amendment" feature:

§134. No Court Business on Judicial Holidays; Exceptions.

(a) **Except as provided in subdivision (c)**, the courts shall be closed for the transaction of judicial business on judicial holidays [1] for **all but** the following purposes:

(1) To give, upon their request, instructions to a jury when deliberating on their verdict.

(2) To receive a verdict or discharge a jury.

(3) For the conduct of arraignments and the exercise of the powers of a magistrate in a criminal action, or in a proceeding of a criminal nature.

(4) For the conduct of Saturday small claims court sessions pursuant to the Small Claims Act [2] **set forth in** Chapter 5.5 (commencing with Section 116.110).

(b) Injunctions and writs of prohibition may be issued and served on any day.

(c) **In any superior, municipal, or justice court, one or more departments of the court may remain open and in session for the transaction of any business which may come before the department in the exercise of the civil or criminal jurisdiction of the court, or both, on a judicial holiday or at any hours of the day or night, or both, as the judges of the court prescribe.**

(d) **The fact that a court is open on a judicial holiday shall not make that day a nonholiday for purposes of computing the time required for the conduct of any proceeding nor for the performance of any act. Any paper lodged with the court at a time when the court is open pursuant to subdivision (c), shall be filed by the court on the next day which is not a judicial holiday, if the document meets appropriate criteria for filing.** Leg.H. 1985 ch. 1450 §2, operative January 1, 1989, 1986 ch. 1398, operative January 1, 1989, 1990 ch. 1305, 1992 ch. 460.

§134. 1992 Deletes. [1] , except [2] ,

To read Section 134 as amended, you read the section as printed, omitting the bracketed figures "[1]" and "[2]":

(a) **Except as provided in subdivision (c),** the courts shall be closed for the transaction of judicial business on judicial holidays for **all but** the following purposes:

(1) To give, upon their request, instructions to a jury when deliberating on their verdict.

(2) To receive a verdict or discharge a jury.

(3) For the conduct of arraignments and the exercise of the powers of a magistrate in a criminal action, or in a proceeding of a criminal nature.

(4) For the conduct of Saturday small claims court sessions pursuant to the Small Claims Act **set forth in** Chapter 5.5 (commencing with Section 116.110).

(b) Injunctions and writs of prohibition may be

issued and served on any day.

(c) In any superior, municipal, or justice court, one or more departments of the court may remain open and in session for the transaction of any business which may come before the department in the exercise of the civil or criminal jurisdiction of the court, or both, on a judicial holiday or at any hours of the day or night, or both, as the judges of the court prescribe.

(d) The fact that a court is open on a judicial holiday shall not make that day a nonholiday for purposes of computing the time required for the conduct of any proceeding nor for the performance of any act. Any paper lodged with the court at a time when the court is open pursuant to subdivision (c), shall be filed by the court on the next day which is not a judicial holiday, if the document meets appropriate criteria for filing.

To reconstruct the section as it read before being amended, you read the section as printed, omitting the words in boldface type and inserting the words appearing in the footnote under Section 134 and referred to by the [1] and [2] in the section:

(a) The courts shall be closed for the transaction of judicial business on judicial holidays, except for the following purposes:

(1) To give, upon their request, instructions to a jury when deliberating on their verdict.

(2) To receive a verdict or discharge a jury.

(3) For the conduct of arraignments and the exercise of the powers of a magistrate in a criminal action, or in a proceeding of a criminal nature.

(4) For the conduct of Saturday small claims court sessions pursuant to the Small Claims Act, Chapter 5.5 (commencing with Section 116.110).

(b) Injunctions and writs of prohibition may be issued and served on any day.

In presenting this Edition, we wish to acknowledge with gratitude the many helpful suggestions received from users of our Codes, and to express the hope that this Edition will serve effectively the needs of bench and bar alike.

THE PUBLISHER

The STANDARD CIVIL CODE

of the

STATE OF CALIFORNIA

2006 EDITION

The Original Civil Code
Adopted March 21, 1872—Effective January 1, 1873
With All Subsequent Legislative Enactments

Table Showing 2005 Changes in the Civil Code
Effective January 1, 2006, unless otherwise noted at end of section

Section	Effect	Chapter	Section	Effect	Chapter
43.55	Amended	706	1378	Amended	37
51	Amended	420	1689.5	Amended	48
51.5	Amended	420	1689.6	Amended	48, 385
51.7	Amended	420	1689.7	Amended	48, 385
51.8	Amended	420	1689.13	Amended	48
52	Amended	123	1689.15	Amended	48, 385
52.5	Added	240	1708.8	Amended	424
53	Amended	420	1746–1746.5	Added	638
798.3	Amended	595	1747.08	Amended	22
798.19.5	Added	35	1747.09	Amended	445
798.25	Amended	22	1748.1	Amended	426
798.36	Amended	24	1789.30	Amended	74
798.55	Amended	24	1798.3	Amended	677
799.1.5	Amended	22	1798.24	Amended	241
945	Amended	37	1798.81.5	Amended	22
945.6	Added	40	1798.83	Amended	22
1102.6c	Added	392	1812.80	Amended	439
1189	Amended	295	1812.84–1812.86	Amended	439
1357.120	Amended	450	1812.96	Added	439
1363	Amended	37	1812.97	Added	439
1363.001	Added	452	1936	Repealed & Amended	22, 82
1363.03	Added	450	1942.3	Amended	595
1363.04	Added	450	2079.10a	Amended	722
1363.07	Added	458	2782	Amended	394
1363.09	Added	450	2924b	Amended	224
1365	Amended	348	2924g	Amended	224
1365.1	Amended	452	2924j	Amended	75
1365.2	Repealed & Added	458	2981	Amended	128
			2982	Amended	128
1365.2.5	Amended	22	2982.2	Added	128
1366.3	Repealed	452	2982.10	Added	128
1367.1	Amended	452	3262	Amended	15
1367.4	Added	452	3439.08	Amended	34
1367.5	Added	452	3439.09	Amended	34
1374	Amended	37	3440.1	Amended	43

CONTENTS

		Sections	
Introduction		1 –	23.6

DIVISION 1. PERSONS

Part 1.	Persons With Unsound Mind	38 –	41
Part 2.	Personal Rights	43 –	53
Part 2.5.	Blind and Other Physically Disabled Persons	54 –	55.2
Part 2.6.	Confidentiality of Medical Information	56 –	56.37
Part 2.9.	California Fair Dealership Law	80 –	86

DIVISION 2. PROPERTY

Part 1.	Property in General	654 –	749
Part 2.	Real or Immovable Property	755 –	945.6
Part 3.	Personal or Movable Property	946 –	998
Part 4.	Acquisition of Property	1000 –	1422

DIVISION 3. OBLIGATIONS

Part 1.	Obligations in General	1427 –	1543
Part 2.	Contracts	1549 –	1701
Part 3.	Obligations Imposed by Law—Fraud—Negligence	1708 –	1725
Part 4.	Obligations Arising From Particular Transactions	1738 –	3272.9

DIVISION 4. GENERAL PROVISIONS

Part 1.	Relief	3274 –	3428
Part 2.	Special Relations of Debtor and Creditor	3429 –	3449
Part 3.	Nuisance	3479 –	3508.2
Part 4.	Maxims of Jurisprudence	3509 –	3548
Part 8.	Automatic Checkout System	7100 –	7106

Part 1.	Relief	3274 – 3428
Part 2.	Special Relations of Debtor and Creditor	3429 – 3449
Part 3.	Nuisance	3479 – 3508.2
Part 4.	Maxims of Jurisprudence	3509 – 3548
Part 8.	Automatic Checkout System	7100 – 7106

CIVIL CODE of CALIFORNIA

An Act to Establish a Civil Code

[Approved March 21, 1872. Effective January 1, 1873.]

[References are to CALIFORNIA FORMS OF PLEADING AND PRACTICE (Matthew Bender); Matthew Bender® Practice Guide: California Civil Discovery; Matthew Bender® Practice Guide: California Landlord-Tenant Litigation; Matthew Bender® Practice Guide: California Pretrial Civil Procedure; Matthew Bender® Practice Guide: California Unfair Competition and Business Torts; Judicial Council of California Civil Jury Instructions (Matthew Bender, Official Publisher); Witkin's *California Procedure*, 4th Ed.; Witkin's *Summary of California Law*, 9th Ed.; Weil & Brown's *California Practice Guide: Civil Procedure Before Trial* (The Rutter Group 2001); and Miller & Starr, *California Real Estate*, 3rd Ed.]

INTRODUCTION

TITLE OF THE ACT

§1. Title and Division of This Act.

1. This Act shall be known as the Civil Code of the State of California, and is in four divisions, as follows:

I. The first relating to persons.

II. The second to property.

III. The third to obligations.

IV. The fourth contains general provisions relating to the three preceding divisions. **Leg.H.** 1872.

PRELIMINARY PROVISIONS

When code took effect. §2.
When retroactive. §3.
Abrogation of common law rule of construction. §4.
Construed as continuations of prior law. §5.
Effect on pending suits. §6.
Holidays. §7.
"Optional bank holidays" defined. §7.1.
Business days. §9.
Excluding holidays in computing time. §10.
Excluding holidays in performing legal duty. §11.
Effect of grant of joint official authority. §12.
Common and technical words and phrases. §13.
Tense, gender, number—Specific words. §14.
Service by certified mail in lieu of registered. §17.
Notice—Actual or constructive. §18.
Notice—Constructive. §19.
General laws in force or repealed by code. §20.
Statute denominated "Civil Code." §21.

§2. When Code Took Effect.

This code takes effect at twelve o'clock, noon on the first day of January, eighteen hundred and seventy-three. **Leg.H.** 1872.

§3. When Retroactive.

No part of it is retroactive, unless expressly so declared. **Leg.H.** 1872.

§4. Abrogation of Common Law Rule of Construction.

The rule of the common law, that statutes in derogation thereof are to be strictly construed, has no application to this code. The code establishes the law of this state respecting the subjects to which it relates, and its provisions are to be liberally construed with a view to effect its objects and to promote justice. **Leg.H.** 1872.

Ref.: W. Cal. Sum., "Torts" §1028.

§5. Construed as Continuations of Prior Law.

The provisions of this code, so far as they are substantially the same as existing statutes or the common law, must be construed as continuations thereof, and not as new enactments. **Leg.H.** 1872.

§6. Effect on Pending Suits.

No action or proceeding commenced before this code and no right accrued, is affected by its provisions. **Leg.H.** 1872.

§7. Holidays.

Holidays within the meaning of this code are every Sunday and such other days as are specified or provided for as holidays in the Government Code of the State of California. **Leg.H.** 1880 p. 9, 1889 p. 47, 1893 p. 186, 1897 p. 14, 1907 p. 565, 1909 p. 23, 1911 p. 520, 1925 ch. 92, 1955 ch. 165.

Ref.: W. Cal. Pro., "Actions" §207; W. Cal. Sum., "Contracts" §710.

§7.1. "Optional Bank Holidays" Defined.

Optional bank holidays within the meaning of Section 9 are:

(a) Any closing of a bank because of an extraordinary situation, as that term is defined in the Bank Extraordinary Situation Closing Act (Chapter 20 (commencing with Section 3600) of Division 1 of the Financial Code).

(b) Every Saturday.

(c) Every Sunday.

(d) January 1st.

(e) The third Monday in January, known as "Dr. Martin Luther King, Jr. Day."

(f) February 12, known as "Lincoln Day."

(g) The third Monday in February.

(h) The last Monday in May.

(i) July 4th.

(j) The first Monday in September.

(k) September 9th, known as "Admission Day."

(*l*) The second Monday in October, known as "Columbus Day."

(m) November 11th, known as "Veteran's Day."

(n) December 25th.

(o) Good Friday from 12 noon until closing.

(p) The Thursday in November appointed as "Thanksgiving Day."

(q) Any Monday following any Sunday on which January 1st, February 12th, July 4th, September 9th, November 11th, or December 25th falls.

(r) Any Friday preceding any Saturday on which July 4th, September 9th, or December 25th falls. **Leg.H.** 1994 ch. 668.

§9. Business Days.

All other days than those mentioned in Section 7 are business days for all purposes; provided, that as to any act appointed by law or contract, or in any other way, to be performed by, at, or through any bank organized under the laws of or doing business in this state, any optional bank holiday as defined in Section 7.1 is not a business day; and provided, that any act appointed by law or contract, or in any other way, to be performed on any day which is an optional bank holiday as defined in Section 7.1, by, at, or through any bank or branch or office thereof, whether acting in its own behalf or in any other capacity whatsoever, may be performed on that optional bank holiday if the bank or branch or office by, at, or through which the act is to be performed is open for the transaction of business on that optional bank holiday, or, at the option of the person obligated to perform the act, it may be performed on the next succeeding business day. **Leg.H.** 1872, 1905 p. 11, 1939 ch. 414, 1955 chs. 198, 599, 1973 ch. 285, 1979 ch. 159, 1981 ch. 67, effective June 16, 1981, 1982 ch. 1203, effective September 22, 1982, 1985 ch. 147, effective July 8, 1985, 1994 ch. 668.

Ref.: W. Cal. Sum., "Contracts" §710.

§10. Excluding Holidays in Computing Time.

The time in which any act provided by law is to be done is computed by excluding the first day and including the last, unless the last day is a holiday, and then it is also excluded. **Leg.H.** 1872.

Ref.: W. Cal. Sum., "Contracts" §710.

§11. Excluding Holidays in Performing Legal Duty.

Whenever any act of a secular nature, other than a work of necessity or mercy, is appointed by law or contract to be performed upon a particular day, which day falls upon a holiday, it may be performed upon the next business day, with the same effect as if it had been performed upon the day appointed. **Leg.H.** 1872.

Ref.: W. Cal. Sum., "Contracts" §710.

§12. Effect of Grant of Joint Official Authority.

Words giving a joint authority to three or more public officers or other persons are construed as giving such authority to a majority of them, unless it is otherwise expressed in the Act giving the authority. **Leg.H.** 1872.

§13. Common and Technical Words and Phrases.

Words and phrases are construed according to the context and the approved usage of the language; but technical words and phrases, and such others as may have acquired a peculiar and appropriate meaning in law, or are defined in the succeeding section, are to be construed according to such peculiar and appropriate meaning or definition. **Leg.H.** 1872.

§14. Tense, Gender, Number—Specific Words.

Words used in this code in the present tense include the future as well as the present; words used in the masculine gender include the feminine and neuter; the singular number includes the plural, and the plural the singular; the word person includes a corporation as well as a natural person; county includes city and county; writing includes printing and typewriting; oath includes affirmation or declaration; and every mode of oral statement, under oath or affirmation, is embraced by the term "testify," and every written one in the term "depose"; signature or subscription includes mark, when the person cannot write, his name being written near it, by a person who writes his own name as a witness; provided, that when a signature is by mark it must in order that the same may be acknowledged or may serve as the signature to any sworn statement be witnessed by two persons who must subscribe their own names as witnesses thereto. The following words have in this code the signification attached to them in this section, unless otherwise apparent from the context:

1. The word "property" includes property real and personal;

2. The words "real property" are coextensive with lands, tenements, and hereditaments;

3. The words "personal property" include money, goods, chattels, things in action, and evidences of debt;

4. The word "month" means a calendar month unless otherwise expressed;

5. The word "will" includes codicil;

6. The word "section" whenever hereinafter employed refers to a section of this code, unless some other code or statute is expressly mentioned. **Leg.H.** 1872, 1903 p. 407.

Ref.: W. Cal. Sum., "Corporations" §1; CACI No. 104 (Matthew Bender).

§17. Service by Certified Mail in Lieu of Registered.

Wherever any notice or other communication is required by this code to be mailed by registered mail, the mailing of such notice or other communication by certified mail shall be deemed to be a sufficient compliance with the requirements of law. **Leg.H.** 1959 ch. 426.

§18. Notice—Actual or Constructive.

Notice is:

1. Actual—which consists in express information of a fact; or,

2. Constructive—which is imputed by law. **Leg.H.** 1872.

§19. Notice—Constructive.

Every person who has actual notice of circumstances sufficient to put a prudent man upon inquiry as to a particular fact, has constructive notice of the fact itself in all cases in which, by prosecuting such inquiry, he might have learned such fact. **Leg.H.** 1872, 1873 p. 182.

§20. General Laws in Force or Repealed by Code.

No statute, law, or rule is continued in force because it is consistent with the provisions of this code on the same subject; but in all cases provided for by this code, all statutes, laws, and rules heretofore in force in this state, whether consistent or not with the provisions of this code, unless expressly continued in force by it, are repealed or abrogated.

This repeal or abrogation does not revive any former law heretofore repealed, nor does it affect any right already existing or accrued, or any action or proceeding already taken, except as in this code provided. **Leg.H.** 1872.

§21. Statute Denominated "Civil Code."

This act, whenever cited, enumerated, referred to, or amended, may be designated simply as "THE CIVIL CODE," adding, when necessary, the number of the section. **Leg.H.** 1872.

DEFINITIONS AND SOURCES OF LAW

Definition of law. §22.
How expressed. §22.1.
Common law—When rule of decision. §22.2.

§22. Definition of Law.

Law is a solemn expression of the will of the supreme power of the State. **Leg.H.** 1951 ch. 655.

§22.1. How Expressed.

The will of the supreme power is expressed:

(a) By the Constitution.

(b) By statutes. **Leg.H.** 1951 ch. 655.

§22.2. Common Law—When Rule of Decision.

The common law of England, so far as it is not repugnant to or inconsistent with the Constitution of the United States, or the Constitution or laws of this State, is the rule of decision in all the courts of this State. **Leg.H.** 1951 ch. 655.

Ref.: W. Cal. Pro., "Appeal" §920.

EFFECT OF THE 1872 CODES

Construction of Codes with relation to 1872 statutes. §23.
1872 statutes prevail over Codes. §23.1.
Construction of codes in relation to each other. §23.2.
Conflicting titles—Which shall prevail. §23.3.
Conflicting chapters—Which shall prevail. §23.4.
Conflicting articles—Which shall prevail. §23.5.
Conflicting sections of same chapter or article—Which shall prevail. §23.6.

§23. Construction of Codes With Relation to 1872 Statutes.

With relation to the laws passed at the 1872 Session of the Legislature, the Political Code, Civil Code, Code of Civil Procedure, and Penal Code, shall be construed as though each had been passed on the first day of the session. **Leg.H.** 1951 ch. 655.

§23.1. 1872 Statutes Prevail Over Codes.

The provisions of any law passed at the 1872 Session of the Legislature which contravene or are inconsistent with the provisions of any of the four codes passed at the 1872 Session prevail. **Leg.H.** 1951 ch. 655.

§23.2. Construction of Codes in Relation to Each Other.

With relation to each other, the provisions of the four codes shall be construed as though all such codes had been passed at the same moment of time and were parts of the same statute. **Leg.H.** 1951 ch. 655.

§23.3. Conflicting Titles—Which Shall Prevail.

If the provisions of any title conflict with or contravene the provisions of another title, the provisions of each title shall prevail as to all matters and questions arising out of the subject matter of the title. **Leg.H.** 1951 ch. 655.

§23.4. Conflicting Chapters—Which Shall Prevail.

If the provisions of any chapter conflict with or contravene the provisions of another chapter of the same title, the provisions of each chapter shall prevail as to all matters and questions arising out of the subject matter of the chapter. **Leg.H.** 1951 ch. 655.

§23.5. Conflicting Articles—Which Shall Prevail.

If the provisions of any article conflict with or contravene the provisions of another article of the same chapter, the provisions of each article shall prevail as to all matters and questions arising out of the subject matter of the article. **Leg.H.** 1951 ch. 655.

§23.6. Conflicting Sections of Same Chapter or Article—Which Shall Prevail.

If conflicting provisions are found in different sections of the same chapter or article, the provisions of the sections last in numerical order shall prevail, unless such construction is inconsistent with the meaning of the chapter or article. **Leg.H.** 1951 ch. 655.

DIVISION 1
PERSONS

Part 1—Persons With Unsound Mind. §§38-41.
Part 2—Personal Rights. §§43-53.
Part 2.5—Blind and Other Physically Disabled Persons. §§54-55.2.
Part 2.6—Confidentiality of Medical Information. §§56-56.37.
Part 2.9—California Fair Dealership Law. §§80-86.

PART 1
Persons With Unsound Mind

Persons without understanding—Capacity to contract—Necessaries. §38.
Contracts before adjudication subject to rescission; rebuttable presumption. §39.
Contracts after adjudication—Establishment of conservatorship. §40.
Liability of incompetents for torts. §41.

§38. Persons Without Understanding—Capacity to Contract—Necessaries.

A person entirely without understanding has no power to make a contract of any kind, but the person is liable for the reasonable value of things furnished to the person necessary for the support of the person or the person's family. **Leg.H.** 1992 ch. 163 §3, operative January 1, 1994.

Ref.: W. Cal. Sum., "Contracts" §§357, 358.

§39. Contracts Before Adjudication Subject to Rescission; Rebuttable Presumption.

(a) A conveyance or other contract of a person of unsound mind, but not entirely without understanding, made before the incapacity of the person has been judicially determined, is subject to rescission, as provided in Chapter 2 (commencing with Section 1688) of Title 5 of Part 2 of Division 3.

(b) A rebuttable presumption affecting the burden of proof that a person is of unsound mind shall exist for purposes of this section if the person is substantially unable to manage his or her own financial resources or resist fraud or undue influence. Substantial inability may not be proved solely by isolated incidents of negligence or improvidence. **Leg.H.** 1992 ch. 163 §3, operative January 1, 1994, 1995 ch. 842.

1995 Notes: This act shall be known and may be cited as the Due Process in Competence Determinations Act. Stats. 1995 ch. 842 §12.

This act shall not apply to proceedings under the Welfare and Institutions Code. Stats. 1995 ch. 842 §13.

Ref.: W. Cal. Sum., "Contracts" §§357, 361.

§40. Contracts After Adjudication—Establishment of Conservatorship.

(a) Subject to Section 1871 of the Probate Code, and subject to Part 1 (commencing wtih Section 5000) of Division 5 of the Welfare and Institutions Code, after his or her incapacity has been judicially determined a person of unsound mind can make no conveyance or other contract, nor delegate any power or waive any right, until his or her restoration to capacity.

(b) Subject to Sections 1873 to 1876, inclusive, of the Probate Code, the establishment of a conservatorship under Division 4 (commencing with Section 1400) of the Probate Code is a judicial determination of the incapacity of the conservatee for the purposes of this section. **Leg.H.** 1992 ch. 163 §3, operative January 1, 1994.

Ref.: W. Cal. Sum., "Contracts" §§357, 359, 360.

§41. Liability of Incompetents for Torts.

A person of unsound mind, of whatever degree, is civilly liable for a wrong done by the person, but is not liable in exemplary damages unless at the time of the act the person was capable of knowing that the act was wrongful. **Leg.H.** 1992 ch. 163 §3, operative January 1, 1994.

Ref.: W. Cal. Sum., "Torts" §§25, 26; CACI No. 403 (Matthew Bender).

PART 2
Personal Rights

LIBEL AND SLANDER; PRIVACY, SECURITY AND EQUALITY

Security from restraint, harm, or defamation. §43.
Unborn child deemed person. §43.1.
Right to breastfeed. §43.3.
No cause of action for fraudulent promise to marry or cohabit after marriage. §43.4.
No cause of action for breach of promise—Other causes excepted. §43.5.
Arrest warrant—No liability—No cause of action against peace officer—Requirements. §43.55.
No cause of action against foster parent for alienation of affection. §43.56.
No cause of action against parent for wrongful life. §43.6.
No liability of committee member of professional society or hospital for nonmalicious action. §43.7.
No liability of person for communication of information evaluating practitioner of healing or veterinary arts. §43.8.
No liability of health care provider for negligence arising from test by multiphasic screening unit. §43.9.
Immunity from liability for committee functions and communication of information by professional society committee member. §43.91.
Psychotherapist's immunity from liability for failure to warn of violent behavior; exception. §43.92.
Cause of action against psychotherapist for sexual contact with patient. §43.93.
Immunity from liability for referrals by professional society. §43.95.
Complaint against medical personnel to be referred to appropriate board; immunity. §43.96.
Hospitals—Limited immunity from liability for actions taken upon recommendation of medical staff. §43.97.
No liability of consultant for communication to Department of Managed Health Care regarding certain health care services. §43.98.
Liability of person or entity under contract with residential building permit applicant for quality review of compliance with state housing law. §43.99.
Defamation. §44.
Libel. §45.
Libel not actionable—When—Special damages to be proven. §45a.
Slander. §46.
Privileged publications or broadcasts—Exceptions. §47.
Defamation action by peace officer. §47.5.
Inference of malice—Exception. §48.
Libel—Demand for correction as condition precedent to action against newspaper. §48a.
Defamation by radio. §48.5.
Action prohibited when in furtherance of child abuse prosecution. §48.7.
Threats communicated against schools. §48.8.
Organizations sponsoring silent witness program are immune from civil suit. §48.9.
Abduction, seduction, injury to servant. §49.
Right to repel invasion of rights by force. §50.
Unruh Civil Rights Act. §51.
Actions requiring copy of petition and brief to be served on State Solicitor General. §51.1.
Housing discrimination prohibited based upon age; application of section—Housing specifications to meet needs of senior citizens. §51.2.
Establishing and preserving accessible housing for senior citizens. §51.3.
Senior housing constructed prior to 1982—Exemption from design requirements. §51.4.
Discrimination or boycott in business transactions prohibited—Parties included. §51.5.
Gender Tax Repeal Act of 1995. §51.6.
Freedom from violence. §51.7.
Discrimination in granting of franchises prohibited. §51.8.
Sexual harassment—Elements of cause of action. §51.9.
Riverside County—Housing discrimination prohibited based upon age. §51.10.
Riverside County—Establishing and preserving accessible housing for senior citizens. §51.11.
Riverside County—Continuing occupancy of certain exempt housing. §51.12.
Penalty for discrimination. §52.
Interference with exercise of civil rights—Remedies. §52.1.
Court of competent jurisdiction for certain actions. §52.2.
Law enforcement officers shall not deprive individuals of constitutionally protected rights, privileges, or immunities. §52.3.
Action for damages against party responsible for gender violence. §52.4.
Action by victim of human trafficking. §52.5.
Discriminatory restrictions on ownership or use of real property void. §53.

§43. Security From Restraint, Harm, or Defamation.

Besides the personal rights mentioned or recognized in the Government Code, every person has, subject to the qualifications and restrictions provided by law, the right of protection from bodily restraint or harm, from personal insult, from defamation, and from injury to his personal relations. **Leg.H.** 1872, 1953 ch. 604.

Ref.: Cal. Fms Pl. & Pr., Ch. 58, "Assault and Battery," Ch. 257, "False Imprisonment," Ch. 297, "Hotels and Motels"; W. Cal. Sum., "Torts" §3.

§43.1. Unborn Child Deemed Person.

A child conceived, but not yet born, is deemed an existing person, so far as necessary for the child's interests in the event of the child's subsequent birth. **Leg.H.** 1992 ch. 163, operative January 1, 1994.

§43.3. Right to Breastfeed.

Notwithstanding any other provision of law, a mother may breastfeed her child in any location, public or private, except the private home or residence of another, where the mother and the child are otherwise authorized to be present. **Leg.H.** 1997 ch. 59.

Ref.: Cal. Fms Pl. & Pr., Ch. 429, "Privacy."

§43.4. No Cause of Action for Fraudulent Promise to Marry or Cohabit After Marriage.

A fraudulent promise to marry or to cohabit after marriage does not give rise to a cause of action for damages. **Leg.H.** 1959 ch. 381.

Ref.: Cal. Fms Pl. & Pr., Ch. 220, "Dissolution of Marriage and Related Proceedings (Pt I)," Ch. 359, "Marriage"; W. Cal. Sum., "Torts" §§691, 692.

§43.5. No Cause of Action for Breach of Promise—Other Causes Excepted.

No cause of action arises for:

(a) Alienation of affection.

(b) Criminal conversation.

(c) Seduction of a person over the age of legal consent.

(d) Breach of promise of marriage. **Leg.H.** 1939 ch. 128.

Ref.: Cal. Fms Pl. & Pr., Ch. 220, "Dissolution of Marriage and Related Proceedings (Pt I)," Ch. 257, "False Imprisonment," Ch. 354, "Loss of Consortium," Ch. 359, "Marriage"; W. Cal. Sum., "Torts" §§692, 695.

§43.55. Arrest Warrant—No Liability—No Cause of Action Against Peace Officer—Requirements.

(a) There shall be no liability on the part of, and no cause of action shall arise against, any peace officer who makes an arrest pursuant to a warrant of arrest regular upon its face if the peace officer in making the arrest acts without malice and in the reasonable belief that the person arrested is the one referred to in the warrant.

(b) As used in this section, a "warrant of arrest regular upon its face" includes both of the following:

(1) A paper arrest warrant that has been issued pursuant to a judicial order.

(2) A judicial order that is entered into an automated warrant system by law enforcement or court personnel authorized to make those entries at or near the time the judicial order is made. Leg.H. 1945 ch. 1117, 1986 ch. 248 (amended and renumbered from §43.5(a)), 2005 ch. 706 (AB 1742) §2.

Ref.: W. Cal. Sum., "Torts" §§325, 394, 395, 396; CACI No. 1406 (Matthew Bender).

§43.56. No Cause of Action Against Foster Parent for Alienation of Affection.

No cause of action arises against a foster parent for alienation of affection of a foster child. **Leg.H.** 1986 ch. 1330, effective September 29, 1986, 1988 ch. 195, effective June 16, 1988, 1990 ch. 216 (renumbered from §43.55).

§43.6. No Cause of Action Against Parent for Wrongful Life.

(a) No cause of action arises against a parent of a child based upon the claim that the child should not have been conceived or, if conceived, should not have been allowed to have been born alive.

(b) The failure or refusal of a parent to prevent the live birth of his or her child shall not be a defense in any action against a third party, nor shall the failure or refusal be considered in awarding damages in any such action.

(c) As used in this section "conceived" means the fertilization of a human ovum by a human sperm. **Leg.H.** 1981 ch. 331.

Ref.: W. Cal. Sum., "Torts" §§798, 799; CACI Nos. 511, 513 (Matthew Bender).

§43.7. No Liability of Committee Member of Professional Society or Hospital for Nonmalicious Action.

(a) There shall be no monetary liability on the part of, and no cause of action for damages shall arise against, any member of a duly appointed mental health professional quality assurance committee that is established in compliance with Section 4070 of the Welfare and Institutions Code, for any act or proceeding undertaken or performed within the scope of the functions of the committee which is formed to review and evaluate the adequacy, appropriateness, or effectiveness of the care and treatment planned for, or provided to, mental health patients in order to improve quality of care by mental health professionals if the committee member acts without malice, has made a reasonable effort to obtain the facts of the matter as to which he or she acts, and acts in reasonable belief that the action taken by him or her is warranted by the facts known to him or her after the reasonable effort to obtain facts.

(b) There shall be no monetary liability on the part of, and no cause of action for damages shall arise against, any professional society, any member of a duly appointed committee of a medical specialty society, or any member of a duly appointed committee of a state or local professional society, or duly appointed member of a committee of a professional staff of a licensed hospital (provided the professional staff operates pursuant to written bylaws that have been approved by the governing board of the hospital), for any act or proceeding undertaken or performed within the scope of the functions of the committee which is formed to maintain the professional standards of the society established by its bylaws, or any member of any peer review committee whose purpose is to review the quality of medical, dental, dietetic, chiropractic, optometric, acupuncture, or veterinary services rendered by physicians and surgeons, dentists, dental hygienists, podiatrists, registered dietitians, chiropractors, optometrists, acupuncturists, veterinarians, or psychologists which committee is composed chiefly of physicians and surgeons, dentists, dental hygienists, podiatrists, registered dietitians, chiropractors, optometrists, acupuncturists, veterinarians, or psychologists for any act or proceeding undertaken or performed in reviewing the quality of medical, dental, dietetic, chiropractic, optometric, acupuncture, or veterinary services rendered by physicians and surgeons, dentists, dental hygienists, podiatrists, registered dietitians, chiropractors, optometrists, acupuncturists, veterinarians, or psychologists or any member of the governing board of a hospital in reviewing the quality of medical services rendered by members of the staff if the professional society, committee, or board member acts without malice, has made a reasonable effort to obtain the facts of the matter as to which he, she, or it acts, and acts in reasonable belief that the action taken by him, her, or it is warranted by the facts known to him, her, or it after the reasonable effort to obtain facts. "Professional society" includes legal, medical, psychological, dental, dental hygiene, dietetic, accounting, optometric, acupuncture, podiatric, pharmaceutic, chiropractic, physical therapist, veterinary, licensed marriage and family therapy, licensed clinical social work, and engineering organizations having as members at least 25 percent of the eligible persons or licentiates in the geographic area served by the particular society. However, if the society has less than 100 members, it shall have as members at least a majority of the eligible persons or licentiates in the geographic area served by the particular society.

"Medical specialty society" means an organization having as members at least 25 percent of the eligible physicians within a given professionally recognized medical specialty in the geographic area served by the particular society.

(c) This section does not affect the official immunity of an officer or employee of a public corporation.

(d) There shall be no monetary liability on the part of, and no cause of action for damages shall arise against, any physician and surgeon, podiatrist, or chiropractor who is a member of an underwriting committee of an interindemnity or reciprocal or interinsurance exchange or mutual company for any act or proceeding undertaken or performed in evaluating physicians and surgeons, podiatrists, or chiropractors for the writing of professional liability insurance, or any act or proceeding undertaken or performed in evaluating physicians and surgeons for the writing of an interindemnity, reciprocal, or interinsurance contract as specified in Section 1280.7 of the Insurance Code, if the evaluating physician or surgeon, podiatrist, or chiropractor acts without malice, has made a reasonable effort to obtain the facts of the matter as to which he or she acts, and acts in reasonable belief that the action taken by him or her is warranted by the facts known to him or her after the reasonable effort to obtain the facts.

(e) This section shall not be construed to confer immunity from liability on any quality assurance committee established in compliance with Section 4070 of the Welfare and Institutions Code or hospital. In any case in which, but for the enactment of the preceding provisions of this section, a cause of action would arise against a quality assurance committee established in compliance with Section 4070 of the Welfare and Institutions Code or hospital, the cause of action shall exist as if the preceding provisions of this section had not been enacted. **Leg.H.** 1961 ch. 623, 1963 ch. 806, 1969 ch. 264, 1973 ch. 191, 1976 ch. 532, 1977 chs. 241, 934, 1978 chs. 268, 503, 1980 ch. 454, 1982 ch. 234, effective June 2, 1982, ch. 705, 1983 chs. 289, 297, 1081 §1.8, 1984 chs. 515, 1012 §2, repealed operative January 1, 1990, ch. 1012 §1, re-operative January 1, 1990, 1986 ch. 669 §§1, 2, 1987 ch. 1169 §1 (deleted re-operative provision), §2 (added future operative date), 1994 ch. 815, 2002 ch. 1013 (SB 2026).

Ref.: Cal. Fms Pl. & Pr., Ch. 295, "Hospitals," Ch. 304, "Insane and Other Incompetent Persons," Ch. 414, "Physicians and Other Medical Personnel"; W. Cal. Sum., "Torts" §513.

§43.8. No Liability of Person for Communication of Information Evaluating Practitioner of Healing or Veterinary Arts.

In addition to the privilege afforded by Section 47, there shall be no monetary liability on the part of, and no cause of action for damages shall arise against, any person on account of the communication of information in the possession of that person to any hospital, hospital medical staff, veterinary hospital staff, professional society, medical, dental, podiatric, or veterinary school, professional licensing board or division, committee or panel of a licensing board, the Senior Assistant Attorney General of the Health Quality Enforcement Section appointed under Section 12529 of the Government Code, peer review committee, quality assurance committees established in compliance with Sections 4070 and 5624 of the Welfare and Institutions Code, or underwriting committee described in Section 43.7 when the communication is intended to aid in the evaluation of the qualifications, fitness, character, or insurability of a practitioner of the healing or veterinary arts. The immunities afforded by this section and by Section 43.7 shall not affect the availability of any absolute privilege which may be afforded by Section 47. **Leg.H.** 1974 ch. 1086, 1975 Second Extra. Sess. ch. 1, 1976 ch. 532, 1977 ch. 934, 1982 ch. 234, effective June 2, 1982, ch. 705, 1983 ch. 1081, 1984 ch. 515, repealed operative January 1, 1990, re-operative January 1, 1990, 1990 ch. 1597, 2002 ch. 664 (AB 3034).

Ref.: Cal. Fms Pl. & Pr., Ch. 414, "Physicians and Other Medical Personnel"; W. Cal. Sum., "Torts" §§513, 514.

§43.9. No Liability of Health Care Provider for Negligence Arising From Test by Multiphasic Screening Unit.

(a) There shall be no liability on the part of, and no cause of action shall accrue against, any health care provider for professional negligence on account of the receipt by such provider of an unsolicited referral, arising from a test performed by a multiphasic screening unit, for any act or omission, including the failure to examine, treat, or refer for examination or treatment any person concerning whom an unsolicited referral has been received. The immunity from liability granted by this subdivision shall only apply where a health provider meets the obligations established in subdivision (c).

(b) Every multiphasic screening unit shall notify each person it tests that the person should contact the health provider to whom the test results are sent within 10 days and that the health provider may not be obligated to interpret the results or provide further care. The multiphasic screening unit shall include the words "PATIENT TEST RESULTS" on the envelope of any test results sent to a health care provider, and shall include the address of the person tested in the test result material sent to the health care provider.

Nothing contained in this section shall relieve any health care provider from liability, if any, when at the time of receipt of the unsolicited referral there exists a provider-patient relationship, or a contract for health care services, or following receipt of such unsolicited referral there is established or reestablished a provider-patient relationship.

(c) A health care provider who receives unsolicited test results from a multiphasic screening unit shall receive immunity from liability pursuant to subdivision (a) only if the provider who receives such test results and does not wish to evaluate them, or evaluates them and takes no further action, either notifies the multiphasic screening unit of that fact or returns the test results within 21 days. If the health care provider reviews the test results and determines that they indicate a substantial risk of serious illness or death the provider shall make a reasonable effort to notify the person tested of the presumptive finding within 14 days after the provider has received the test results.

(d) For the purposes of this section:

(1) "Health care provider" means any person licensed or certified pursuant to Division 2 (commencing with Section 500) of the Business and Professions Code, or licensed pursuant to the Osteopathic Initiative Act or the Chiropractic Initiative Act, or licensed pursuant to Chapter 2.5 (commencing with Section 1440) of Division 2 of the Health and Safety Code, and any clinic, health dispensary, or health facility licensed pursuant to Division 2 (com-

mencing with Section 1200) of the Health and Safety Code. "Health care provider" also includes the legal representatives of a health care provider.

(2) "Professional negligence" means an action for personal injury or wrongful death proximately caused by a health care provider's negligent act or omission to act in the rendering of professional services, provided that such services are within the scope of services for which the health care provider is licensed and are not within any restriction imposed by the licensing agency or any licensed hospital.

(3) "Unsolicited referral" means any written report regarding the health, physical or mental condition of any person which was forwarded or delivered to a health care provider without prior request by such provider.

(4) A "multiphasic screening unit" means a facility which does not prescribe or treat patients but performs diagnostic testing only. **Leg.H.** 1978 ch. 1296, 1980 ch. 676.

Note: Sections 43.55 and 43.56 appear following §43.5.

§43.91. Immunity From Liability for Committee Functions and Communication of Information by Professional Society Committee Member.

(a) There shall be no monetary liability on the part of, and no cause of action shall arise against, any member of a duly appointed committee of a professional society which comprises a substantial percentage of the persons licensed pursuant to Part 1 (commencing with Section 10000) of Division 4 of the Business and Professions Code and situated in the geographic area served by the particular society, for any act or proceeding undertaken or performed within the scope of the functions of any such committee which is formed to maintain the professional standards of the society established by its bylaws, if such member acts without malice, has made a reasonable effort to obtain the facts of the matter as to which he acts, and acts in reasonable belief that the action taken by him is warranted by the facts known to him after such reasonable effort to obtain facts.

(b) There shall be no monetary liability on the part of, and no cause of action for damages shall arise against, any person on account of the communication of information in the possession of such person to any committee specified in subdivision (a) when such communication is intended to aid in the evaluation of the qualifications, fitness or character of a member or applicant for membership in any such professional society, and does not represent as true any matter not reasonably believed to be true.

(c) The immunities afforded by this section shall not affect the availability of any absolute privilege which may be afforded by Section 47.

(d) This section shall not be construed to confer immunity from liability on any professional society. In any case in which, but for the enactment of this section, a cause of action would arise against a professional society, such cause of action shall exist as if this section had not been enacted. **Leg.H.** 1980 ch. 492.

§43.92. Psychotherapist's Immunity From Liability for Failure to Warn of Violent Behavior; Exception.

(a) There shall be no monetary liability on the part of, and no cause of action shall arise against, any person who is a psychotherapist as defined in Section 1010 of the Evidence Code in failing to warn of and protect from a patient's threatened violent behavior or failing to predict and warn of and protect from a patient's violent behavior except where the patient has communicated to the psychotherapist a serious threat of physical violence against a reasonably identifiable victim or victims.

(b) If there is a duty to warn and protect under the limited circumstances specified above, the duty shall be discharged by the psychotherapist making reasonable efforts to communicate the threat to the victim or victims and to a law enforcement agency. **Leg.H.** 1985 ch. 737.

Ref.: Cal. Fms Pl. & Pr., Ch. 304, "Insane and Other Incompetent Persons"; CACI No. 503 (Matthew Bender).

§43.93. Cause of Action Against Psychotherapist for Sexual Contact With Patient.

(a) For the purposes of this section the following definitions are applicable:

(1) "Psychotherapy" means the professional treatment, assessment, or counseling of a mental or emotional illness, symptom, or condition.

(2) "Psychotherapist" means a physician and surgeon specializing in the practice of psychiatry, a psychologist, a psychological assistant, a marriage and family therapist, a registered marriage and family therapist intern or trainee, an educational psychologist, an associate clinical social worker, or a licensed clinical social worker.

(3) "Sexual contact" means the touching of an intimate part of another person. "Intimate part" and "touching" have the same meanings as defined in subdivisions (f) and (d), respectively, of Section 243.4 of the Penal Code. For the purposes of this section, sexual contact includes sexual intercourse, sodomy, and oral copulation.

(4) "Therapeutic relationship" exists during the time the patient or client is rendered professional service by the therapist.

(5) "Therapeutic deception" means a representation by a psychotherapist that sexual contact with the psychotherapist is consistent with or part of the patient's or former patient's treatment.

(b) A cause of action against a psychotherapist for sexual contact exists for a patient or former patient for injury caused by sexual contact with the psychotherapist, if the sexual contact occurred under any of the following conditions:

(1) During the period the patient was receiving psychotherapy from the psychotherapist.

(2) Within two years following termination of therapy.

(3) By means of therapeutic deception.

(c) The patient or former patient may recover damages from a psychotherapist who is found liable for sexual contact. It is not a defense to the action that sexual contact with a patient occurred outside a therapy or treatment session or that it occurred off the premises regularly used by the psychotherapist for therapy or treatment sessions. No cause of action shall exist between spouses within a marriage.

(d) In an action for sexual contact, evidence of the plaintiff's sexual history is not subject to discovery and is not admissible as evidence except in either of the following situations:

(1) The plaintiff claims damage to sexual functioning.

(2) The defendant requests a hearing prior to conducting discovery and makes an offer of proof of the relevancy of the history, and the court finds that the history is relevant and the probative value of the history outweighs its prejudicial effect.

The court shall allow the discovery or introduction as evidence only of specific information or examples of the plaintiff's conduct that are determined by the court to be relevant. The court's order shall detail the information or conduct that is subject to discovery. **Leg.H.** 1987 ch. 1474, 1992 ch. 890, 1993 ch. 589, 2002 ch. 1013 (SB 2026).

§43.95. Immunity From Liability for Referrals by Professional Society.

(a) There shall be no monetary liability on the part of, and no cause of action for damages shall arise against, any professional society or any nonprofit corporation authorized by a professional society to operate a referral service, or their agents, employees, or members, for referring any member of the public to any professional member of the society or service, or for acts of negligence or conduct constituting unprofessional conduct committed by a professional to whom a member of the public was referred, so long as any of the foregoing persons or entities has acted without malice, and the referral was made at no cost added to the initial referral fee as part of a public service referral system organized under the auspices of the professional society. Further, there shall be no monetary liability on the part of, and no cause of action for damages shall arise against, any professional society for providing a telephone information library available for use by the general public without charge, nor against any nonprofit corporation authorized by a professional society for providing a telephone information library available for use by the general public without charge. "Professional society" includes legal, psychological, architectural, medical, dental, dietetic, accounting, optometric, podiatric, pharmaceutic, chiropractic, veterinary, licensed marriage and family therapy, licensed clinical social work, and engineering organizations having as members at least 25 percent of the eligible persons or licentiates in the geographic area served by the particular society. However, if the society has less than 100 members, it shall have as members at least a majority of the eligible persons or licentiates in the geographic area served by the particular society. "Professional society" also includes organizations with referral services that have been authorized by the State Bar of California and operated in accordance with its Minimum Standards for a Lawyer Referral Service in California, and organizations that have been established to provide free assistance or representation to needy patients or clients.

(b) This section shall not apply whenever the professional society, while making a referral to a professional member of the society, fails to disclose the nature of any disciplinary action of which it has actual knowledge taken by a state licensing agency against that professional member. However, there shall be no duty to disclose a disciplinary action in either of the following cases:

(1) Where a disciplinary proceeding results in no disciplinary action being taken against the professional to whom a member of the public was referred.

(2) Where a period of three years has elapsed since the professional to whom a member of the public was referred has satisfied any terms, conditions, or sanctions imposed upon the professional as disciplinary action; except that if the professional is an attorney, there shall be no time limit on the duty to disclose. **Leg.H.** 1987 ch. 727 §4, 1988 ch. 312 §2, 2002 ch. 1013 (SB 2026).

Ref.: Cal. Fms Pl. & Pr., Ch. 61, "Associations and Clubs."

§43.96. Complaint Against Medical Personnel to Be Referred to Appropriate Board; Immunity.

(a) Any medical or podiatric society, health facility licensed or certified under Division 2 (commencing with Section 1200) of the Health and Safety Code, state agency as defined in Section 11000 of the Government Code, or local government agency that receives written complaints related to the professional competence or professional conduct of a physician and surgeon or doctor of podiatric medicine from the public shall inform the complainant that the Medical Board of California or the California Board of Podiatric Medicine, as the case may be, is the only authority in the state that may take disciplinary action against the license of the named licensee, and shall provide to the complainant the address and toll-free telephone number of the applicable state board.

(b) The immunity provided in Section 2318 of the Business and Professions Code and in Section 47 shall apply to complaints and information made or provided to a board pursuant to this section. **Leg.H.** 1993 ch. 1267, 1994 ch. 1206, 1995 ch. 708.

§43.97. Hospitals—Limited Immunity From Liability for Actions Taken Upon Recommendation of Medical Staff.

(a) There shall be no monetary liability on the part of, and no cause of action for damages, other than economic or pecuniary damages, shall arise against a hospital for any action taken upon the recommendation of its medical staff, or against any other person or organization for any action taken, or restriction imposed, which is required to be reported pursuant to Section 805 of the Business and Professions Code, provided that the action or restriction is reported in accordance with Section 805 of the Business and Professions Code. This section shall not apply to an action knowingly and intentionally taken for the purpose of injuring a person affected by the action, or infringing upon a person's rights. **Leg.H.** 1981 ch. 926, 1986 ch. 1274.

1986 Note: It appears that the Legislature inadvertently retained the lettering of subdivision (a), after it deleted subdivision (b).

Ref.: Cal. Fms Pl. & Pr., Ch. 414, "Physicians and Other Medical Personnel."

§43.98. No Liability of Consultant for Communication to Department of Managed Health Care Regarding Certain Health Care Services.

(a) There shall be no monetary liability on the part of, and no cause of action shall arise against, any consultant on account of any communication by that consultant to the Director of the Department of Managed Health Care or any other officer, employee, agent, contractor, or consultant of the Department of Managed Health Care, when that communication is for the purpose of determining whether health care services have been or are being arranged or provided in accordance with the Knox-Keene Health Care Service Plan Act of 1975 (Chapter 2.2 (commencing with Section 1340) of Division 2 of the Health and Safety Code) and any regulation adopted thereunder and the consultant does all of the following:

(1) Acts without malice.

(2) Makes a reasonable effort to obtain the facts of the matter communicated.

(3) Acts with a reasonable belief that the communication is warranted by the facts actually known to the consultant after a reasonable effort to obtain the facts.

(4) Acts pursuant to a contract entered into on or after January 1, 1998, between the Commissioner of Corporations and a state licensing board or committee, including, but not limited to, the Medical Board of California, or pursuant to a contract entered into on or after January 1, 1998, with the Commissioner of Corporations pursuant to Section 1397.6 of the Health and Safety Code.

(5) Acts pursuant to a contract entered into on or after July 1, 2000, between the Director of the Department of Managed Health Care and a state licensing board or committee, including, but not limited to, the Medical Board of California, or pursuant to a contract entered into on or after July 1, 1999, with the Director of the Department of Managed Health Care pursuant to Section 1397.6 of the Health and Safety Code.

(b) The immunities afforded by this section shall not affect the availability of any other privilege or immunity which may be afforded under this part. Nothing in this section shall be construed to alter the laws regarding the confidentiality of medical records. **Leg.H.** 1997 ch. 139, 1999 ch. 525, operative July 1, 2000, 2000 ch. 857.

§43.99. Liability of Person or Entity Under Contract With Residential Building Permit Applicant for Quality Review of Compliance With State Housing Law.

(a) There shall be no monetary liability on the part of, and no cause of action for damages shall arise against, any person or other legal entity that is under contract with an applicant for a residential building permit to provide independent quality review of the plans and specifications provided with the application in order to determine compliance with all applicable requirements imposed pursuant to the State Housing Law (Part 1.5 (commencing with Section 17910) of Division 13 of the Health and Safety Code), or any rules or regulations adopted pursuant to that law, or under contract with that applicant to provide independent quality review of the work of improvement to determine compliance with these plans and specifications, if the person or other legal entity meets the requirements of this section and one of the following applies:

(1) The person, or a person employed by any other legal entity, performing the work as described in this subdivision, has completed not less than five years of verifiable experience in the appropriate field and has obtained certification as a building inspector, combination inspector, or combination dwelling inspector from the International Conference of Building Officials (ICBO) and has successfully passed the technical written examination promulgated by ICBO for those certification categories.

(2) The person, or a person employed by any other legal entity, performing the work as described in this subdivision, has completed not less than five years of verifiable experience in the appropriate field and is a registered professional engineer, licensed general contractor, or a licensed architect rendering independent quality review of the work of improvement or plan examination services within the scope of his or her registration or licensure.

(3) The immunity provided under this section does not apply to any action initiated by the applicant who retained the qualified person.

(4) A "qualified person" for purposes of this section means a person holding a valid certification as one of those inspectors.

(b) Except for qualified persons, this section shall not relieve from, excuse, or lessen in any manner, the responsibility or liability of any person, company, contractor, builder, developer, architect, engineer, designer, or other individual or entity who develops, improves, owns, operates, or manages any residential building for any damages to persons or property caused by construction or design defects. The fact that an inspection by a qualified person has taken place may not be introduced as evidence in a construction defect action, including any reports or other items generated by the qualified person. This subdivision shall not apply in any action initiated by the applicant who retained the qualified person.

(c) Nothing in this section, as it relates to construction inspectors or plans examiners, shall be construed to alter the requirements for licensure, or the jurisdiction, authority, or scope of practice, of architects pursuant to Chapter 3 (commencing with Section 5500) of Division 3 of the Business and Professions Code, professional engineers pursuant to Chapter 7 (commencing with Section 6700) of Division 3 of the Business and Professions Code, or general contractors pursuant to Chapter 9 (commencing with Section 7000) of Division 3 of the Business and Professions Code.

(d) Nothing in this section shall be construed to alter the immunity of employees of the Department of Housing and Community Development under the Tort Claims Act (Division 3.6 (commencing with Section 810) of Title 1 of the Government Code) when acting pursuant to Section 17965 of the Health and Safety Code.

(e) The qualifying person shall engage in no other construction, design, planning, supervision, or activities of any kind on the work of improvement, nor provide quality review services for any other party on the work of improvement.

(f) The qualifying person, or other legal entity, shall maintain professional errors and omissions insurance coverage in an amount not less than two million dollars ($2,000,000).

(g) The immunity provided by subdivision (a) does not inure to the benefit of the qualified person for damages caused to the applicant solely by the negligence or willful misconduct of the qualified person resulting from the provision of services under the contract with the applicant. **Leg.H.** 2002 ch. 722 (SB 800).

§44. Defamation.

Defamation is effected by either of the following:
(a) Libel.
(b) Slander. **Leg.H.** 1872, 1980 ch. 676.

Ref.: CACI No. 1700 (Matthew Bender).

§45. Libel.

Libel is a false and unprivileged publication by writing, printing, picture, effigy, or other fixed representation to the eye, which exposes any person to hatred, contempt, ridicule, or obloquy, or which causes him to be shunned or avoided, or which has a tendency to injure him in his occupation. **Leg.H.** 1872.

Ref.: Cal. Fms Pl. & Pr., Ch. 340, "Libel and Slander"; MB Prac. Guide: Cal. Unfair Comp. & Bus. Torts, §9.07; W. Cal. Pro., "Pleading" §694; W. Cal. Sum., "Torts" §480; CACI Nos. 1700, 1702, 1704 (Matthew Bender).

§45a. Libel Not Actionable—When—Special Damages to Be Proven.

A libel which is defamatory of the plaintiff without the necessity of explanatory matter, such as an inducement, innuendo or other extrinsic fact, is said to be a libel on its face. Defamatory language not libelous on its face is not actionable unless the plaintiff alleges and proves that he has suffered special damage as a proximate result thereof. Special damage is defined in Section 48a of this code. **Leg.H.** 1945 ch. 1489.

Ref.: Cal. Fms Pl. & Pr., Ch. 340, "Libel and Slander"; MB Prac. Guide: Cal. Unfair Comp. & Bus. Torts, §9.07; W. Cal. Pro., "Pleading" §691; W. Cal. Sum., "Torts" §§481, 488, 586; CACI Nos. 1701, 1703, 1705 (Matthew Bender).

§46. Slander.

Slander is a false and unprivileged publication, orally uttered, and also communications by radio or any mechanical or other means which:

1. Charges any person with crime, or with having been indicted, convicted, or punished for crime;

2. Imputes in him the present existence of an infectious, contagious, or loathsome disease;

3. Tends directly to injure him in respect to his office, profession, trade or business, either by imputing to him general disqualification in those respects which the office or other occupation peculiarly requires, or by imputing something with reference to his office, profession, trade, or business that has a natural tendency to lessen its profits;

4. Imputes to him impotence or a want of chastity; or

5. Which, by natural consequence, causes actual damage. **Leg.H.** 1872, 1945 ch. 1489.

Ref.: Cal. Fms Pl. & Pr., Ch. 340, "Libel and Slander"; MB Prac. Guide: Cal. Unfair Comp. & Bus. Torts, §9.07; W. Cal. Pro., "Pleading" §606; W. Cal. Sum., "Torts" §§471, 472, 480, 490, 491; CACI Nos. 1700, 1702, 1704 (Matthew Bender).

§47. Privileged Publications or Broadcasts—Exceptions.

A privileged publication or broadcast is one made:
(a) In the proper discharge of an official duty.
(b) In any (1) legislative proceeding, (2) judicial proceeding, (3) in any other official proceeding authorized by law, or (4) in the initiation or course of any other proceeding authorized by law and reviewable pursuant to Chapter 2 (commencing with Section 1084) of Title 1 of Part 3 of the Code of Civil Procedure, except as follows:

(1) An allegation or averment contained in any pleading or affidavit filed in an action for marital dissolution or legal separation made of or concerning a person by or against whom no affirmative relief is prayed in the action shall not be a privileged publication or broadcast as to the person making the allegation or averment within the meaning of this section unless the pleading is verified or affidavit sworn to, and is made without malice, by one having reasonable and probable cause for believing the truth of the allegation or averment and unless the allegation or averment is material and relevant to the issues in the action.

(2) This subdivision does not make privileged any communication made in furtherance of an act of intentional destruction or alteration of physical evidence undertaken for the purpose of depriving a party to litigation of the use of that evidence, whether or not the content of the communication is the subject of a subsequent publication or broadcast which is privileged pursuant to this section. As used in this paragraph, "physical evidence" means evidence specified in Section 250 of the Evidence Code or evidence that is property of any type specified in Chapter 14 (commencing with Section 2031.010) of Title 4 of Part 4 of the Code of Civil Procedure.

(3) This subdivision does not make privileged any communication made in a judicial proceeding knowingly concealing the existence of an insurance policy or policies.

(4) A recorded lis pendens is not a privileged publication unless it identifies an action previously filed with a court of competent jurisdiction which affects the title or right of possession of real property, as authorized or required by law.

(c) In a communication, without malice, to a person interested therein, (1) by one who is also interested, or (2) by one who stands in such a relation to the person interested as to afford a reasonable ground for supposing the motive for the communication to be innocent, or (3) who is requested by the person interested to give the information. This subdivision applies to and includes a communication concerning the job performance or qualifications of an applicant for employment, based upon credible evidence, made without malice, by a current or former employer of the applicant to, and upon request of, one whom the employer reasonably believes is a prospective employer of the applicant. This subdivision authorizes a current or former employer, or the employer's agent, to answer whether or not the employer would rehire a current or former employee. This subdivision shall not apply to a communication concerning the speech or activities of an applicant for employment if the speech or activities are constitutionally protected, or otherwise protected by Section 527.3 of the Code of Civil Procedure or any other provision of law.

(d) (1) By a fair and true report in, or a communication to, a public journal, of (A) a judicial, (B) legislative, or (C) other public official proceeding, or (D) of anything said in the course thereof, or (E) of a verified charge or complaint made by any person to a public official, upon which complaint a warrant has been issued.

(2) Nothing in paragraph (1) shall make privileged any communication to a public journal that does any of the following:

(A) Violates Rule 5-120 of the State Bar Rules of Professional Conduct.

(B) Breaches a court order.

(C) Violates any requirement of confidentiality imposed by law.

(e) By a fair and true report of (1) the proceedings of a public meeting, if the meeting was lawfully convened for a lawful purpose and open to the public, or (2) the publication of the matter complained of was for the public benefit. **Leg.H.** 1872, 1874 p. 184, 1905 p. 168, 1927 ch. 866, 1945 ch. 1489, 1979 ch. 184, 1990 ch. 1491, 1991 ch. 432, 1992 ch. 615, 1994 chs. 364, 700 §2.5, 1996 ch. 1055 §2, 2002 ch. 1029 (AB 2868), effective September 28, 2002, 2004 ch. 182 (AB 3081), operative July 1, 2005.

1996 Note: In amending Section 47 of the Civil Code by this act, it is the intent of the Legislature to abrogate the decision in *Shahvar v. Superior Court* (1994), 25 Cal. App. 4th 653, to preserve the scarce resources of California's courts, to avoid using the courts for satellite litigation, and to increase public participation in the political, legislative, and judicial processes. It is not the intent of the Legislature to limit in any manner the application of subdivision (b) or (d) of Section 47 of the Civil Code. Specifically, it is not the intent of the Legislature to affect case law holding that certain prelitigation statements are privileged as described in, for example, *Lerette v. Dean Witter Organization, Inc.*, 60 Cal. App. 3d 573; *Martin v. Kearney*, 51 Cal. App. 3d 309; *Ascherman v. Natanson*, 23 Cal. App. 3d 861; and the Second Restatement of Torts, Section 586. Stats. 1996 ch. 1055 §1.

1994 Note: It is the intent of the Legislature in amending Section 47 of the Civil Code to overturn the decision in *California Dredging Company v. Insurance Company of North America*, 18 Cal. App. 4th 572. Stats. 1994 ch. 700 §1.

Ref.: Cal. Fms Pl. & Pr., Ch. 340, "Libel and Slander," Ch. 348, "Lis Pendens," Ch. 357, "Malicious Prosecution and Abuse of Process," Ch. 362, "Mental Suffering and Emotional Distress," Ch. 429, "Privacy"; MB Prac. Guide: Cal. Unfair Comp. & Bus. Torts, §§2.43[1], 4.2, 6.38[1], 9.19; W. Cal. Pro., "Pleading" §1027; W. Cal. Sum., "Torts" §§307A, 324, 415, 432, 440, 470, 499 et seq., 500–503, 505, 505A, 506A, 509–514, 523–528, 530–532, 548, 575, 581, 597, 667, 1332, 1947; CACI Nos. 1501, 1520, 1605, 1723, 2711 (Matthew Bender).

§47.5. Defamation Action by Peace Officer.

Notwithstanding Section 47, a peace officer may bring an action for defamation against an individual who has filed a complaint with that officer's employing agency alleging misconduct, criminal conduct, or incompetence, if that complaint is false, the complaint was made with knowledge that it was false and that it was made with spite, hatred, or ill will. Knowledge that the complaint was false may be proved by a showing that the complainant had no reasonable grounds to believe the statement was true and that the complainant exhibited a reckless disregard for ascertaining the truth. **Leg.H.** 1982 ch. 1588.

Ref.: W. Cal. Sum., "Torts" §512.

§48. Inference of Malice—Exception.

In the case provided for in subdivision (c) of Section 47, malice is not inferred from the communication. **Leg.H.** 1872, 1895 p. 167, 1945 p. 1489, 2003 ch. 62 (SB 600).

Ref.: Cal. Fms Pl. & Pr., Ch. 340, "Libel and Slander"; W. Cal. Sum., "Torts" §521.

§48a. Libel—Demand for Correction as Condition Precedent to Action Against Newspaper.

1. In any action for damages for the publication of a libel in a newspaper, or of a slander by radio broadcast, plaintiff shall recover no more than special damages unless a correction be demanded and be not published or broadcast, as hereinafter provided. Plaintiff shall serve upon the publisher, at the place of publication or broadcaster at the place of broadcast, a written notice specifying the statements claimed to be libelous and demanding that the same be corrected. Said notice and demand must be served within 20 days after knowledge of the publication or broadcast of the statements claimed to be libelous.

2. If a correction be demanded within said period and be not published or broadcast in substantially as conspicuous a manner in said newspaper or on said broadcasting station as were the statements claimed to be libelous, in a regular issue thereof published or broadcast within three weeks after such service, plaintiff, if he pleads and proves such notice, demand and failure to correct, and if his cause of action be maintained, may recover general, special and exemplary damages; provided that no exemplary damages may be recovered unless the plaintiff shall prove that defendant made the publication or broadcast with actual malice and then only in the discretion of the court or jury, and actual malice shall not be inferred or presumed from the publication or broadcast.

3. A correction published or broadcast in substantially as conspicuous a manner in said newspaper or on said broadcasting station as the statements claimed in the complaint to be libelous, prior to receipt of a demand therefor, shall be of the same force and effect as though such correction had been published or broadcast within three weeks after a demand therefor.

4. As used herein, the terms "general damages," "special damages," "exemplary damages" and "actual malice," are defined as follows:

(a) "General damages" are damages for loss of reputation, shame, mortification and hurt feelings;

(b) "Special damages" are all damages which plaintiff alleges and proves that he has suffered in respect to his property, business, trade, profession or occupation, including such amounts of money as the plaintiff alleges and proves he has expended as a result of the alleged libel, and no other;

(c) "Exemplary damages" are damages which may in the discretion of the court or jury be recovered in addition to general and special damages for the sake of example and by way of punishing a defendant who has made the publication or broadcast with actual malice;

(d) "Actual malice" is that state of mind arising from hatred or ill will toward the plaintiff; provided, however, that such a state of mind occasioned by a good faith belief on the part of the defendant in the truth of the libelous publication or broadcast at the time it is published or broadcast shall not constitute actual malice. **Leg.H.** 1931 ch. 1018, 1945 ch. 1489.

Ref.: Cal. Fms Pl. & Pr., Ch. 340, "Libel and Slander"; MB Prac. Guide: Cal. Unfair Comp. & Bus. Torts, §§9.07, 9.19; W. Cal. Pro., "Appeal" §§972, 973, "Pleading" §694; W. Cal. Sum., "Torts" §§521, 557–566, 586, 1435–1436; CACI Nos. 1701, 1703, 1705, 1722, 1802 (Matthew Bender).

§48.5. Defamation by Radio.

(1) The owner, licensee or operator of a visual or sound radio broadcasting station or network of stations, and the agents or employees of any such owner, licensee or operator, shall not be liable for any damages for any defamatory statement or matter published or uttered in or as a part of a visual or sound radio broadcast by one other than such owner, licensee or operator, or agent or employee thereof, if it shall be alleged and proved by such owner, licensee or operator, or agent or employee thereof, that such owner, licensee or operator, or such agent or employee, has exercised due care to prevent the publication or utterance of such statement or matter in such broadcast.

(2) If any defamatory statement or matter is published or uttered in or as a part of a broadcast over the facilities of a network of visual or sound radio broadcasting stations, the owner, licensee or operator of any such station, or network of stations, and the agents or employees thereof, other than the owner, licensee or operator of the station, or network of stations, originating such broadcast, and the agents or employees thereof, shall in no event be liable for any damages for any such defamatory statement or matter.

(3) In no event, however, shall any owner, licensee or operator of such station or network of stations, or the agents or employees thereof, be liable for any damages for any defamatory statement or matter published or uttered, by one other than such owner, licensee or operator, or agent or employee thereof, in or as a part of a visual or sound radio broadcast by or on behalf of any candidate for public office, which broadcast cannot be censored by reason of the provisions of federal statute or regulation of the Federal Communications Commission.

(4) As used in this Part 2, the terms "radio," "radio broadcast," and "broadcast," are defined to include both visual and sound radio broadcasting.

(5) Nothing in this section contained shall deprive any such owner, licensee or operator, or the agent or employee thereof, of any rights under any other section of this Part 2. **Leg.H.** 1949 ch. 1258.

Ref.: Cal. Fms Pl. & Pr., Ch. 340, "Libel and Slander"; MB Prac. Guide: Cal. Unfair Comp. & Bus. Torts, §9.07; W. Cal. Sum., "Torts" §472.

§48.7. Action Prohibited When in Furtherance of Child Abuse Prosecution.

(a) No person charged by indictment, information, or other accusatory pleading of child abuse may bring a civil libel or slander action against the minor, the parent or guardian of the minor, or any witness, based upon any statements made by the minor, parent or guardian, or witness which are reasonably believed to be in furtherance of the prosecution of the criminal charges while the charges are pending before a trial court. The charges are not pending within the meaning of this section after dismissal, after pronouncement of judgment, or during an appeal from a judgment.

Any applicable statue of limitations shall be tolled during the period that such charges are pending before a trial court.

(b) Whenever any complaint for libel or slander is filed which is subject to the provisions of this section, no responsive pleading shall be required to be filed until 30 days after the end of the period set forth in subdivision (a).

(c) Every complaint for libel or slander based on a statement that the plaintiff committed an act of child abuse shall state that the complaint is not barred by subdivision (a). A failure to include that statement shall be grounds for a demurrer.

(d) Whenever a demurrer against a complaint for libel or slander is sustained on the basis that the complaint was filed in violation of this section, attorney's fees and costs shall be awarded to the prevailing party.

(e) Whenever a prosecutor is informed by a minor, parent, guardian, or witness that a complaint against one of those persons has been filed which may be subject to the provisions of this section, the prosecutor shall provide that person with a copy of this section.

(f) As used in this section, child abuse has the meaning set forth in Section 11165 of the Penal Code. **Leg.H.** 1981 ch. 253.

Ref.: Cal. Fms Pl. & Pr., Ch. 340, "Libel and Slander."

§48.8. Threats Communicated Against Schools.

(a) A communication by any person to a school principal, or a communication by a student attending the school to the student's teacher or to a school counselor or school nurse and any report of that communication to the school principal, stating that a specific student or other specified person has made a threat to commit violence or potential violence on the school grounds involving the use of a firearm or other deadly or dangerous weapon, is a communication on a matter of public concern and is subject to liability in defamation only upon a showing by clear and convincing evidence that the communication or report was made with knowledge of its falsity or with reckless disregard for the truth or falsity of the communication. Where punitive damages are alleged, the provisions of Section 3294 shall also apply.

(b) As used in this section, "school" means a public or private school providing instruction in kindergarten or grades 1 to 12, inclusive. **Leg.H.** 2001 ch. 570.

§48.9. Organizations Sponsoring Silent Witness Program Are Immune From Civil Suit.

(a) An organization which sponsors or conducts an anonymous witness program, and its employees and agents, shall not be liable in a civil action for damages resulting from its receipt of information regarding possible criminal activity or from dissemination of that information to a law enforcement agency.

(b) The immunity provided by this section shall apply to any civil action for damages, including, but not limited to, a defamation action or an action for damages resulting from retaliation against a person who provided information.

(c) The immunity provided by this section shall not apply in any of the following instances:

(1) The information was disseminated with actual knowledge that it was false.

(2) The name of the provider of the information was disseminated without that person's authorization and the dissemination was not required by law.

(3) The name of the provider of information was obtained and the provider was not informed by the organization that the disclosure of his or her name may be required by law.

(d) As used in this section, an "anonymous witness program" means a program whereby information relating to alleged criminal activity is received from persons, whose names are not released without their authorization unless required by law, and disseminated to law enforcement agencies. **Leg.H.** 1983 ch. 495.

§49. Abduction, Seduction, Injury to Servant.

The rights of personal relations forbid:

(a) The abduction or enticement of a child from a parent, or from a guardian entitled to its custody;

(b) The seduction of a person under the age of legal consent;

(c) Any injury to a servant which affects his ability to serve his master, other than seduction, abduction or criminal conversation. **Leg.H.** 1872, 1905 p. 68, 1939 chs. 128, 1103.

Ref.: Cal. Fms Pl. & Pr., Ch. 394, "Parent and Child"; W. Cal. Pro., "Appeal" §§972, 973; W. Cal. Sum., "Torts" §§631, 640, 641.

§50. Right to Repel Invasion of Rights by Force.

Any necessary force may be used to protect from wrongful injury the person or property of oneself, or of a wife, husband, child, parent, or other relative, or member of one's family, or of a ward, servant, master, or guest. **Leg.H.** 1872, 1874 p. 184.

Ref.: Cal. Fms Pl. & Pr., Ch. 58, "Assault and Battery"; W. Cal. Sum., "Torts" §369; CACI No. 1304 (Matthew Bender).

§51. Unruh Civil Rights Act.

(a) This section shall be known, and may be cited, as the Unruh Civil Rights Act.

(b) All persons within the jurisdiction of this state are free and equal, and no matter what their sex, race, color, religion, ancestry, national origin, disability, [1] medical condition, **marital status, or sexual orientation** are entitled to the full and equal accommodations, advantages, facilities, privileges, or services in all business establishments of every kind whatsoever.

(c) This section shall not be construed to confer any right or privilege on a person that is conditioned or limited by law or that is applicable alike to persons of every sex, color, race, religion, ancestry, national origin, disability, [2] medical condition, **marital status, or sexual orientation**.

(d) Nothing in this section shall be construed to require any construction, alteration, repair, structural or otherwise, or modification of any sort whatsoever, beyond that construction, alteration, repair, or modification that is otherwise required by other provisions of law, to any new or existing establishment, facility, building, improvement, or any other structure, nor shall anything in this section be construed to augment, restrict, or alter in any way the authority of the State Architect to require construction, alteration, repair, or modifications that the State Architect otherwise possesses pursuant to other laws.

(e) For purposes of this section:

(1) "Disability" means any mental or physical disability as defined in [3] **Sections 12926 and 12926.1** of the Government Code.

(2) "Medical condition" has the same meaning as defined in subdivision (h) of Section 12926 of the Government Code.

(3) **"Religion" includes all aspects of religious belief, observance, and practice.**

(4) **"Sex" has the same meaning as defined in subdivision (p) of Section 12926 of the Government Code.**

(5) **"Sex, race, color, religion, ancestry, national origin, disability, medical condition, marital status, or sexual orientation" includes a perception that the person has any particular characteristic or characteristics within the listed categories or that the person is associated with a person who has, or is perceived to have, any particular characteristic or characteristics within the listed categories.**

(6) **"Sexual orientation" has the same meaning as defined in subdivision (q) of Section 12926 of the Government Code.**

(f) A violation of the right of any individual under the Americans with Disabilities Act of 1990 (Public Law 101-336) shall also constitute a violation of this section. **Leg.H.** 1905 p. 553, 1919 p. 309, 1923 ch. 235, 1959 ch. 1866, 1961 ch. 1187, 1974 ch. 1193, 1987 ch. 159, 1992 ch. 913, 1998 ch. 195, 2000 ch. 1049, 2005 ch. 420 (AB 1400) §3.

§51. 2005 Deletes. [1] or [2] or [3] Section

2005 Notes: This act shall be known and may be cited as "The Civil Rights Act of 2005." Stats. 2005 ch. 420 (AB 1400) §1.

The Legislature affirms that the bases of discrimination prohibited by the Unruh Civil Rights Act include, but are not limited to, marital status and sexual orientation, as defined herein. By specifically enumerating these bases in the Unruh Civil Rights Act, the Legislature intends to clarify the existing law, rather than to change the law, as well as the principle that the bases enumerated in the act are illustrative rather than restrictive. Stats. 2005 ch. 420 (AB 1400) §2(c).

It is the intent of the Legislature that the amendments made to the Unruh Civil Rights Act by this act do not affect the California Supreme Court's rulings in *Marina Point, Ltd. v. Wolfson* (1982) 30 Cal.3d 721 and *O'Connor v. Village Green Owners Association* (1983) 33 Cal.3d 790. Stats. 2005 ch. 420 (AB 1400) §2(d).

Ref.: Cal. Fms Pl. & Pr., Ch. 116, "Civil Rights: Discrimination in Business Establishments," Ch. 117, "Civil Rights: Housing Discrimination," Ch. 117A, "Civil Rights: Interference With Civil Rights by Threats, Intimidation, Coercion or Violence," Ch. 547, "Theatres, Shows, and Amusement Places"; W. Cal. Pro., "Pleading" §137; W. Cal. Sum., "Constitutional Law" §§272A, 383, 746–755; MB Prac. Guide: Landlord-Tenant, Ch. 2; CACI Nos. 3020, VF-3010 (Matthew Bender).

§51.1. Actions Requiring Copy of Petition and Brief to Be Served on State Solicitor General.

If a violation of Section 51, 51.5, 51.7, 51.9, or 52.1 is alleged or the application or construction of any of these sections is in issue in any proceeding in the Supreme Court of California, a state court of appeal, or the appellate division of a superior court, each party shall serve a copy of the party's brief or petition and brief, on the State Solicitor General at the Office of the Attorney General. No brief may be accepted for filing unless the proof of service shows service on the State Solicitor General. Any party failing to comply with this requirement shall be given a reasonable opportunity to cure the failure before the court imposes any sanction and, in that instance, the court shall allow the Attorney General reasonable additional time to file a brief in the matter. **Leg.H.** 2002 ch. 244 (AB 2524).

§51.2. Housing Discrimination Prohibited Based Upon Age; Application of Section—Housing Specifications to Meet Needs of Senior Citizens.

(a) Section 51 shall be construed to prohibit a business establishment from discriminating in the sale or rental of housing based upon age. Where accommodations are designed to meet the physical and social needs of senior citizens, a business establishment may establish and preserve that housing for senior citizens, pursuant to Section 51.3, except housing as to which Section 51.3 is preempted by the prohibition in the federal Fair Housing Amendments Act of 1988 (P.L. 100-430) and implementing regulations against discrimination on the basis of familial status. For accommodations constructed before February 8, 1982, that meet all the criteria for senior citizen housing specified in Section 51.3, a business establishment may establish and preserve that housing development for senior citizens without the housing development being designed to meet physical and social needs of senior citizens.

(b) This section is intended to clarify the holdings in *Marina Point, Ltd. v. Wolfson* (1982) 30 Cal. 3d 72 and *O'Connor v. Village Green Owners Association* (1983) 33 Cal. 3d 790.

(c) This section shall not apply to the County of Riverside.

(d) A housing development for senior citizens constructed on or after January 1, 2001, shall be presumed to be designed to meet the physical and social needs of senior citizens if it includes all of the following elements:

(1) Entryways, walkways, and hallways in the common areas of the development, and doorways and paths of access to and within the housing units, shall be as wide as required by current laws applicable to new multifamily housing construction for provision of access to persons using a standard-width wheelchair.

(2) Walkways and hallways in the common areas of the development shall be equipped with standard height railings or grab bars to assist persons who have difficulty with walking.

(3) Walkways and hallways in the common areas shall have lighting conditions which are of sufficient brightness to assist persons who have difficulty seeing.

(4) Access to all common areas and housing units within the development shall be provided without use of stairs, either by means of an elevator or sloped walking ramps.

(5) The development shall be designed to encourage social contact by providing at least one common room and at least some common open space.

(6) Refuse collection shall be provided in a manner that requires a minimum of physical exertion by residents.

(7) The development shall comply with all other applicable requirements for access and design imposed by law, including, but not limited to, the Fair Housing Act (42 U.S.C. Sec. 3601 et seq.), the Americans with Disabilities Act (42 U.S.C. Sec. 12101 et seq.), and the regulations promulgated at Title 24 of the California Code of Regulations that relate to access for persons with disabilities or handicaps. Nothing in this section shall be construed to limit or reduce any right or obligation applicable under those laws. **Leg.H.** 1984 ch. 787, 1989 ch. 501, 1993 ch. 830, effective October 6, 1993, 1996 ch. 1147, 1999 ch. 324, 2000 ch. 1004, 2002 ch. 726 (AB 2787).

§51.3. Establishing and Preserving Accessible Housing for Senior Citizens.

(a) The Legislature finds and declares that this section is essential to establish and preserve specially designed accessible housing for senior citizens. There are senior citizens who need special living environments and services, and find that there is an inadequate supply of this type of housing in the state.

(b) For the purposes of this section, the following definitions apply:

(1) "Qualifying resident" or "senior citizen" means a person 62 years of age or older, or 55 years of age or older in a senior citizen housing development.

(2) "Qualified permanent resident" means a person who meets both of the following requirements:

(A) Was residing with the qualifying resident or senior citizen prior to the death, hospitalization, or other prolonged absence of, or the dissolution of marriage with, the qualifying resident or senior citizen.

(B) Was 45 years of age or older, or was a spouse, cohabitant, or person providing primary physical or economic support to the qualifying resident or senior citizen.

(3) "Qualified permanent resident" also means a disabled person or person with a disabling illness or injury who is a child or grandchild of the senior citizen or a qualified permanent resident as defined in paragraph (2) who needs to live with the senior citizen or qualified permanent resident because of the disabling condition, illness, or injury. For purposes of this section, "disabled" means a person who has a disability as defined in subdivision (b) of Section 54. A "disabling injury or illness" means an illness or injury which results in a condition meeting the definition of disability set forth in subdivision (b) of Section 54.

(A) For any person who is a qualified permanent resident under this paragraph whose disabling condition ends, the owner, board of directors, or other governing body may require the formerly disabled resident to cease residing in the development upon receipt of six months' written notice; provided, however, that the owner, board of directors, or other governing body may allow the person to remain a resident for up to one year after the disabling condition ends.

(B) The owner, board of directors, or other governing body of the senior citizen housing development may take action to prohibit or terminate occupancy by a person who is a qualified permanent resident under this paragraph if the owner, board of directors, or other governing body finds, based on credible and objective evidence, that the person is likely to pose a significant threat to the health or safety of others that cannot be ameliorated by means of a reasonable accommodation; provided, however, that the action to prohibit or terminate the occupancy may be taken only after doing both of the following:

(i) Providing reasonable notice to and an opportunity to be heard for the disabled person whose occupancy is being challenged, and reasonable notice to the coresident parent or grandparent of that person.

(ii) Giving due consideration to the relevant, credible, and objective information provided in the hearing. The evidence shall be taken and held in a confidential manner, pursuant to a closed session, by the owner, board of directors, or other governing body in order to preserve the privacy of the affected persons.

The affected persons shall be entitled to have present at the hearing an attorney or any other person authorized by them to speak on their behalf or to assist them in the matter.

(4) "Senior citizen housing development" means a residential development developed, substantially rehabilitated, or substantially renovated for, senior citizens that has at least 35 dwelling units. Any senior citizen housing development which is required to obtain a public report under Section 11010 of the Business and Professions Code and which submits its application for a public report after July 1, 2001, shall be required to have been issued a public report as a senior citizen housing development under Section 11010.05 of the Business and Professions Code. No housing development constructed prior to January 1, 1985, shall fail to qualify as a senior citizen housing development because it was not originally developed or put to use for occupancy by senior citizens.

(5) "Dwelling unit" or "housing" means any residential accommodation other than a mobilehome.

(6) "Cohabitant" refers to persons who live together as husband and wife, or persons who are domestic partners within the meaning of Section 297 of the Family Code.

(7) "Permitted health care resident" means a person hired to provide live-in, long-term, or terminal health care to a qualifying resident, or a family member of the qualifying resident providing that care. For the purposes of this section, the care provided by a permitted health care resident must be substantial in nature and must provide either assistance with necessary daily activities or medical treatment, or both.

A permitted health care resident shall be entitled to continue his or her occupancy, residency, or use of the dwelling unit as a permitted resident in the absence of the senior citizen from the dwelling unit only if both of the following are applicable:

(A) The senior citizen became absent from the dwelling due to hospitalization or other necessary medical treatment and expects to return to his or her residence within 90 days from the date the absence began.

(B) The absent senior citizen or an authorized person acting for the senior citizen submits a written request to the owner, board of directors, or governing board stating that the senior citizen desires that the permitted health care resident be allowed to remain in order to be present when the senior citizen returns to reside in the development.

Upon written request by the senior citizen or an authorized person acting for the senior citizen, the owner, board of directors, or governing board shall have the discretion to allow a permitted health care resident to remain for a time period longer than 90 days from the date that the senior citizen's absence began, if it appears that the senior citizen will return within a period of time not to exceed an additional 90 days.

(c) The covenants, conditions, and restrictions and other documents or written policy shall set forth the limitations on occupancy, residency, or use on the basis of age. Any such limitation shall not be more exclusive than to require that one person in residence in each dwelling unit may be required to be a senior citizen and that each other resident in the same dwelling unit may be required to be a qualified permanent resident, a permitted health care resident, or a person under 55 years of age whose occupancy is permitted under subdivision (h) of this section or under subdivision (b) of Section 51.4. That limitation may be less exclusive, but shall at least require that the persons commencing any occupancy of a dwelling unit include a senior citizen who intends to reside in the unit as his or her primary residence on a permanent basis. The application of the rules set forth in this subdivision regarding limitations on occupancy may result in less than all of the dwellings being actually occupied by a senior citizen.

(d) The covenants, conditions, and restrictions or other documents or written policy shall permit temporary residency, as a guest of a senior citizen or qualified permanent resident, by a person of less than 55 years of age for periods of time, not less than 60 days in any year, that are specified in the covenants, conditions, and restrictions or other documents or written policy.

(e) Upon the death or dissolution of marriage, or upon hospitalization, or other prolonged absence of the qualifying resident, any qualified permanent resident shall be entitled to continue his or her occupancy, residency, or use of the dwelling unit as a permitted resident. This subdivision shall not apply to a permitted health care resident.

(f) The condominium, stock cooperative, limited-equity housing cooperative, planned development, or multiple-family residential rental property shall have been developed for, and initially been put to use as, housing for senior citizens, or shall have been substantially rehabilitated or renovated for, and immediately afterward put to use as, housing for senior citizens, as provided in this section; provided, however, that no housing development constructed prior to January 1, 1985, shall fail to qualify as a senior citizen housing development because it was not originally developed for or originally put to use for occupancy by senior citizens.

(g) The covenants, conditions, and restrictions or other documents or written policies applicable to any condominium, stock cooperative, limited-equity housing cooperative, planned development, or multiple-family residential property that contained age restrictions on January 1, 1984, shall be enforceable only to the extent permitted by this section, notwithstanding lower age restrictions contained in those documents or policies.

(h) Any person who has the right to reside in, occupy, or use the housing or an unimproved lot subject to this section on January 1, 1985, shall not be deprived of the right to continue that residency, occupancy, or use as the result of the enactment of this section.

(i) The covenants, conditions, and restrictions or other documents or written policy of the senior citizen housing development shall permit the occupancy of a dwelling unit by a permitted health care resident during any period that the person is actually providing live-in, long-term, or hospice health care to a qualifying resident for compensation. For purposes of this subdivision, the term "for compensation" shall include provisions of lodging and food in exchange for care.

(j) Notwithstanding any other provision of this section, this section shall not apply to the County of Riverside. **Leg.H.** 1984 ch. 1333, 1985 ch. 1505, 1989 ch. 190, 1994 ch. 464, 1995 ch. 147, 1996 ch. 1147, 1999 ch. 324, 2000 ch. 1004 §3.

Ref.: Cal. Fms Pl. & Pr., Ch. 117, "Civil Rights: Housing Discrimination," Ch. 124, "Condominiums and Other Common Interest Developments," Ch. 184, "Deeds"; W. Cal. Sum., "Constitutional Law" §754.

§51.4. Senior Housing Constructed Prior to 1982—Exemption From Design Requirements.

(a) The Legislature finds and declares that the requirements for senior housing under Sections 51.2 and 51.3 are more stringent than the requirements for that housing under the federal Fair Housing Amendments Act of 1988 (Public Law 100-430) in recognition of the acute shortage of housing for families with children in California. The Legislature further finds and declares that the special design requirements for senior housing under Sections 51.2 and 51.3 may pose a hardship to some housing developments which were constructed before the decision in *Marina Point Ltd. v. Wolfson* (1982), 30 Cal. 3d 72. The Legislature further finds and declares that the requirement for specially designed accommodations in senior housing under Sections 51.2 and 51.3 provides important benefits to senior citizens and also ensures that housing exempt from the prohibition of age discrimination is carefully tailored to meet the compelling societal interest in providing senior housing.

(b) Any person who resided in, occupied, or used, prior to January 1, 1990, a dwelling in a senior citizen housing development which relied on the exemption to the special design requirement provided by this section prior to January 1, 2001, shall not be deprived of the right to continue that residency, occupancy, or use as the result of the changes made to this section by the enactment of Senate Bill 1382 or Senate Bill 2011 at the 1999–2000 Regular Session of the Legislature.

(c) This section shall not apply to the County of Riverside. **Leg.H.** 1989 ch. 501, 1991 ch. 59, effective June 14, 1991, 1996 ch. 1147, 2000 ch. 1004 §4.

§51.5. Discrimination or Boycott in Business Transactions Prohibited—Parties Included.

(a) No business establishment of any kind whatsoever shall discriminate against, boycott or blacklist, or refuse to buy from, contract with, sell to, or trade with any person in this state [1] **on account of any characteristic listed or defined in subdivision (b) or (e) of Section 51,** or of the person's partners, members, stockholders, directors, officers, managers, superintendents, agents, employees, business associates, suppliers, or customers, because the person is perceived to have one or more of those characteristics, or because the person is associated with a person who has, or is perceived to have, any of those characteristics.

(b) As used in this section, "person" includes any person, firm, association, organization, partnership, business trust, corporation, limited liability company, or company.

(c) This section shall not be construed to require any construction, alteration, repair, structural or otherwise, or modification of any sort whatsoever, beyond that construction, alteration, repair, or modification that is otherwise required by other provisions of law, to any new or existing establishment, facility, building, improvement, or any other structure, nor shall this section be construed to augment, restrict, or alter in any way the authority of the State Architect to require construction, alteration, repair, or modifications that the State Architect otherwise possesses pursuant to other laws.

[2] **Leg.H.** 1976 ch. 366, 1987 ch. 159, 1992 ch. 913, 1994 ch. 1010, 1998 ch. 195, 1999 ch. 591, 2000 ch. 1049, 2005 ch. 420 (AB 1400) §4.

§51.5. **2005 Deletes.** [1] because of the race, creed, religion, color, national origin, sex, disability, or medical condition of the person [2] (d) For purposes of this section: (1) "Disability" means any mental or physical disability as defined in Section 12926 of the Government Code. (2) "Medical condition" has the same meaning as defined in subdivision (h) of Section 12926 of the Government Code.

2005 Notes: This act shall be known and may be cited as "The Civil Rights Act of 2005." Stats. 2005 ch. 420 (AB 1400) §1.

The Legislature affirms that the bases of discrimination prohibited by the Unruh Civil Rights Act include, but are not limited to, marital status and sexual orientation, as defined herein. By specifically enumerating these bases in the Unruh Civil Rights Act, the Legislature intends to clarify the existing law, rather than to change the law, as well as the principle that the bases enumerated in the act are illustrative rather than restrictive. Stats. 2005 ch. 420 (AB 1400) §2(c).

It is the intent of the Legislature that the amendments made to the Unruh Civil Rights Act by this act do not affect the California Supreme Court's rulings in *Marina Point, Ltd. v. Wolfson* (1982) 30 Cal.3d 721 and *O'Connor v. Village Green Owners Association* (1983) 33 Cal.3d 790. Stats. 2005 ch. 420 (AB 1400) §2(d).

1999 Note: The amendments made by Chapter 591 to Section 51.5 of the Civil Code do not constitute a change in, but are declaratory of existing law. Stats 1999 ch. 591 §16.

Ref.: Cal. Fms Pl. & Pr., Ch. 116, "Civil Rights: Discrimination in Business Establishments," Ch. 117A, "Civil Rights: Interference With Civil Rights by Threats, Intimidation, Coercion or Violence"; W. Cal. Pro. "Pleading" §137; MB Prac. Guide: Landlord-Tenant, Ch. 2; CACI Nos. 3021, VF-3011 (Matthew Bender).

§51.6. Gender Tax Repeal Act of 1995.

(a) This section shall be known, and may be cited, as the Gender Tax Repeal Act of 1995.

(b) No business establishment of any kind whatsoever may discriminate, with respect to the price charged for services of similar or like kind, against a person because of the person's gender.

(c) Nothing in subdivision (b) prohibits price differences based specifically upon the amount of time, difficulty, or cost of providing the services.

(d) Except as provided in subdivision (f), the remedies for a violation of this section are the remedies provided in subdivision (a) of Section 52. However, an action under this section is independent of any other remedy or procedure that may be available to an aggrieved party.

(e) This act does not alter or affect the provisions of the Health and Safety Code, the Insurance Code, or other laws that govern health care service plan or insurer underwriting or rating practices.

(f) (1) The following business establishments shall clearly and conspicuously disclose to the customer in writing the pricing for each standard service provided:

(A) Tailors or businesses providing aftermarket clothing alterations.

(B) Barbers or hair salons.

(C) Dry cleaners and laundries providing services to individuals.

(2) The price list shall be posted in an area conspicuous to customers. Posted price lists shall be in no less than 14-point boldface type and clearly and completely display pricing for every standard service offered by the business under paragraph (1).

(3) The business establishment shall provide the customer with a complete written price list upon request.

(4) The business establishment shall display in a conspicuous place at least one clearly visible sign, printed in no less than 24-point boldface type, which reads: "CALIFORNIA LAW PROHIBITS ANY BUSINESS ESTABLISHMENT FROM DISCRIMINATING, WITH RESPECT TO THE PRICE CHARGED FOR SERVICES OF SIMILAR OR LIKE KIND, AGAINST A PERSON BECAUSE OF THE PERSON'S GENDER. A COMPLETE PRICE LIST IS AVAILABLE UPON REQUEST."

(5) A business establishment that fails to correct a violation of this subdivision within 30 days of receiving written notice of the violation is liable for a civil penalty of one thousand dollars ($1,000).

(6) For the purposes of this subdivision, "standard service" means the 15 most frequently requested services provided by the business. **Leg.H.** 1995 ch. 866, 2001 ch. 312.

Ref.: CACI Nos. 3022, VF-3012 (Matthew Bender).

§51.7. Freedom From Violence.

(a) All persons within the jurisdiction of this state have the right to be free from any violence, or intimidation by threat of violence, committed against their persons or property because of [1] political affiliation, [2] **or on account of any characteristic listed or defined in subdivision (b) or (e) of Section 51**, or position in a labor dispute, or because another person perceives them to have one or more of those characteristics. The identification in this subdivision of particular bases of discrimination is illustrative rather than restrictive.

(b) This section does not apply to statements concerning positions in a labor dispute which are made during otherwise lawful labor picketing.

[3] **Leg.H.** 1976 ch. 1293, 1984 ch. 1437, 1985 ch. 497, 1987 ch. 1277, 1994 ch. 407, 2005 ch. 420 (AB 1400) §5.

§51.7. 2005 Deletes. [1] their race, color, religion, ancestry, national origin, [2] sex, sexual orientation, age, disability [3] (b) As used in this section, "sexual orientation" means heterosexuality, homosexuality, or bisexuality.

2005 Notes: This act shall be known and may be cited as "The Civil Rights Act of 2005." Stats. 2005 ch. 420 (AB 1400) §1.

The Legislature affirms that the bases of discrimination prohibited by the Unruh Civil Rights Act include, but are not limited to, marital status and sexual orientation, as defined herein. By specifically enumerating these bases in the Unruh Civil Rights Act, the Legislature intends to clarify the existing law, rather than to change the law, as well as the principle that the bases enumerated in the act are illustrative rather than restrictive. Stats. 2005 ch. 420 (AB 1400) §2(c).

It is the intent of the Legislature that the amendments made to the Unruh Civil Rights Act by this act do not affect the California Supreme Court's rulings in *Marina Point, Ltd. v. Wolfson* (1982) 30 Cal.3d 721 and *O'Connor v. Village Green Owners Association* (1983) 33 Cal.3d 790. Stats. 2005 ch. 420 (AB 1400) §2(d).

Ref.: Cal. Fms Pl. & Pr., Ch. 117A, "Civil Rights: Interference With Civil Rights by Threats, Intimidation, Coercion or Violence"; W. Cal. Pro., "Pleading" §137; W. Cal. Sum., "Constitutional Law" §775; CACI Nos. 3023, 3027, VF-3013 (Matthew Bender).

§51.8. Discrimination in Granting of Franchises Prohibited.

(a) No franchisor shall discriminate in the granting of franchises solely [1] **on account of any characteristic listed or defined in subdivision (b) or (e) of Section 51** of the franchisee and the [2] composition of a neighborhood or geographic area **reflecting any characteristic listed or defined in subdivision (b) or (e) of Section 51** in which the franchise is located. Nothing in this section shall be interpreted to prohibit a franchisor from granting a franchise to prospective franchisees as part of a program or programs to make franchises available to persons lacking the capital, training, business experience, or other qualifications ordinarily required of franchisees, or any other affirmative action program adopted by the franchisor.

(b) Nothing in this section shall be construed to require any construction, alteration, repair, structural or otherwise, or modification of any sort whatsoever, beyond that construction, alteration, repair, or modification that is otherwise required by other provisions of law, to any new or existing establishment, facility, building, improvement, or any other structure, nor shall anything in this section be construed to augment, restrict, or alter in any way the authority of the State Architect to require construction, alteration, repair, or modifications that the State Architect otherwise possesses pursuant to other laws. **Leg.H.** 1980 ch. 1303, 1987 ch. 159, 1992 ch. 913, 1998 ch. 195, 2005 ch. 420 (AB 1400) §6.

§51.8. 2005 Deletes. [1] because of the race, color, religion, sex, national origin, or disability [2] racial, ethnic, religious, national origin, or disability

2005 Notes: This act shall be known and may be cited as "The Civil Rights Act of 2005." Stats. 2005 ch. 420 (AB 1400) §1.

The Legislature affirms that the bases of discrimination prohibited by the Unruh Civil Rights Act include, but are not limited to, marital status and sexual orientation, as defined herein. By specifically enumerating these bases in the Unruh Civil Rights Act, the Legislature intends to clarify the existing law, rather than to change the law, as well as the principle that the bases enumerated in the act are illustrative rather than restrictive. Stats. 2005 ch. 420 (AB 1400) §2(c).

It is the intent of the Legislature that the amendments made to the Unruh Civil Rights Act by this act do not affect the California Supreme Court's rulings in *Marina Point, Ltd. v. Wolfson* (1982) 30 Cal.3d 721 and *O'Connor v. Village Green Owners Association* (1983) 33 Cal.3d 790. Stats. 2005 ch. 420 (AB 1400) §2(d).

Ref.: Cal. Fms Pl. & Pr., Ch. 515, "Securities and Franchise Regulation."

§51.9. Sexual Harassment—Elements of Cause of Action.

(a) A person is liable in a cause of action for sexual harassment under this section when the plaintiff proves all of the following elements:

(1) There is a business, service, or professional relationship between the plaintiff and defendant. Such a relationship may exist between a plaintiff and a person, including, but not limited to, any of the following persons:

(A) Physician, psychotherapist, or dentist. For purposes of this section, "psychotherapist" has the same meaning as set forth in paragraph (1) of subdivision (c) of Section 728 of the Business and Professions Code.

(B) Attorney, holder of a master's degree in social work, real estate agent, real estate appraiser, accountant, banker, trust officer, financial planner loan officer, collection service, building contractor, or escrow loan officer.

(C) Executor, trustee, or administrator.

(D) Landlord or property manager.

(E) Teacher.

(F) A relationship that is substantially similar to any of the above.

(2) The defendant has made sexual advances, solicitations, sexual requests, demands for sexual compliance by the plaintiff, or engaged in other verbal, visual, or physical conduct of a sexual nature or of a hostile nature based on gender, that were unwelcome and pervasive or severe.

(3) There is an inability by the plaintiff to easily terminate the relationship.

(4) The plaintiff has suffered or will suffer economic loss or disadvantage or personal injury, including, but not limited to, emotional distress or the violation of a statutory or constitutional right, as a result of the conduct described in paragraph (2).

(b) In an action pursuant to this section, damages shall be awarded as provided by subdivision (b) of Section 52.

(c) Nothing in this section shall be construed to limit application of any other remedies or rights provided under the law.

(d) The definition of sexual harassment and the standards for determining liability set forth in this section shall be limited to determining liability only with regard to a cause of action brought under this section. **Leg.H.** 1994 ch. 710, 1996 ch. 150, 1999 ch. 964.

Ref.: MB Prac. Guide: Landlord-Tenant, Ch. 2; CACI Nos. 3024, 3027, VF-3013, VF-3014 (Matthew Bender).

§51.10. Riverside County—Housing Discrimination Prohibited Based Upon Age.

(a) Section 51 shall be construed to prohibit a business establishment from discriminating in the sale or rental of housing based upon age. A business establishment may establish and preserve housing for senior citizens, pursuant to Section 51.11, except housing as to which Section 51.11 is preempted by the prohibition in the federal Fair Housing Amendments Act of 1988 (P.L. 100-430) and implementing regulations against discrimination on the basis of familial status.

(b) This section is intended to clarify the holdings in *Marina Point, Ltd. v. Wolfson* (1982) 30 Cal. 3d 721, and *O'Connor v. Village Green Owners Association* (1983) 33 Cal. 3d 790.

(c) This section shall only apply to the County of Riverside. **Leg.H.** 1996 ch. 1147, 2004 ch. 183 (AB 3082).

§51.11. Riverside County—Establishing and Preserving Accessible Housing for Senior Citizens.

(a) The Legislature finds and declares that this section is essential to establish and preserve housing for senior citizens. There are senior citizens who need special living environments, and find that there is an inadequate supply of this type of housing in the state.

(b) For the purposes of this section, the following definitions apply:

(1) "Qualifying resident" or "senior citizen" means a person 62 years of age or older, or 55 years of age or older in a senior citizen housing development.

(2) "Qualified permanent resident" means a person who meets both of the following requirements:

(A) Was residing with the qualifying resident or senior citizen prior to the death, hospitalization, or other prolonged absence of, or the dissolution of marriage with, the qualifying resident or senior citizen.

(B) Was 45 years of age or older, or was a spouse, cohabitant, or person providing primary physical or economic support to the qualifying resident or senior citizen.

(3) "Qualified permanent resident" also means a disabled person or person with a disabling illness or injury who is a child or grandchild of the senior citizen or a qualified permanent resident as defined in paragraph (2) who needs to live with the senior citizen or qualified permanent resident because of the disabling condition, illness, or injury. For purposes of this section, "disabled" means a person who has a disability as defined in subdivision (b) of Section 54. A "disabling injury or illness" means an illness or injury which results in a condition meeting the definition of disability set forth in subdivision (b) of Section 54.

(A) For any person who is a qualified permanent resident under paragraph (3) whose disabling condition ends, the owner, board of directors, or other governing body may require the formerly disabled resident to cease residing in the development upon receipt of six months' written notice; provided, however, that the owner, board of directors, or other governing body may allow the person to remain a resident for up to one year, after the disabling condition ends.

(B) The owner, board of directors, or other governing body of the senior citizen housing development may take action to prohibit or terminate occupancy by a person who is a qualified permanent resident under paragraph (3) if the owner, board of directors, or other governing body finds, based on credible and objective evidence, that the person is likely to pose a significant threat to the health or safety of others that cannot be ameliorated by means of a reasonable accommodation; provided, however, that action to prohibit or terminate the occupancy may be taken only after doing both of the following:

(i) Providing reasonable notice to and an opportunity to be heard for the disabled person whose occupancy is being challenged, and reasonable notice to the coresident parent or grandparent of that person.

(ii) Giving due consideration to the relevant, credible, and objective information provided in that hearing. The evidence shall be taken and held in a confidential manner, pursuant to a closed session, by the owner, board of directors, or other governing body in order to preserve the privacy of the affected persons.

The affected persons shall be entitled to have present at the hearing an attorney or any other person authorized by them to speak on their behalf or to assist them in the matter.

(4) "Senior citizen housing development" means a residential development developed with more than 20 units as a senior community by its developer and zoned as a senior community by a local governmental entity, or characterized as a senior community in its governing documents, as these are defined in Section 1351, or qualified as a senior community under the federal Fair Housing Amendments Act of 1988, as amended. Any senior citizen housing development which is required to obtain a public report under Section 11010 of the Business and Professions Code and which submits its application for a public report after July 1, 2001, shall be required to have been issued a public report as a senior citizen housing development under Section 11010.05 of the Business and Professions Code.

(5) "Dwelling unit" or "housing" means any residential accommodation other than a mobilehome.

(6) "Cohabitant" refers to persons who live together as husband and wife, or persons who are domestic partners within the meaning of Section 297 of the Family Code.

(7) "Permitted health care resident" means a person hired to provide live-in, long-term, or terminal health care to a qualifying resident, or a family member of the qualifying resident providing that care. For the purposes of this section, the care provided by a permitted health care resident must be substantial in nature and must provide either assistance with necessary daily activities or medical treatment, or both.

A permitted health care resident shall be entitled to continue his or her occupancy, residency, or use of the dwelling unit as a permitted resident in the absence of the senior citizen from the dwelling unit only if both of the following are applicable:

(A) The senior citizen became absent from the dwelling due to hospitalization or other necessary medical treatment and expects to return to his or her residence within 90 days from the date the absence began.

(B) The absent senior citizen or an authorized person acting for the senior citizen submits a written request to the owner, board of directors, or governing board stating that the senior citizen desires that the permitted health care resident be allowed to remain in order to be present when the senior citizen returns to reside in the development.

Upon written request by the senior citizen or an authorized person acting for the senior citizen, the owner, board of directors, or governing board shall have the discretion to allow a permitted health care resident to remain for a time period longer than 90 days from the date that the senior citizen's absence began, if it appears that the senior citizen will return within a period of time not to exceed an additional 90 days.

(c) The covenants, conditions, and restrictions and other documents or written policy shall set forth the limitations on occupancy, residency, or use on the basis of age. Any such limitation shall not be more exclusive than to require that one person in residence in each dwelling unit may be required to be a senior citizen and that each other resident in the same dwelling unit may be required to be a qualified permanent resident, a permitted health care resident, or a person under 55 years of age whose occupancy is permitted under subdivision (g) of this section or subdivision (b) of Section 51.12. That limitation may be less exclusive, but shall at least require that the persons commencing any occupancy of a dwelling unit include a senior citizen who intends to reside in the unit as his or her primary residence on a permanent basis. The application of the rules set forth in this subdivision regarding limitations on occupancy may result in less than all of the dwellings being actually occupied by a senior citizen.

(d) The covenants, conditions, and restrictions or other documents or written policy shall permit temporary residency, as a guest of a senior citizen or qualified permanent resident, by a person of less than 55 years of age for periods of time, not more than 60 days in any year, that are specified in the covenants, conditions, and restrictions or other documents or written policy.

(e) Upon the death or dissolution of marriage, or upon hospitalization, or other prolonged absence of the qualifying resident, any qualified permanent resident shall be entitled to continue his or her occupancy, residency, or use of the dwelling unit as a permitted resident. This subdivision shall not apply to a permitted health care resident.

(f) The covenants, conditions, and restrictions or other documents or written policies applicable to any condominium, stock cooperative, limited-equity housing cooperative, planned development, or multiple-family residential property that contained age restrictions on January 1, 1984, shall be enforceable only to the extent permitted by this section, notwithstanding lower age restrictions contained in those documents or policies.

(g) Any person who has the right to reside in, occupy, or use the housing or an unimproved lot subject to this section on or after January 1, 1985, shall not be deprived of the right to continue that residency, occupancy, or use as the result of the enactment of this section by Chapter 1147 of the Statutes of 1996.

(h) A housing development may qualify as a senior citizen housing development under this section even though, as of January 1, 1997, it does not meet the definition of a senior citizen housing development specified in subdivision (b), if the development complies with that definition for every unit that becomes occupied after January 1, 1997, and if the development was once within that definition, and then became noncompliant with the definition as the result of any one of the following:

(1) The development was ordered by a court or a local, state, or federal enforcement agency to allow persons other than qualifying residents, qualified permanent residents, or permitted health care residents to reside in the development.

(2) The development received a notice of a pending or proposed action in, or by, a court, or a local, state, or federal enforcement agency, which action could have resulted in the development being ordered by a court or a state or federal enforcement agency to allow persons other than qualifying residents, qualified permanent residents, or permitted health care residents to reside in the development.

(3) The development agreed to allow persons other than qualifying residents, qualified permanent residents, or permitted health care residents to reside in the development by entering into a stipulation, conciliation agreement, or settlement agreement with a local, state, or federal enforcement agency or with a private party who had filed, or indicated an intent to file, a complaint against the development with a local, state, or federal enforcement agency, or file an action in a court.

(4) The development allowed persons other than qualifying residents, qualified permanent residents, or permitted health care residents to reside in the development on the advice of counsel in order to prevent the possibility of an action being filed by a private party or by a local, state, or federal enforcement agency.

(i) The covenants, conditions, and restrictions or other documents or written policy of the senior citizen housing development shall permit the occupancy of a dwelling unit by a permitted health care resident during any period that the person is actually providing live-in, long-term, or hospice health care to a qualifying resident for compensation.

(j) This section shall only apply to the County of Riverside. **Leg.H.** 1996 ch. 1147, 1999 ch. 324, 2000 ch. 1004 §5.

Ref.: Cal. Fms Pl. & Pr., Ch. 117, "Civil Rights: Housing Discrimination."

§51.12. Riverside County—Continuing Occupancy of Certain Exempt Housing.

(a) The Legislature finds and declares that the requirements for senior housing under Sections 51.10 and 51.11 are more stringent than the requirements for that housing under the federal Fair Housing Amendments Act of 1988 (Public Law 100-430).

(b) Any person who resided in, occupied, or used, prior to January 1, 1990, a dwelling in a senior citizen housing development which relied on the exemption to the special design requirement provided by Section 51.4 as that section read prior to January 1, 2001, shall not be deprived of the right to continue that residency, or occupancy, or use as the result of the changes made to this section by the enactment of Senate Bill 1382 or Senate Bill 2011 at the 1999–2000 Regular Session of the Legislature.

(c) This section shall only apply to the County of Riverside. **Leg.H.** 1996 ch. 1147, 2000 ch. 1004.

§52. Penalty for Discrimination.

(a) Whoever denies, aids or incites a denial, or makes any discrimination or distinction contrary to Section 51, 51.5, or 51.6, is liable for each and every offense for the actual damages, and any amount that may be determined by a jury, or a court sitting without a jury, up to a maximum of three times the amount of actual damage but in no case less than four thousand dollars ($4,000), and any attorney's fees that may be determined by the court in addition thereto, suffered by any person denied the rights provided in Section 51, 51.5, or 51.6.

(b) Whoever denies the right provided by Section 51.7 or 51.9, or aids, incites, or conspires in that denial, is liable for each and every offense for the actual damages suffered by any person denied that right and, in addition, the following:

(1) An amount to be determined by a jury, or a court sitting without a jury, for exemplary damages.

(2) A civil penalty of twenty-five thousand dollars ($25,000) to be awarded to the person denied the right provided by Section 51.7 in any action brought by the person denied the right, or by the Attorney General, a district attorney, or a city attorney. **An action for that penalty brought pursuant to Section 51.7 shall be commenced within three years of the alleged practice.**

(3) Attorney's fees as may be determined by the court.

(c) Whenever there is reasonable cause to believe that any person or group of persons is engaged in conduct of resistance to the full enjoyment of any of the rights described in this section, and that conduct is of that nature and is intended to deny the full exercise of those rights, the Attorney General, any district attorney or city attorney, or any person aggrieved by the conduct may bring a civil action in the appropriate court by filing with it a complaint. The complaint shall contain the following:

(1) The signature of the officer, or, in his or her absence, the individual acting on behalf of the officer, or the signature of the person aggrieved.

(2) The facts pertaining to the conduct.

(3) A request for preventive relief, including an application for a permanent or temporary injunction, restraining order, or other order against the person or persons responsible for the conduct, as the complainant deems necessary to ensure the full enjoyment of the rights described in this section.

(d) Whenever an action has been commenced in any court seeking relief from the denial of equal protection of the laws under the Fourteenth Amendment to the Constitution of the United States on account of race, color, religion, sex, national origin, or disability, the Attorney General or any district attorney or city attorney for or in the name of the people of the State of California may intervene in the action upon timely application if the Attorney General or any district attorney or city attorney certifies that the case is of general public importance. In that action, the people of the State of California shall be entitled to the same relief as if it had instituted the action.

(e) Actions brought pursuant to this section are independent of any other actions, remedies, or procedures that may be available to an aggrieved party pursuant to any other law.

(f) Any person claiming to be aggrieved by an alleged unlawful practice in violation of Section 51 or 51.7 may also file a verified complaint with the Department of Fair Employment and Housing pursuant to Section 12948 of the Government Code.

(g) This section does not require any construction, alteration, repair, structural or otherwise, or modification of any sort whatsoever, beyond that construction, alteration, repair, or modification that is otherwise required by other provisions of law, to any new or existing establishment, facility, building, improvement, or any other structure, nor does this section augment, restrict, or alter in any way the authority of the State Architect to require construction, alteration, repair, or modifications that the State Architect otherwise possesses pursuant to other laws.

(h) For the purposes of this section, "actual damages" means special and general damages. This subdivision is declaratory of existing law. **Leg.H.** 1905 p. 553, 1919 p. 309, 1923 ch. 235, 1959 ch. 1866, 1974 ch. 1193, 1976 chs. 366, 1293, 1978 ch. 1212, 1981 ch. 521, effective September 16, 1981, 1986 ch. 244, 1987 ch. 159, 1989 ch. 459, 1991 chs. 607, 839 §2, 1992 ch. 913, 1994 ch. 535, 1998 ch. 195, 1999 ch. 964, 2000 ch. 98, 2001 ch. 261, 2005 ch. 123 (AB 378) §1.

1991 Note: It is the intent of the Legislature to modify the prerequisite for injunctive relief under Section 52 of the Civil Code. By providing a civil remedy for the classes of persons specifically identified in Sections 51, 51.7, and 52 of the Civil Code, the Legislature does not intend to limit the availability of this remedy for any other form of discrimination which is prohibited by these sections. Stats. 1991 ch. 839 §3.

Ref.: Cal. Fms Pl. & Pr., Ch. 116, "Civil Rights: Discrimination in Business Establishments," Ch. 117A, "Civil Rights: Interference With Civil Rights by Threats, Intimidation, Coercion or Violence"; W. Cal. Pro., "Pleading" §137; W. Cal. Sum., "Constitutional Law" §755; CACI Nos. 3020, 3021, 3023, 3025–3027, VF-3010 (Matthew Bender).

§52.1. Interference With Exercise of Civil Rights—Remedies.

(a) If a person or persons, whether or not acting under color of law, interferes by threats, intimidation, or coercion, or attempts to interfere by threats, intimidation, or coercion, with the exercise or enjoyment by any individual or individuals of rights secured by the Constitution or laws of the United States, or of the rights secured by the Constitution or laws of this state, the Attorney General, or any district attorney or city attorney may bring a civil action for injunctive and other appropriate equitable relief in the name of the people of the State of California, in order to protect the peaceable exercise or enjoyment of the right or rights secured. An action brought by the Attorney General, any district attorney, or any city attorney may also seek a civil penalty of twenty-five thousand dollars ($25,000). If this civil penalty is requested, it shall be assessed individually against each person who is determined to have violated this section and the penalty shall be awarded to each individual whose rights under this section are determined to have been violated.

(b) Any individual whose exercise or enjoyment of rights secured by the Constitution or laws of the United States, or of rights secured by the Constitution or laws of this state, has been interfered with, or attempted to be interfered with, as described in subdivision (a), may institute and prosecute in his or her own name and on his or her own behalf a civil action for damages, including, but not limited to, damages under Section 52, injunctive relief, and other appropriate equitable relief to protect the peaceable exercise or enjoyment of the right or rights secured.

(c) An action brought pursuant to subdivision (a) or (b) may be filed either in the superior court for the county in which the conduct complained of occurred or in the superior court for the county in which a person whose conduct complained of resides or has his or her place of business. An action brought by the Attorney General pursuant to subdivision (a) also may be filed in the superior court for any county wherein the Attorney General has an office, and in that case, the jurisdiction of the court shall extend throughout the state.

(d) If a court issues a temporary restraining order or a preliminary or permanent injunction in an action brought pursuant to subdivision (a) or (b), ordering a defendant to refrain from conduct or activities, the order issued shall include the following statement: VIOLATION OF THIS ORDER IS A CRIME PUNISHABLE UNDER SECTION 422.77 OF THE PENAL CODE.

(e) The court shall order the plaintiff or the attorney for the plaintiff to deliver, or the clerk of the court to mail, two copies of any order, extension, modification, or termination thereof granted pursuant to this section, by the close of the business day on which the order, extension, modification, or termination was granted, to each local law enforcement agency having jurisdiction over the residence of the plaintiff and any other locations where the court determines that acts of violence against the plaintiff are likely to occur. Those local law enforcement agencies shall be designated by the plaintiff or the attorney for the plaintiff. Each appropriate law enforcement agency receiving any order, extension, or modification of any order issued pursuant to this section shall serve forthwith one copy thereof upon the defendant. Each appropriate law enforcement agency shall provide to any law enforcement officer responding to the scene of reported violence, information as to the existence of, terms, and current status of, any order issued pursuant to this section.

(f) A court shall not have jurisdiction to issue an order or injunction under this section, if that order or injunction would be prohibited under Section 527.3 of the Code of Civil Procedure.

(g) An action brought pursuant to this section is independent of any other action, remedy, or procedure that may be available to an aggrieved individual under any other provision of law, including, but not limited to, an action, remedy, or procedure brought pursuant to Section 51.7.

(h) In addition to any damages, injunction, or other equitable relief awarded in an action brought pursuant to subdivision (b), the court may award the petitioner or plaintiff reasonable attorney's fees.

(i) A violation of an order described in subdivision (d) may be punished either by prosecution under Section 422.77 of the Penal Code, or by a proceeding for contempt brought pursuant to Title 5 (commencing with Section 1209) of Part 3 of the Code of Civil Procedure. However, in any proceeding pursuant to the Code of Civil Procedure, if it is determined that the person proceeded against is guilty of the contempt charged, in addition to any other relief, a fine may be imposed not exceeding one thousand dollars ($1,000), or the person may be ordered imprisoned in a county jail not exceeding six months, or the court may order both the imprisonment and fine.

(j) Speech alone is not sufficient to support an action brought pursuant to subdivision (a) or (b), except upon a showing that the speech itself threatens violence against a specific person or group of persons; and the person or group of persons against whom the threat is directed reasonably fears that, because of the speech, violence will be committed against them or their property and that the person threatening violence had the apparent ability to carry out the threat.

(k) No order issued in any proceeding brought pursuant to subdivision (a) or (b) shall restrict the content of any person's speech. An order restricting the time, place, or manner of any person's speech shall do so only to the extent reasonably necessary to protect the peaceable exercise or enjoyment of constitutional or statutory rights, consistent with the constitutional rights of the person sought to be enjoined. **Leg.H.** 1987 ch. 1277, 1990 ch. 392, 1991 ch. 607, 2000 ch. 98, 2001 ch. 261, 2002 ch. 784 (SB 1316), 2004 ch. 700 (SB 1234).

2000 Note: (a) The Legislature hereby finds and declares all of the following:

(1) Section 52.1 of the Civil Code guarantees the exercise or enjoyment by any individual or individuals of rights secured by the Constitution or laws of the United States, or of the rights secured by the Constitution or laws of this state without regard to his or her membership in a protected class identified by its race, color, religion, or sex, among other things.

(2) The decision in *Boccato v. City of Hermosa Beach* (1994) 29 Cal.App.4th 1797 misconstrued Section 52.1 of the Civil Code to require that an individual who brings an action, or on whose behalf an action is brought, pursuant to that section, be a member of one of those specified protected classes.

(b) It is the intent of the Legislature in enacting this act to clarify that an action brought pursuant to Section 52.1 of the Civil Code does not require the individual whose rights are secured by the Constitution or laws of the United States, or of the rights secured by the Constitution or laws of California to be a member of a protected class identified by its race, color, religion, or sex, among other things. Stats. 2000 ch. 98 §1.

Ref.: Cal. Fms Pl. & Pr., Ch. 117A, "Civil Rights: Interference With Civil Rights by Threats, Intimidation, Coercion or Violence"; W. Cal. Sum., "Constitutional Law" §775; CACI Nos. 3025, VF-3015 (Matthew Bender).

§52.2. Court of Competent Jurisdiction for Certain Actions.

An action pursuant to Section 52 or 54.3 may be brought in any court of competent jurisdiction. A "court of competent jurisdiction" shall include small claims court if the amount of the damages sought in the action does not exceed five thousand dollars ($5,000). **Leg.H.** 1998 ch. 195.

Ref.: Rutter Civ. P. Before Trial, 3:42.

§52.3. Law Enforcement Officers Shall Not Deprive Individuals of Constitutionally Protected Rights, Privileges, or Immunities.

(a) No governmental authority, or agent of a governmental authority, or person acting on behalf of a governmental authority, shall engage in a pattern or practice of conduct by law enforcement officers that deprives any person of rights, privileges, or immunities secured or protected by the Constitution or laws of the United States or by the Constitution or laws of California.

(b) The Attorney General may bring a civil action in the name of the people to obtain appropriate equitable and declaratory relief to eliminate the pattern or practice of conduct specified in subdivision (a), whenever the Attorney General has reasonable cause to believe that a violation of subdivision (a) has occurred. **Leg.H.** 2000 ch. 622.

Ref.: Cal. Fms Pl. & Pr., Ch. 113, "Civil Rights: The Post-Civil War Civil Rights Statutes."

§52.4. Action for Damages Against Party Responsible for Gender Violence.

(a) Any person who has been subjected to gender violence may bring a civil action for damages against any responsible party. The plaintiff may seek actual damages, compensatory damages, punitive damages, injunctive relief, any combination of those, or any other appropriate relief. A prevailing plaintiff may also be awarded attorney's fees and costs.

(b) An action brought pursuant to this section shall be commenced within three years of the act, or if the victim was a minor when the act occurred, within eight years after the date the plaintiff attains the age of majority or within three years after the date the plaintiff discovers or reasonably should have discovered the psychological injury or illness occurring after the age of majority that was caused by the act, whichever date occurs later.

(c) For purposes of this section, "gender violence," is a form of sex discrimination and means any of the following:

(1) One or more acts that would constitute a criminal offense under state law that has as an element the use, attempted use, or threatened use of physical force against the person or property of another, committed at least in part based on the gender of the victim, whether or not those acts have resulted in criminal complaints, charges, prosecution, or conviction.

(2) A physical intrusion or physical invasion of a sexual nature under coercive conditions, whether or not those acts have resulted in criminal complaints, charges, prosecution, or conviction.

(d) Notwithstanding any other laws that may establish the liability of an employer for the acts of an employee, this section does not establish any civil liability of a person because of his or her status as an employer, unless the employer personally committed an act of gender violence. **Leg.H.** 2002 ch. 842 (AB 1928).

§52.5. Action by Victim of Human Trafficking.

(a) A victim of human trafficking, as defined in Section 236.1 of the Penal Code, may bring a civil action for actual damages, compensatory damages, punitive damages, injunctive relief, any combination of those, or any other appropriate relief. A prevailing plaintiff may also be awarded attorney's fees and costs.

(b) In addition to the remedies specified herein, in any action under subdivision (a), the plaintiff may be awarded up to three times his or her actual damages or ten thousand dollars ($10,000), whichever is greater. In addition, punitive damages may also be awarded upon proof of the defendant's malice, oppression, fraud, or duress in committing the act of human trafficking.

(c) An action brought pursuant to this section shall be commenced within five years of the date on which the trafficking victim was freed from the trafficking situation, or if the victim was a minor when the act of human trafficking against the victim occurred, within eight years after the date the plaintiff attains the age of majority.

(d) If a person entitled to sue is under a disability at the time the cause of action accrues, so that it is impossible or impracticable for him or her to bring an action, then the time of the disability is not part of the time limited for the commencement of the action. Disability will toll the running of the statute of limitation for this action.

(1) Disability includes being a minor, insanity, imprisonment, or other incapacity or incompetence.

(2) The statute of limitations shall not run against an incompetent or minor plaintiff simply because a guardian ad litem has been appointed. A guardian ad litem's failure to bring a plaintiff's action within the applicable limitation period will not prejudice the plaintiff's right to do so after his or her disability ceases.

(3) A defendant is estopped to assert a defense of the statute of limitations when the expiration of the statute is due to conduct by the defendant inducing the plaintiff to delay the filing of the action, or due to threats made by the defendant causing duress upon the plaintiff.

(4) The suspension of the statute of limitations due to disability, lack of knowledge, or estoppel applies to all other related claims arising out of the trafficking situation.

(5) The running of the statute of limitations is postponed during the pendency of any criminal proceedings against the victim.

(e) The running of the statute of limitations may be suspended where a person entitled to sue could not have reasonably discovered the cause of action due to circumstances resulting from the trafficking situation, such as psychological trauma, cultural and linguistic isolation, and the inability to access services.

(f) A prevailing plaintiff may also be awarded reasonable attorney's fees and litigation costs including, but not limited to, expert witness fees and expenses as part of the costs.

(g) Any restitution paid by the defendant to the victim shall be credited against any judgment, award, or settlement obtained pursuant to this section. Any judgment, award, or settlement obtained pursuant to an action under this section shall be subject to the provisions of Section 13963 of the Government Code.

(h) Any civil action filed under this section shall be stayed during the pendency of any criminal action arising out of the same occurrence in which the claimant is the victim. As used in this section, a "criminal action"
includes investigation and prosecution, and is pending until a final adjudication in the trial court, or dismissal. **Leg.H.** 2005 ch. 240 (AB 22) §2.

2005 Note: Nothing in this act shall be construed as prohibiting or precluding prosecution under any other provision of law or to prevent punishment pursuant to any other provision of law that imposes a greater or more severe punishment than provided for in this act. Stats. 2005 ch. 240 (AB 22) §13.

§53. Discriminatory Restrictions on Ownership or Use of Real Property Void.

(a) Every provision in a written instrument relating to real property [1] **that** purports to forbid or restrict the conveyance, encumbrance, leasing, or mortgaging of that real property to any person [2] **because of any characteristic listed or defined in subdivision (b) or (e) of Section 51** is void, and every restriction or prohibition as to the use or occupation of real property because of [3] **any characteristic listed or defined in subdivision (b) or (e) of Section 51** is void.

(b) Every restriction or prohibition, whether by way of covenant, condition upon use or occupation, or upon transfer of title to real property, which restriction or prohibition directly or indirectly limits the acquisition, use or occupation of that property because of [4] **any characteristic listed or defined in subdivision (b) or (e) of Section 51** is void.

(c) In any action to declare that a restriction or prohibition specified in subdivision (a) or (b) is void, the court shall take judicial notice of the recorded instrument or instruments containing the prohibitions or restrictions in the same manner that it takes judicial notice of the matters listed in Section 452 of the Evidence Code. **Leg.H.** 1961 ch. 1877, 1965 ch. 299, operative January 1, 1967, 1974 ch. 1193, 1987 ch. 159, 1992 ch. 913, 2005 ch. 420 (AB 1400) §7.

§53. 2005 Deletes. [1] which [2] of a specified sex, race, color, religion, ancestry, national origin, or disability, [3] the user's or occupier's sex, race, color, religion, ancestry, national origin, or disability [4] the acquirer's, user's, or occupier's sex, race, color, religion, ancestry, national origin, or disability

2005 Notes: This act shall be known and may be cited as "The Civil Rights Act of 2005." Stats. 2005 ch. 420 (AB 1400) §1.

The Legislature affirms that the bases of discrimination prohibited by the Unruh Civil Rights Act include, but are not limited to, marital status and sexual orientation, as defined herein. By specifically enumerating these bases in the Unruh Civil Rights Act, the Legislature intends to clarify the existing law, rather than to change the law, as well as the principle that the bases enumerated in the act are illustrative rather than restrictive. Stats. 2005 ch. 420 (AB 1400) §2(c).

It is the intent of the Legislature that the amendments made to the Unruh Civil Rights Act by this act do not affect the California Supreme Court's rulings in *Marina Point, Ltd. v. Wolfson* (1982) 30 Cal.3d 721 and *O'Connor v. Village Green Owners Association* (1983) 33 Cal.3d 790. Stats. 2005 ch. 420 (AB 1400) §2(d).

Ref.: Cal. Fms Pl. & Pr., Ch. 116, "Civil Rights: Discrimination in Business Establishments," Ch. 117, "Civil Rights: Housing Discrimination," Ch. 184, "Deeds."

PART 2.5
Blind and Other Physically Disabled Persons

Equal rights to public facilities. §54.
Right to full and equal access to public facilities. §54.1.
Guide dog, signal dog, or service dog permitted. §54.2.
Denial or interference with admittance—Punishment. §54.3.
As pedestrian failure to carry white cane or use guide dog not negligence. §54.4.
White Cane Safety Day. §54.5.
"Visually impaired" defined. §54.6.
Guide dogs, signal dogs, or service dogs in zoos or wild animal parks. §54.7.
Assistive listening or computer-aided transcription systems in court proceedings. §54.8.
Injunction by aggrieved person. §55.
Injunction by public officials. §55.1.
Actions requiring copy of petition and brief to be served on State Solicitor General. §55.2.

§54. Equal Rights to Public Facilities.

(a) Individuals with disabilities or medical conditions have the same right as the general public to the full and free use of the streets, highways, sidewalks, walkways, public buildings, medical facilities, including hospitals, clinics, and physicians' offices, public facilities, and other public places.

(b) For purposes of this section:

(1) "Disability" means any mental or physical disability as defined in Section 12926 of the Government Code.

(2) "Medical condition" has the same meaning as defined in subdivision (h) of Section 12926 of the Government Code.

(c) A violation of the right of an individual under the Americans with Disabilities Act of 1990 (Public Law 101-336) also constitutes a violation of this section. **Leg.H.** 1968 ch. 461, 1992 ch. 913, 1994 ch. 1257, 1996 ch. 498, 2000 ch. 1049.

Ref.: Cal. Fms Pl. & Pr., Ch. 116, "Civil Rights: Discrimination in Business Establishments," Ch. 117, "Civil Rights: Housing Discrimination"; W. Cal. Sum., "Constitutional Law" §773.

§54.1. Right to Full and Equal Access to Public Facilities.

(a) (1) Individuals with disabilities shall be entitled to full and equal access, as other members of the general public, to accommodations, advantages, facilities, medical facilities, including hospitals, clinics, and physicians' offices, and privileges of all common carriers, airplanes, motor vehicles, railroad trains, motorbuses, streetcars, boats, or any other public conveyances or modes of transportation (whether private, public, franchised, licensed, contracted, or otherwise provided), telephone facilities, adoption agencies, private schools, hotels, lodging places, places of public accommodation, amusement, or resort, and other places to which the general public is invited, subject only to the conditions and limitations established by law, or state or federal regulation, and applicable alike to all persons.

(2) As used in this section, "telephone facilities" means tariff items and other equipment and services that have been approved by the Public Utilities Commission to be used by individuals with disabilities in a manner feasible and compatible with the existing telephone network provided by the telephone companies.

(3) "Full and equal access," for purposes of this section in its application to transportation, means access that meets the standards of Titles II and III of the Americans with Disabilities Act of 1990 (Public Law 101-336) and federal regulations adopted pursuant thereto, except that, if the laws of this state prescribe higher standards, it shall mean access that meets those higher standards.

(b) (1) Individuals with disabilities shall be entitled to full and equal access, as other members of the general public, to all housing accommodations offered for rent, lease, or compensation in this state, subject to the conditions and limitations established by law, or state or federal regulation, and applicable alike to all persons.

(2) "Housing accommodations" means any real property, or portion thereof, that is used or occupied, or is intended, arranged, or designed to be used or occupied, as the home, residence, or sleeping place of one or more human beings, but shall not include any accommodations included within subdivision (a) or any single-family residence the occupants of which rent, lease, or furnish for compensation not more than one room therein.

(3) (A) Any person renting, leasing, or otherwise providing real property for compensation shall not refuse to permit an individual with a disability, at that person's expense, to make reasonable modifications of the existing rented premises if the modifications are necessary to afford the person full enjoyment of the premises. However, any modifications under this paragraph may be conditioned on the disabled tenant entering into an agreement to restore the interior of the premises to the condition existing prior to the modifications. No additional security may be required on account of an election to make modifications to the rented premises under this paragraph, but the lessor and tenant may negotiate, as part of the agreement to restore the premises, a provision requiring the disabled tenant to pay an amount into an escrow account, not to exceed a reasonable estimate of the cost of restoring the premises.

(B) Any person renting, leasing, or otherwise providing real property for compensation shall not refuse to make reasonable accommodations in rules, policies, practices, or services, when those accommodations may be necessary to afford individuals with a disability equal opportunity to use and enjoy the premises.

(4) Nothing in this subdivision shall require any person renting, leasing, or providing for compensation real property to modify his or her property in any way or provide a higher degree of care for an individual with a disability than for an individual who is not disabled.

(5) Except as provided in paragraph (6), nothing in this part shall require any person renting, leasing, or providing for compensation real property, if that person refuses to accept tenants who have dogs, to accept as a tenant an individual with a disability who has a dog.

(6) (A) It shall be deemed a denial of equal access to housing accommodations within the meaning of this subdivision for any person, firm, or corporation to refuse

to lease or rent housing accommodations to an individual who is blind or visually impaired on the basis that the individual uses the services of a guide dog, an individual who is deaf or hearing impaired on the basis that the individual uses the services of a signal dog, or to an individual with any other disability on the basis that the individual uses the services of a service dog, or to refuse to permit such an individual who is blind or visually impaired to keep a guide dog, an individual who is deaf or hearing impaired to keep a signal dog, or an individual with any other disability to keep a service dog on the premises.

(B) Except in the normal performance of duty as a mobility or signal aid, nothing contained in this paragraph shall be construed to prevent the owner of a housing accommodation from establishing terms in a lease or rental agreement that reasonably regulate the presence of guide dogs, signal dogs, or service dogs on the premises of a housing accommodation, nor shall this paragraph be construed to relieve a tenant from any liability otherwise imposed by law for real and personal property damages caused by such a dog when proof of the same exists.

(C) (i) As used in this subdivision, "guide dog" means any guide dog that was trained by a person licensed under Chapter 9.5 (commencing with Section 7200) of Division 3 of the Business and Professions Code or as defined in the regulations implementing Title III of the Americans with Disabilities Act of 1990 (Public Law 101-336).

(ii) As used in this subdivision, "signal dog" means any dog trained to alert an individual who is deaf or hearing impaired to intruders or sounds.

(iii) As used in this subdivision, "service dog" means any dog individually trained to the requirements of the individual with a disability, including, but not limited to, minimal protection work, rescue work, pulling a wheelchair, or fetching dropped items.

(7) It shall be deemed a denial of equal access to housing accommodations within the meaning of this subdivision for any person, firm, or corporation to refuse to lease or rent housing accommodations to an individual who is blind or visually impaired, an individual who is deaf or hearing impaired, or other individual with a disability on the basis that the individual with a disability is partially or wholly dependent upon the income of his or her spouse, if the spouse is a party to the lease or rental agreement. Nothing in this subdivision, however, shall prohibit a lessor or landlord from considering the aggregate financial status of an individual with a disability and his or her spouse.

(c) Visually impaired or blind persons and persons licensed to train guide dogs for individuals who are visually impaired or blind pursuant to Chapter 9.5 (commencing with Section 7200) of Division 3 of the Business and Professions Code or guide dogs as defined in the regulations implementing Title III of the Americans with Disabilities Act of 1990 (Public Law 101-336), and persons who are deaf or hearing impaired and persons authorized to train signal dogs for individuals who are deaf or hearing impaired, and other individuals with a disability and persons authorized to train service dogs for individuals with a disability, may take dogs, for the purpose of training them as guide dogs, signal dogs, or service dogs in any of the places specified in subdivisions (a) and (b). These persons shall ensure that the dog is on a leash and tagged as a guide dog, signal dog, or service dog by identification tag issued by the county clerk, animal control department, or other agency, as authorized by Chapter 3.5 (commencing with Section 30850) of Division 14 of the Food and Agricultural Code. In addition, the person shall be liable for any provable damage done to the premises or facilities by his or her dog.

(d) A violation of the right of an individual under the Americans with Disabilities Act of 1990 (Public Law 101-336) also constitutes a violation of this section, and nothing in this section shall be construed to limit the access of any person in violation of that act.

(e) Nothing in this section shall preclude the requirement of the showing of a license plate or disabled placard when required by enforcement units enforcing disabled persons parking violations pursuant to Sections 22507.8 and 22511.8 of the Vehicle Code. **Leg.H.** 1968 ch. 461, 1969 ch. 832, 1972 ch. 819, 1974 ch. 108, 1976 chs. 971, 972 §1.5, 1977 ch. 700, 1978 ch. 380, 1979 ch. 293, 1980 ch. 773, 1988 ch. 1595 §2, 1992 ch. 913, 1993 chs. 1149, 1214 §1.5, 1994 ch. 1257, 1996 ch. 498.

Ref.: Cal. Fms Pl. & Pr., Ch. 116, "Civil Rights: Discrimination in Business Establishments," Ch. 117, "Civil Rights: Housing Discrimination"; W. Cal. Sum., "Constitutional Law" §773; MB Prac. Guide: Landlord-Tenant, Ch. 2.

§54.2. Guide Dog, Signal Dog, or Service Dog Permitted.

(a) Every individual with a disability has the right to be accompanied by a guide dog, signal dog, or service dog, especially trained for the purpose, in any of the places specified in Section 54.1 without being required to pay an extra charge or security deposit for the guide dog, signal dog, or service dog. However, the individual shall be liable for any damage done to the premises or facilities by his or her dog.

(b) Individuals who are blind or otherwise visually impaired and persons licensed to train guide dogs for individuals who are blind or visually impaired pursuant to Chapter 9.5 (commencing with Section 7200) of Division 3 of the Business and Professions Code or as defined in regulations implementing Title III of the Americans with Disabilities Act of 1990 (Public Law 101-336), and individuals who are deaf or hearing impaired and persons authorized to train signal dogs for individuals who are deaf or hearing impaired, and individuals with a disability and persons who are authorized to train service dogs for the individuals with a disability may take dogs, for the purpose of training them as guide dogs, signal dogs, or service dogs in any of the places specified in Section 54.1 without being required to pay an extra charge or security deposit for the guide dog, signal dog, or service dog. However, the person shall be liable for any damage done to the premises or facilities by his or her dog. These persons shall ensure the dog is on a leash and tagged as a guide dog, signal dog, or service dog by an identification tag issued by the county clerk, animal control department, or other agency, as authorized by Chapter 3.5 (commencing with Section 30850) of Title 14 of the Food and Agricultural Code.

A violation of the right of an individual under the Americans with Disabilities Act of 1990 (Public Law 101-

336) also constitutes a violation of this section, and nothing in this section shall be construed to limit the access of any person in violation of that act.

(c) As used in this section, the terms "guide dog," "signal dog," and "service dog" have the same meanings as specified in Section 54.1.

(d) Nothing in this section precludes the requirement of the showing of a license plate or disabled placard when required by enforcement units enforcing disabled persons parking violations pursuant to Sections 22507.8 and 22511.8 of the Vehicle Code. **Leg.H.** 1968 ch. 461, 1972 ch. 819, 1979 ch. 293, 1980 ch. 773, 1988 ch. 1595, 1992 ch. 913, 1994 ch. 1257, 1996 ch. 498.

Ref.: Cal. Fms Pl. & Pr., Ch. 116, "Civil Rights: Discrimination in Business Establishments."

§54.3. Denial or Interference With Admittance—Punishment.

(a) Any person or persons, firm or corporation who denies or interferes with admittance to or enjoyment of the public facilities as specified in Sections 54 and 54.1 or otherwise interferes with the rights of an individual with a disability under Sections 54, 54.1 and 54.2 is liable for each offense for the actual damages and any amount as may be determined by a jury, or the court sitting without a jury, up to a maximum of three times the amount of actual damages but in no case less than one thousand dollars ($1,000), and attorney's fees as may be determined by the court in addition thereto, suffered by any person denied any of the rights provided in Sections 54, 54.1, and 54.2. "Interfere," for purposes of this section, includes, but is not limited to, preventing or causing the prevention of a guide dog, signal dog, or service dog from carrying out its functions in assisting a disabled person.

(b) Any person who claims to be aggrieved by an alleged unlawful practice in violation of Section 54, 54.1, or 54.2 may also file a verified complaint with the Department of Fair Employment and Housing pursuant to Section 12948 of the Government Code. The remedies in this section are nonexclusive and are in addition to any other remedy provided by law, including, but not limited to, any action for injunctive or other equitable relief available to the aggrieved party or brought in the name of the people of this state or of the United States.

(c) A person may not be held liable for damages pursuant to both this section and Section 52 for the same act or failure to act. **Leg.H.** 1968 ch. 461, 1976 chs. 971, 972 §2.5, 1977 ch. 881, effective September 16, 1977, 1981 ch. 395, 1992 ch. 913, 1994 ch. 1257, 1996 ch. 498.

Ref.: Cal. Fms Pl. & Pr., Ch. 116, "Civil Rights: Discrimination in Business Establishments."

§54.4. As Pedestrian Failure to Carry White Cane or Use Guide Dog Not Negligence.

A blind or otherwise visually impaired pedestrian shall have all of the rights and privileges conferred by law upon other persons in any of the places, accommodations, or conveyances specified in Sections 54 and 54.1, notwithstanding the fact that the person is not carrying a predominantly white cane (with or without a red tip), or using a guide dog. The failure of a blind or otherwise visually impaired person to carry such a cane or to use such a guide dog shall not constitute negligence per se. **Leg.H.** 1968 ch. 461, 1994 ch. 1257.

Ref.: Cal. Fms Pl. & Pr., Ch. 116, "Civil Rights: Discrimination in Business Establishments."

§54.5. White Cane Safety Day.

Each year, the Governor shall publicly proclaim October 15 as White Cane Safety Day. He or she shall issue a proclamation in which:

(a) Comments shall be made upon the significance of this chapter.

(b) Citizens of the state are called upon to observe the provisions of this chapter and to take precautions necessary to the safety of disabled persons.

(c) Citizens of the state are reminded of the policies with respect to disabled persons declared in this chapter and he urges the citizens to cooperate in giving effect to them.

(d) Emphasis shall be made on the need of the citizenry to be aware of the presence of disabled persons in the community and to keep safe and functional for the disabled the streets, highways, sidewalks, walkways, public buildings, public facilities, other public places, places of public accommodation, amusement and resort, and other places to which the public is invited, and to offer assistance to disabled persons upon appropriate occasions.

(e) It is the policy of this state to encourage and enable disabled persons to participate fully in the social and economic life of the state and to engage in remunerative employment. **Leg.H.** 1968 ch. 461, 1994 ch. 1257.

§54.6. "Visually Impaired" Defined.

As used in this part, "visually impaired" includes blindness and means having central visual acuity not to exceed 20/200 in the better eye, with corrected lenses, as measured by the Snellen test, or visual acuity greater than 20/200, but with a limitation in the field of vision such that the widest diameter of the visual field subtendsan angle is not greater than 20 degrees. **Leg.H.** 1968 ch. 461, 1994 ch. 1257.

§54.7. Guide Dogs, Signal Dogs, or Service Dogs in Zoos or Wild Animal Parks.

(a) Notwithstanding any other provision of law, the provisions of this part shall not be construed to require zoos or wild animal parks to allow guide dogs, signal dogs, or service dogs to accompany individuals with a disability in areas of the zoo or park where zoo or park animals are not separated from members of the public by a physical barrier. As used in this section, "physical barrier" does not include an automobile or other conveyance.

(b) Any zoo or wild animal park that does not permit guide dogs, signal dogs, or service dogs to accompany individuals with a disability therein shall maintain, free of charge, adequate kennel facilities for the use of guide dogs, signal dogs, or service dogs belonging to these persons. These facilities shall be of a character commensurate with the anticipated daily attendance of individuals with a disability. The facilities shall be in an area not accessible to the general public, shall be equipped with water and utensils for the consumption thereof, and shall otherwise be safe, clean, and comfortable.

(c) Any zoo or wild animal park that does not permit guide dogs to accompany blind or visually impaired persons therein shall provide free transportation to blind or visually impaired persons on any mode of transportation provided for members of the public.

Each zoo or wild animal park that does not permit service dogs to accompany individuals with a disability shall provide free transportation to individuals with a disability on any mode of transportation provided for a member of the public in cases where the person uses a wheelchair and it is readily apparent that the person is unable to maintain complete or independent mobility without the aid of the service dog.

(d) Any zoo or wild animal park that does not permit guide dogs to accompany blind or otherwise visually impaired persons therein shall provide sighted escorts for blind or otherwise visually impaired persons if they are unaccompanied by a sighted person.

(e) As used in this section, "wild animal park" means any entity open to the public on a regular basis, licensed by the United States Department of Agriculture under the Animal Welfare Act as an exhibit, and operating for the primary purposes of conserving, propagating, and exhibiting wild and exotic animals, and any marine, mammal, or aquatic park open to the general public. **Leg.H.** 1979 ch. 525, 1988 ch. 1595, 1994 ch. 1257.

Ref.: Cal. Fms Pl. & Pr., Ch. 116, "Civil Rights: Discrimination in Business Establishments."

§54.8. Assistive Listening or Computer-Aided Transcription Systems in Court Proceedings.

(a) In any civil or criminal proceeding, including, but not limited to, traffic, small claims court, family court proceedings and services, and juvenile court proceedings, in any court-ordered or court-provided alternative dispute resolution, including mediation and arbitration, or in any administrative hearing of a public agency, where a party, witness, attorney, judicial employee, judge, juror, or other participant who is hearing impaired, the individual who is hearing impaired, upon his or her request, shall be provided with a functioning assistive listening system or a computer-aided transcription system. Any individual requiring this equipment shall give advance notice of his or her need to the appropriate court or agency at the time the hearing is set or not later than five days before the hearing.

(b) Assistive listening systems include, but are not limited to, special devices which transmit amplified speech by means of audio-induction loops, radio frequency systems (AM or FM), or infrared transmission. Personal receivers, headphones, and neck loops shall be available upon request by individuals who are hearing impaired.

(c) If a computer-aided transcription system is requested, sufficient display terminals shall be provided to allow the individual who is hearing impaired to read the real-time transcript of the proceeding without difficulty.

(d) A sign shall be posted in a prominent place indicating the availability of, and how to request, an assistive listening system and a computer-aided transcription system. Notice of the availability of the systems shall be posted with notice of trials.

(e) Each superior court shall have at least one portable assistive listening system for use in any court facility within the county. When not in use, the system shall be stored in a location determined by the court.

(f) The Judicial Council shall develop and approve official forms for notice of the availability of assistive listening systems and computer-aided transcription systems for individuals who are hearing impaired. The Judicial Council shall also develop and maintain a system to record utilization by the courts of these assistive listening systems and computer-aided transcription systems.

(g) If the individual who is hearing impaired is a juror, the jury deliberation room shall be equipped with an assistive listening system or a computer-aided transcription system upon the request of the juror.

(h) A court reporter may be present in the jury deliberating room during a jury deliberation if the services of a court reporter for the purpose of operating a computer-aided transcription system are required for a juror who is hearing impaired.

(i) In any of the proceedings referred to in subdivision (a), or in any administrative hearing of a public agency, in which the individual who is hearing impaired is a party, witness, attorney, judicial employee, judge, juror, or other participant, and has requested use of an assistive listening system or computer-aided transcription system, the proceedings shall not commence until the system is in place and functioning.

(j) As used in this section, "individual who is hearing impaired" means an individual with a hearing loss, who, with sufficient amplification or a computer-aided transcription system, is able to fully participate in the proceeding.

(k) In no case shall this section be construed to prescribe a lesser standard of accessibility or usability than that provided by Title II of the Americans with Disabilities Act of 1990 (Public Law 101-336) and federal regulations adopted pursuant to that act. **Leg.H.** 1989 ch. 1002, 1992 ch. 913, 1993 ch. 1214, 2001 ch. 824.

§55. Injunction by Aggrieved Person.

Any person who is aggrieved or potentially aggrieved by a violation of Section 54 or 54.1 of this code, Chapter 7 (commencing with Section 4450) of Division 5 of Title 1 of the Government Code, or Part 5.5 (commencing with Section 19955) of Division 13 of the Health and Safety Code may bring an action to enjoin the violation. The prevailing party in the action shall be entitled to recover reasonable attorney's fees. **Leg.H.** 1974 ch. 1443.

Ref.: Cal. Fms Pl. & Pr., Ch. 112, "Civil Rights: Government-Funded Programs and Activities," Ch. 116, "Civil Rights: Discrimination in Business Establishments."

§55.1. Injunction by Public Officials.

In addition to any remedies available under the federal Americans with Disabilities Act of 1990, Public Law 101-336 (42 U.S.C. Sec. 12102), or other provisions of law, the district attorney, the city attorney, the Department of Rehabilitation acting through the Attorney General, or the Attorney General may bring an action to enjoin any violation of Section 54 or 54.1. **Leg.H.** 1976 ch. 869, 1994 ch. 1257.

Ref.: Cal. Fms Pl. & Pr., Ch. 116, "Civil Rights: Discrimination in Business Establishments."

§55.2. Actions Requiring Copy of Petition and Brief to Be Served on State Solicitor General.

If a violation of Section 54, 54.1, 54.2, or 54.3 is alleged or the application or construction of any of these sections is in issue in any proceeding in the Supreme Court of California, a state court of appeal, or the appellate division of a superior court, each party shall serve a copy of the party's brief or petition and brief, on the State Solicitor General at the Office of the Attorney General.

No brief may be accepted for filing unless the proof of service shows service on the State Solicitor General. Any party failing to comply with this requirement shall be given a reasonable opportunity to cure the failure before the court imposes any sanction and, in that instance, the court shall allow the Attorney General reasonable additional time to file a brief in the matter. **Leg.H.** 2002 ch. 244 (AB 2524).

PART 2.6
Confidentiality of Medical Information

Chap. 1. Definitions. §§56-56.07.
Chap. 2. Disclosure of Medical Information by Providers. §§56.10-56.16.
Chap. 2.5. Disclosure of Genetic Test Results by a Health Care Service Plan. §56.17.
Chap. 3. Use and Disclosure of Medical Information by Employers. §§56.20-56.245.
Chap. 4. Relationship of Chapters 2 and 3. §56.25.
Chap. 5. Use and Disclosure of Medical and Other Information by Third Party Administrators and Others. §§56.26, 56.265.
Chap. 6. Relationship to Existing Law. §§56.27-56.31.
Chap. 7. Violations. §§56.35-56.37.

CHAPTER 1
DEFINITIONS

Title of part. §56.
Definitions. §56.05.
Medical information corporations—Confidentiality and disclosure requirements. §56.06.
Access to records kept by corporation. §56.07.

§56. Title of Part.

This part may be cited as the Confidentiality of Medical Information Act. Leg.H. 1981 ch. 782.

§56.05. Definitions.

For purposes of this part:

(a) "Authorization" means permission granted in accordance with Section 56.11 or 56.21 for the disclosure of medical information.

(b) "Authorized recipient" means any person who is authorized to receive medical information pursuant to Section 56.10 or 56.20.

(c) "Contractor" means any person or entity that is a medical group, independent practice association, pharmaceutical benefits manager, or a medical service organization and is not a health care service plan or provider of health care. "Contractor" does not include insurance institutions as defined in subdivision (k) of Section 791.02 of the Insurance Code or pharmaceutical benefits managers licensed pursuant to the Knox-Keene Health Care Service Plan Act of 1975 (Chapter 2.2 (commencing with Section 1340) of Division 2 of the Health and Safety Code).

(d) "Health care service plan" means any entity regulated pursuant to the Knox-Keene Health Care Service Plan Act of 1975 (Chapter 2.2 (commencing with Section 1340) of Division 2 of the Health and Safety Code).

(e) "Licensed health care professional" means any person licensed or certified pursuant to Division 2 (commencing with Section 500) of the Business and Professions Code, the Osteopathic Initiative Act or the Chiropractic Initiative Act, or Division 2.5 (commencing with Section 1797) of the Health and Safety Code.

(f) "Marketing" means to make a communication about a product or service that encourages recipients of the communication to purchase or use the product or service.

"Marketing" does not include any of the following:

(1) Communications made orally or in writing for which the communicator does not receive direct or indirect remuneration, including, but not limited to, gifts, fees, payments, subsidies, or other economic benefits, from a third party for making the communication.

(2) Communications made to current enrollees solely for the purpose of describing a provider's participation in an existing health care provider network or health plan network of a Knox-Keene licensed health plan to which the enrollees already subscribe; communications made to current enrollees solely for the purpose of describing if, and the extent to which, a product or service, or payment for a product or service, is provided by a provider, contractor, or plan or included in a plan of benefits of a Knox-Keene licensed health plan to which the enrollees already subscribe; or communications made to plan enrollees describing the availability of more cost-effective pharmaceuticals.

(3) Communications that are tailored to the circumstances of a particular individual to educate or advise the individual about treatment options, and otherwise maintain the individual's adherence to a prescribed course of medical treatment, as provided in Section 1399.901 of the Health and Safety Code, for a chronic and seriously debilitating or life-threatening condition as defined in subdivisions (d) and (e) of Section 1367.21 of the Health and Safety Code, if the health care provider, contractor, or health plan receives direct or indirect remuneration, including, but not limited to, gifts, fees, payments, subsidies, or other economic benefits, from a third party for making the communication, if all of the following apply:

(A) The individual receiving the communication is notified in the communication in typeface no smaller than 14-point type of the fact that the provider, contractor, or health plan has been remunerated and the source of the remuneration.

(B) The individual is provided the opportunity to opt out of receiving future remunerated communications.

(C) The communication contains instructions in typeface no smaller than 14-point type describing how the individual can opt out of receiving further communications by calling a toll-free number of the health care provider, contractor, or health plan making the remunerated communications. No further communication may be made to an individual who has opted out after 30 calendar days from the date the individual makes the opt out request.

(g) "Medical information" means any individually identifiable information, in electronic or physical form, in possession of or derived from a provider of health care, health care service plan, pharmaceutical company, or contractor regarding a patient's medical history, mental or physical condition, or treatment. "Individually identifiable" means that the medical information includes or contains any element of personal identifying information sufficient to allow identification of the individual, such as the patient's name, address, electronic mail address, telephone number, or social security number, or other information that, alone or in combination with other publicly available information, reveals the individual's identity.

(h) "Patient" means any natural person, whether or not still living, who received health care services from a provider of health care and to whom medical information pertains.

(i) "Pharmaceutical company" means any company or business, or an agent or representative thereof, that manufactures, sells, or distributes pharmaceuticals, medications, or prescription drugs. "Pharmaceutical company" does not include a pharmaceutical benefits manager, as included in subdivision (c), or a provider of health care.

(j) "Provider of health care" means any person licensed or certified pursuant to Division 2 (commencing with Section 500) of the Business and Professions Code; any person licensed pursuant to the Osteopathic Initiative Act or the Chiropractic Initiative Act; any person certified pursuant to Division 2.5 (commencing with Section 1797) of the Health and Safety Code; any clinic, health dispensary, or health facility licensed pursuant to Division 2 (commencing with Section 1200) of the Health and Safety Code. "Provider of health care" does not include insurance institutions as defined in subdivision (k) of Section 791.02 of the Insurance Code. **Leg.H.** 1981 ch. 782, 1984 ch. 1391, 1999 ch. 526, 2000 ch. 1067, 2002 ch. 853 (AB 2191), 2003 ch. 562 (AB 715).

§56.06. Medical Information Corporations—Confidentiality and Disclosure Requirements.

(a) Any corporation organized for the primary purpose of maintaining medical information in order to make the information available to the patient or to a provider of health care at the request of the patient or a provider of health care, for purposes of diagnosis or treatment of the patient, shall be deemed to be a provider of health care subject to the requirements of this part. However, nothing in this section shall be construed to make a corporation specified in this subdivision a provider of health care for purposes of any law other than this part, including laws that specifically incorporate by reference the definitions of this part.

(b) Any corporation described in subdivision (a) shall maintain the same standards of confidentiality required of a provider of health care with respect to medical information disclosed to the corporation.

(c) Any corporation described in subdivision (a) shall be subject to the penalties for improper use and disclosure of medical information prescribed in this part. **Leg.H.** 1993 ch. 1004.

§56.07. Access to Records Kept by Corporation.

(a) Except as provided in subdivision (c), upon the patient's written request, any corporation described in Section 56.06, or any other entity that compiles or maintains medical information for any reason, shall provide the patient, at no charge, with a copy of any medical profile, summary, or information maintained by the corporation or entity with respect to the patient.

(b) A request by a patient pursuant to this section shall not be deemed to be an authorization by the patient for the release or disclosure of any information to any person or entity other than the patient.

(c) This section shall not apply to any patient records that are subject to inspection by the patient pursuant to Section 123110 of the Health and Safety Code and shall not be deemed to limit the right of a health care provider to charge a fee for the preparation of a summary of patient records as provided in Section 123130 of the Health and Safety Code. This section shall not apply to a health care service plan licensed pursuant to Chapter 2.2 (commencing with Section 1340) of Division 2 of the Health and Safety Code or a disability insurer licensed pursuant to the Insurance Code. This section shall not apply to medical information compiled or maintained by a fire and casualty insurer or its retained counsel in the regular course of investigating or litigating a claim under a policy of insurance that it has written. For the purposes of this section, a fire and casualty insurer is an insurer writing policies that may be sold by a fire and casualty licensee pursuant to Section 1625 of the Insurance Code. **Leg.H.** 2000 ch. 1066.

Ref.: Cal. Fms Pl. & Pr., Ch. 429, "Privacy."

CHAPTER 2
DISCLOSURE OF MEDICAL INFORMATION BY PROVIDERS

When medical information may be disclosed. §56.10.
Preservation of confidentiality of records. §56.101.
Pharmaceutical company cannot require patient to sign form permitting disclosure of medical information as condition of receiving pharmaceuticals; exceptions. §56.102.
Release of information on psychotherapy. §56.104.
Authorization to disclose medical information in connection with settlement or compromise of medical malpractice case. §56.105.
Requirements for authorizing release of medical information. §56.11.
Furnishing copy of authorization to patient. §56.12.
Confidentiality of released medical information. §56.13.
Provider non-liability for unauthorized use of medical information §56.14.
Cancellation or modification of authorization. §56.15.
Disclosure of nonmedical information permitted. §56.16.

§56.10. Enacted 1981. Repealed operative January 1, 2003, by its own provisions. 2000 ch. 1068 §1.8.
Another §56.10 follows.

§56.10. When Medical Information May Be Disclosed.

(a) No provider of health care, health care service plan, or contractor shall disclose medical information regarding a patient of the provider of health care or an enrollee or subscriber of a health care service plan without first obtaining an authorization, except as provided in subdivision (b) or (c).

(b) A provider of health care, a health care service plan, or a contractor shall disclose medical information if the disclosure is compelled by any of the following:

(1) By a court pursuant to an order of that court.

(2) By a board, commission, or administrative agency for purposes of adjudication pursuant to its lawful authority.

(3) By a party to a proceeding before a court or administrative agency pursuant to a subpoena, subpoena duces tecum, notice to appear served pursuant to Section 1987 of the Code of Civil Procedure, or any provision authorizing discovery in a proceeding before a court or administrative agency.

(4) By a board, commission, or administrative agency pursuant to an investigative subpoena issued under Article 2 (commencing with Section 11180) of Chapter 2 of Part 1 of Division 3 of Title 2 of the Government Code.

(5) By an arbitrator or arbitration panel, when arbitration is lawfully requested by either party, pursuant to a subpoena duces tecum issued under Section 1282.6 of the Code of Civil Procedure, or any other provision authorizing discovery in a proceeding before an arbitrator or arbitration panel.

(6) By a search warrant lawfully issued to a governmental law enforcement agency.

(7) By the patient or the patient's representative pursuant to Chapter 1 (commencing with Section 123100) of Part 1 of Division 106 of the Health and Safety Code.

(8) By a coroner, when requested in the course of an investigation by the coroner's office for the purpose of identifying the decedent or locating next of kin, or when investigating deaths that may involve public health concerns, organ or tissue donation, child abuse, elder abuse, suicides, poisonings, accidents, sudden infant death, suspicious deaths, unknown deaths, or criminal deaths, or when otherwise authorized by the decedent's representative. Medical information requested by the coroner under this paragraph shall be limited to information regarding the patient who is the decedent and who is the subject of the investigation and shall be disclosed to the coroner without delay upon request.

(9) When otherwise specifically required by law.

(c) A provider of health care or a health care service plan may disclose medical information as follows:

(1) The information may be disclosed to providers of health care, health care service plans, contractors, or other health care professionals or facilities for purposes of diagnosis or treatment of the patient. This includes, in an emergency situation, the communication of patient information by radio transmission or other means between emergency medical personnel at the scene of an emergency, or in an emergency medical transport vehicle, and emergency medical personnel at a health facility licensed pursuant to Chapter 2 (commencing with Section 1250) of Division 2 of the Health and Safety Code.

(2) The information may be disclosed to an insurer, employer, health care service plan, hospital service plan, employee benefit plan, governmental authority, contractor, or any other person or entity responsible for paying for health care services rendered to the patient, to the extent necessary to allow responsibility for payment to be determined and payment to be made. If (A) the patient is, by reason of a comatose or other disabling medical condition, unable to consent to the disclosure of medical information and (B) no other arrangements have been made to pay for the health care services being rendered to the patient, the information may be disclosed to a governmental authority to the extent necessary to determine the patient's eligibility for, and to obtain, payment under a governmental program for health care services provided to the patient. The information may also be disclosed to another provider of health care or health care service plan as necessary to assist the other provider or health care service plan in obtaining payment for health care services rendered by that provider of health care or health care service plan to the patient.

(3) The information may be disclosed to any person or entity that provides billing, claims management, medical data processing, or other administrative services for providers of health care or health care service plans or for any of the persons or entities specified in paragraph (2). However, no information so disclosed shall be further disclosed by the recipient in any way that would be violative of this part.

(4) The information may be disclosed to organized committees and agents of professional societies or of medical staffs of licensed hospitals, licensed health care service plans, professional standards review organizations, independent medical review organizations and their selected reviewers, utilization and quality control peer review organizations as established by Congress in Public Law 97-248 in 1982, contractors, or persons or organizations insuring, responsible for, or defending professional liability that a provider may incur, if the committees, agents, health care service plans, organizations, reviewers, contractors, or persons are engaged in reviewing the competence or qualifications of health care professionals or in reviewing health care services with respect to medical necessity, level of care, quality of care, or justification of charges.

(5) The information in the possession of any provider of health care or health care service plan may be reviewed by any private or public body responsible for licensing or accrediting the provider of health care or health care service plan. However, no patient-identifying medical information may be removed from the premises except as expressly permitted or required elsewhere by law, nor shall that information be further disclosed by the recipient in any way that would violate this part.

(6) The information may be disclosed to the county coroner in the course of an investigation by the coroner's office when requested for all purposes not included in paragraph (8) of subdivision (b).

(7) The information may be disclosed to public agencies, clinical investigators, including investigators conducting epidemiologic studies, health care research organizations, and accredited public or private nonprofit educational or health care institutions for bona fide research purposes. However, no information so disclosed shall be further disclosed by the recipient in any way that would disclose the identity of any patient or be violative of this part.

(8) A provider of health care or health care service plan that has created medical information as a result of employment-related health care services to an employee conducted

at the specific prior written request and expense of the employer may disclose to the employee's employer that part of the information that:

(A) Is relevant in a lawsuit, arbitration, grievance, or other claim or challenge to which the employer and the employee are parties and in which the patient has placed in issue his or her medical history, mental or physical condition, or treatment, provided that information may only be used or disclosed in connection with that proceeding.

(B) Describes functional limitations of the patient that may entitle the patient to leave from work for medical reasons or limit the patient's fitness to perform his or her present employment, provided that no statement of medical cause is included in the information disclosed.

(9) Unless the provider of health care or health care service plan is notified in writing of an agreement by the sponsor, insurer, or administrator to the contrary, the information may be disclosed to a sponsor, insurer, or administrator of a group or individual insured or uninsured plan or policy that the patient seeks coverage by or benefits from, if the information was created by the provider of health care or health care service plan as the result of services conducted at the specific prior written request and expense of the sponsor, insurer, or administrator for the purpose of evaluating the application for coverage or benefits.

(10) The information may be disclosed to a health care service plan by providers of health care that contract with the health care service plan and may be transferred among providers of health care that contract with the health care service plan, for the purpose of administering the health care service plan. Medical information may not otherwise be disclosed by a health care service plan except in accordance with the provisions of this part.

(11) Nothing in this part shall prevent the disclosure by a provider of health care or a health care service plan to an insurance institution, agent, or support organization, subject to Article 6.6 (commencing with Section 791) of Part 2 of Division 1 of the Insurance Code, of medical information if the insurance institution, agent, or support organization has complied with all requirements for obtaining the information pursuant to Article 6.6 (commencing with Section 791) of Part 2 of Division 1 of the Insurance Code.

(12) The information relevant to the patient's condition and care and treatment provided may be disclosed to a probate court investigator engaged in determining the need for an initial conservatorship or continuation of an existent conservatorship, if the patient is unable to give informed consent, or to a probate court investigator, probation officer, or domestic relations investigator engaged in determining the need for an initial guardianship or continuation of an existent guardianship.

(13) The information may be disclosed to an organ procurement organization or a tissue bank processing the tissue of a decedent for transplantation into the body of another person, but only with respect to the donating decedent, for the purpose of aiding the transplant. For the purpose of this paragraph, the terms "tissue bank" and "tissue" have the same meaning as defined in Section 1635 of the Health and Safety Code.

(14) The information may be disclosed when the disclosure is otherwise specifically authorized by law, such as the voluntary reporting, either directly or indirectly, to the federal Food and Drug Administration of adverse events related to drug products or medical device problems.

(15) Basic information, including the patient's name, city of residence, age, sex, and general condition, may be disclosed to a state or federally recognized disaster relief organization for the purpose of responding to disaster welfare inquiries.

(16) The information may be disclosed to a third party for purposes of encoding, encrypting, or otherwise anonymizing data. However, no information so disclosed shall be further disclosed by the recipient in any way that would be violative of this part, including the unauthorized manipulation of coded or encrypted medical information that reveals individually identifiable medical information.

(17) For purposes of disease management programs and services as defined in Section 1399.901 of the Health and Safety Code, information may be disclosed as follows: (A) to any entity contracting with a health care service plan or the health care service plan's contractors to monitor or administer care of enrollees for a covered benefit, provided that the disease management services and care are authorized by a treating physician, or (B) to any disease management organization, as defined in Section 1399.900 of the Health and Safety Code, that complies fully with the physician authorization requirements of Section 1399.902 of the Health and Safety Code, provided that the health care service plan or its contractor provides or has provided a description of the disease management services to a treating physician or to the health care service plan's or contractor's network of physicians. Nothing in this paragraph shall be construed to require physician authorization for the care or treatment of the adherents of any well-recognized church or religious denomination who depend solely upon prayer or spiritual means for healing in the practice of the religion of that church or denomination.

(d) Except to the extent expressly authorized by the patient or enrollee or subscriber or as provided by subdivisions (b) and (c), no provider of health care, health care service plan, contractor, or corporation and its subsidiaries and affiliates shall intentionally share, sell, use for marketing, or otherwise use any medical information for any purpose not necessary to provide health care services to the patient.

(e) Except to the extent expressly authorized by the patient or enrollee or subscriber or as provided by subdivisions (b) and (c), no contractor or corporation and its subsidiaries and affiliates shall further disclose medical information regarding a patient of the provider of health care or an enrollee or subscriber of a health care service plan or insurer or self-insured employer received under this section to any person or entity that is not engaged in providing direct health care services to the patient or his or her provider of health care or health care service plan or insurer or self-insured employer. **Leg.H.** 2000 ch. 1068 §1.16, 2002 ch. 123 (AB 1958), 2003 ch. 562 (AB 715).

Ref.: Cal. Fms Pl. & Pr., Ch. 429, "Privacy," Ch. 535, "Subpoena."

§56.101. Preservation of Confidentiality of Records.

Every provider of health care, health care service plan, pharmaceutical company, or contractor who creates, maintains, preserves, stores, abandons, destroys, or disposes of medical records shall do so in a manner that preserves the confidentiality of the information contained therein. Any provider of health care, health care service plan, pharmaceutical company, or contractor who negligently creates, maintains, preserves, stores, abandons, destroys, or disposes of medical records shall be subject to the remedies and penalties provided under subdivisions (b) and (c) of Section 56.36. **Leg.H.** 1999 ch. 526, 2000 ch. 1067, 2002 ch. 853 (AB 2191).

§56.102. Pharmaceutical Company Cannot Require Patient to Sign Form Permitting Disclosure of Medical Information as Condition of Receiving Pharmaceuticals; Exceptions.

(a) A pharmaceutical company may not require a patient, as a condition of receiving pharmaceuticals, medications, or prescription drugs, to sign an authorization, release, consent, or waiver that would permit the disclosure of medical information that otherwise may not be disclosed under Section 56.10 or any other provision of law, unless the disclosure is for one of the following purposes:

(1) Enrollment of the patient in a patient assistance program or prescription drug discount program.

(2) Enrollment of the patient in a clinical research project.

(3) Prioritization of distribution to the patient of a prescription medicine in limited supply in the United States.

(4) Response to an inquiry from the patient communicated in writing, by telephone, or by electronic mail.

(b) Except as provided in subdivision (a) or Section 56.10, a pharmaceutical company may not disclose medical information provided to it without first obtaining a valid authorization from the patient. **Leg.H.** 2002 ch. 853 (AB 2191).

§56.104. Release of Information on Psychotherapy.

(a) Notwithstanding subdivision (c) of Section 56.10, except as authorized in paragraph (1) of subdivision (c) of Section 56.10, no provider of health care, health care service plan, or contractor may release medical information to persons or entities authorized by law to receive that information pursuant to subdivision (c) of Section 56.10, if the requested information specifically relates to the patient's participation in outpatient treatment with a psychotherapist, unless the person or entity requesting that information submits to the patient pursuant to subdivision (b) and to the provider of health care, health care service plan, or contractor a written request, signed by the person requesting the information or an authorized agent of the entity requesting the information, that includes all of the following:

(1) The specific information relating to a patient's participation in outpatient treatment with a psychotherapist being requested and its specific intended use or uses.

(2) The length of time during which the information will be kept before being destroyed or disposed of. A person or entity may extend that timeframe, provided that the person or entity notifies the provider, plan, or contractor of the extension. Any notification of an extension shall include the specific reason for the extension, the intended use or uses of the information during the extended time, and the expected date of the destruction of the information.

(3) A statement that the information will not be used for any purpose other than its intended use.

(4) A statement that the person or entity requesting the information will destroy the information and all copies in the person's or entity's possession or control, will cause it to be destroyed, or will return the information and all copies of it before or immediately after the length of time specified in paragraph (2) has expired.

(b) The person or entity requesting the information shall submit a copy of the written request required by this section to the patient within 30 days of receipt of the information requested, unless the patient has signed a written waiver in the form of a letter signed and submitted by the patient to the provider of health care or health care service plan waiving notification.

(c) For purposes of this section, "psychotherapist" means a person who is both a "psychotherapist" as defined in Section 1010 of the Evidence Code and a "provider of health care" as defined in subdivision (i) of Section 56.05.

(d) This section does not apply to the disclosure or use of medical information by a law enforcement agency or a regulatory agency when required for an investigation of unlawful activity or for licensing, certification, or regulatory purposes, unless the disclosure is otherwise prohibited by law.

(e) Nothing in this section shall be construed to grant any additional authority to a provider of health care, health care service plan, or contractor to disclose information to a person or entity without the patient's consent. **Leg.H.** 1999 ch. 527, 2004 ch. 463 (SB 598).

§56.105. Authorization to Disclose Medical Information in Connection With Settlement or Compromise of Medical Malpractice Case.

Whenever, prior to the service of a complaint upon a defendant in any action arising out of the professional negligence of a person holding a valid physician's and surgeon's certificate issued pursuant to Chapter 5 (commencing with Section 2000) of Division 2 of the Business and Professions Code, a demand for settlement or offer to compromise is made on a patient's behalf, the demand or offer shall be accompanied by an authorization to disclose medical information to persons or organizations insuring, responsible for, or defending professional liability that the certificate holder may incur. The authorization shall be in accordance with Section 56.11 and shall authorize disclosure of that information that is necessary to investigate issues of liability and extent of potential damages in evaluating the merits of the demand for settlement or offer to compromise.

Notice of any request for medical information made pursuant to an authorization as provided by this section shall be given to the patient or the patient's legal representative. The notice shall describe the inclusive subject matter and dates of the materials requested and shall also authorize the patient or the patient's legal representative to receive, upon request, copies of the information at his or her expense.

Nothing in this section shall be construed to waive or limit any applicable privileges set forth in the Evidence Code except for the disclosure of medical information subject to the patient's authorization. Nothing in this section shall be construed as authorizing a representative of any person from whom settlement has been demanded to communicate in violation of the physician-patient privilege with a treating physician except for the medical information request.

The requirements of this section are independent of the requirements of Section 364 of the Code of Civil Procedure. **Leg.H.** 1985 ch. 484, 1991 ch. 591.

§56.11. Requirements for Authorizing Release of Medical Information.

Any person or entity that wishes to obtain medical information pursuant to subdivision (a) of Section 56.10, other than a person or entity authorized to receive medical information pursuant to subdivision (b) or (c) of Section 56.10, shall obtain a valid authorization for the release of this information.

An authorization for the release of medical information by a provider of health care, health care service plan, pharmaceutical company, or contractor shall be valid if it:

(a) Is handwritten by the person who signs it or is in a typeface no smaller than 14-point type.

(b) Is clearly separate from any other language present on the same page and is executed by a signature which serves no other purpose than to execute the authorization.

(c) Is signed and dated by one of the following:

(1) The patient. A patient who is a minor may only sign an authorization for the release of medical information obtained by a provider of health care, health care service plan, pharmaceutical company, or contractor in the course of furnishing services to which the minor could lawfully have consented under Part 1 (commencing with Section 25) or Part 2.7 (commencing with Section 60).

(2) The legal representative of the patient, if the patient is a minor or an incompetent. However, authorization may not be given under this subdivision for the disclosure of medical information obtained by the provider of health care, health care service plan, pharmaceutical company, or contractor in the course of furnishing services to which a minor patient could lawfully have consented under Part 1 (commencing with Section 25) or Part 2.7 (commencing with Section 60).

(3) The spouse of the patient or the person financially responsible for the patient, where the medical information is being sought for the sole purpose of processing an application for health insurance or for enrollment in a nonprofit hospital plan, a health care service plan, or an employee benefit plan, and where the patient is to be an enrolled spouse or dependent under the policy or plan.

(4) The beneficiary or personal representative of a deceased patient.

(d) States the specific uses and limitations on the types of medical information to be disclosed.

(e) States the name or functions of the provider of health care, health care service plan, pharmaceutical company, or contractor that may disclose the medical information.

(f) States the name or functions of the persons or entities authorized to receive the medical information.

(g) States the specific uses and limitations on the use of the medical information by the persons or entities authorized to receive the medical information.

(h) States a specific date after which the provider of health care, health care service plan, pharmaceutical company, or contractor is no longer authorized to disclose the medical information.

(i) Advises the person signing the authorization of the right to receive a copy of the authorization. **Leg.H.** 1981 ch. 782, 1999 ch. 526, 2000 ch. 1066, 2002 ch. 853 (AB 2191), 2003 ch. 562 (AB 715).

§56.12. Furnishing Copy of Authorization to Patient.

Upon demand by the patient or the person who signed an authorization, a provider of health care, health care service plan, pharmaceutical company, or contractor possessing the authorization shall furnish a true copy thereof. **Leg.H.** 1981 ch. 782, 1999 ch. 526, 2002 ch. 853 (AB 2191).

§56.13. Confidentiality of Released Medical Information.

A recipient of medical information pursuant to an authorization as provided by this chapter or pursuant to the provisions of subdivision (c) of Section 56.10 may not further disclose that medical information except in accordance with a new authorization that meets the requirements of Section 56.11, or as specifically required or permitted by other provisions of this chapter or by law. **Leg.H.** 1981 ch. 782.

§56.14. Provider Non-Liability for Unauthorized Use of Medical Information.

A provider of health care, health care service plan, or contractor that discloses medical information pursuant to the authorizations required by this chapter shall communicate to the person or entity to which it discloses the medical information any limitations in the authorization regarding the use of the medical information. No provider of health care, health care service plan, or contractor that has attempted in good faith to comply with this provision shall be liable for any unauthorized use of the medical information by the person or entity to which the provider, plan, or contractor disclosed the medical information. **Leg.H.** 1981 ch. 782, 1999 ch. 526.

§56.15. Cancellation or Modification of Authorization.

Nothing in this part shall be construed to prevent a person who could sign the authorization pursuant to subdivision (c) of Section 56.11 from cancelling or modifying an authorization. However, the cancellation or modification shall be effective only after the provider of health care actually receives written notice of the cancellation or modification. **Leg.H.** 1981 ch. 782.

§56.16. Disclosure of Nonmedical Information Permitted.

Unless there is specific written request by the patient to the contrary, nothing in this part shall be construed to prevent a provider, upon an inquiry concerning a specific patient, from releasing at its discretion any of the following information: the patient's name, address, age, and sex; a general description of the reason for treatment (whether an injury, a burn, poisoning, or some unrelated condition); the general nature of the injury, burn, poisoning, or other condition; the general condition of the patient; and any information that is not medical information as defined in subdivision (c) of Section 56.05. **Leg.H.** 1981 ch. 782.

CHAPTER 2.5
DISCLOSURE OF GENETIC TEST RESULTS BY A HEALTH CARE SERVICE PLAN

§56.17. Insurers Prohibited From Offering or Providing Different Terms, Conditions, or Benefits Based on Genetic Characteristics; Penalties; Disclosure of Test Results for Genetic Characteristic—Civil and Criminal Liability.

(a) This section shall apply to the disclosure of genetic test results contained in an applicant's or enrollee's medical records by a health care service plan.

(b) Any person who negligently discloses results of a test for a genetic characteristic to any third party in a manner that identifies or provides identifying characteristics of the person to whom the test results apply, except pursuant to a written authorization as described in subdivision (g), shall be assessed a civil penalty in an amount not to exceed one thousand dollars ($1,000) plus court costs, as determined by the court, which penalty and costs shall be paid to the subject of the test.

(c) Any person who willfully discloses the results of a test for a genetic characteristic to any third party in a manner that identifies or provides identifying characteristics of the person to whom the test results apply, except pursuant to a written authorization as described in subdivision (g), shall be assessed a civil penalty in an amount not less than one thousand dollars ($1,000) and no more than five thousand dollars ($5,000) plus court costs, as determined by the court, which penalty and costs shall be paid to the subject of the test.

(d) Any person who willfully or negligently discloses the results of a test for a genetic characteristic to a third party in a manner that identifies or provides identifying characteristics of the person to whom the test results apply, except pursuant to a written authorization as described in subdivision (g), that results in economic, bodily, or emotional harm to the subject of the test, is guilty of a misdemeanor punishable by a fine not to exceed ten thousand dollars ($10,000).

(e) In addition to the penalties listed in subdivisions (b) and (c), any person who commits any act described in subdivision (b) or (c) shall be liable to the subject for all actual damages, including damages for economic, bodily, or emotional harm which is proximately caused by the act.

(f) Each disclosure made in violation of this section is a separate and actionable offense.

(g) The applicant's "written authorization," as used in this section, shall satisfy the following requirements:

(1) Is written in plain language and is in a typeface no smaller than 14-point type.

(2) Is dated and signed by the individual or a person authorized to act on behalf of the individual.

(3) Specifies the types of persons authorized to disclose information about the individual.

(4) Specifies the nature of the information authorized to be disclosed.

(5) States the name or functions of the persons or entities authorized to receive the information.

(6) Specifies the purposes for which the information is collected.

(7) Specifies the length of time the authorization shall remain valid.

(8) Advises the person signing the authorization of the right to receive a copy of the authorization. Written authorization is required for each separate disclosure of the test results.

(h) This section shall not apply to disclosures required by the Department of Health Services necessary to monitor compliance with Chapter 1 (commencing with Section 124975) of Part 5 of Division 106 of the Health and Safety Code, nor to disclosures required by the Department of Managed Care necessary to administer and enforce compliance with Section 1374.7 of the Health and Safety Code.

(i) For purposes of this section, "genetic characteristic" has the same meaning as that set forth in subdivision (d) of Section 1374.7 of the Health and Safety Code. **Leg.H.** 1995 ch. 695, 1996 ch. 1023, effective September 29, 1996, ch. 532, operative January 1, 1997 (ch. 532 prevails), 1999 chs. 311, 525, operative July 1, 2000, 2000 chs. 857, 941, 2003 ch. 562 (AB 715).

CHAPTER 3
USE AND DISCLOSURE OF MEDICAL INFORMATION BY EMPLOYERS

Employer's duty to ensure confidentiality of medical information; employee's right to refuse release of such information. §56.20.
Requirements for authorized release of medical information. §56.21.
Furnishing copy of authorization to patient. §56.22.
Employer's non-liability for unauthorized use of medical information. §56.23.
Cancellation or modification of authorization. §56.24.
Confidentiality of released medical information. §56.245.

§56.20. Employer's Duty to Ensure Confidentiality of Medical Information; Employee's Right to Refuse Release of Such Information.

(a) Each employer who receives medical information shall establish appropriate procedures to ensure the confidentiality and protection from unauthorized use and disclosure of that information. These procedures may include, but are not limited to instruction regarding confidentiality of employees and agents handling files containing medical information, and security systems restricting access to files containing medical information.

(b) No employee shall be discriminated against in terms or conditions of employment due to that employee's refusal to sign an authorization under this part. However, nothing in this section shall prohibit an employer from taking such action as is necessary in the absence of medical information due to an employee's refusal to sign an authorization under this part.

(c) No employer shall use, disclose, or knowingly permit its employees or agents to use or disclose medical information which the employer possesses pertaining to its employees without the patient having first signed an authorization under Section 56.11 or Section 56.21 permitting such use or disclosure, except as follows:

(1) The information may be disclosed if the disclosure is compelled by judicial or administrative process or by any other specific provision of law.

(2) That part of the information which is relevant in a lawsuit, arbitration, grievance, or other claim or challenge to which the employer and employee are parties and in which the patient has placed in issue his or her medical history, mental or physical condition, or treatment may be used or disclosed in connection with that proceeding.

(3) The information may be used only for the purpose of administering and maintaining employee benefit plans, including health care plans and plans providing short-term and long-term disability income, workers' compensation and for determining eligibility for paid and unpaid leave from work for medical reasons.

(4) The information may be disclosed to a provider of health care or other health care professional or facility to aid the diagnosis or treatment of the patient, where the patient or other person specified in subdivision (c) of Section 56.21 is unable to authorize the disclosure.

(d) If an employer agrees in writing with one or more of its employees or maintains a written policy which provides that particular types of medical information shall not be used or disclosed by the employer in particular ways, the employer shall obtain an authorization for such uses or disclosures even if an authorization would not otherwise be required by subdivision (c). **Leg.H.** 1981 ch. 782.

§56.21. Requirements for Authorized Release of Medical Information.

An authorization for an employer to disclose medical information shall be valid if it:

(a) Is handwritten by the person who signs it or is a in typeface no smaller than 14-point type.

(b) Is clearly separate from any other language present on the same page and is executed by a signature which serves no purpose other than to execute the authorization.

(c) Is signed and dated by one of the following:

(1) The patient, except that a patient who is a minor may only sign an authorization for the disclosure of medical information obtained by a provider of health care in the course of furnishing services to which the minor could lawfully have consented under Part 1 (commencing with Section 25) or Part 2.7 (commencing with Section 60) of Division 1.

(2) The legal representative of the patient, if the patient is a minor or incompetent. However, authorization may not be given under this subdivision for the disclosure of medical information which pertains to a competent minor and which was created by a provider of health care in the course of furnishing services to which a minor patient could lawfully have consented under Part 1 (commencing with Section 25) or Part 2.7 (commencing with Section 60) of Division 1.

(3) The beneficiary or personal representative of a deceased patient.

(d) States the limitations, if any, on the types of medical information to be disclosed.

(e) States the name or functions of the employer or person authorized to disclose the medical information.

(f) States the names or functions of the persons or entities authorized to receive the medical information.

(g) States the limitations, if any, on the use of the medical information by the persons or entities authorized to receive the medical information.

(h) States a specific date after which the employer is no longer authorized to disclose the medical information.

(i) Advises the person who signed the authorization of the right to receive a copy of the authorization. **Leg.H.** 1981 ch. 782, 2003 ch. 562 (AB 715).

2003 Note: The Legislature inadvertently created the phrase ". . . is a in typeface . . ." in subsection (a). It is the Publisher's belief the Legislature intended to create the phrase ". . . is in a typeface . . .".

§56.22. Furnishing Copy of Authorization to Patient.

Upon demand by the patient or the person who signed an authorization, an employer possessing the authorization shall furnish a true copy thereof. **Leg.H.** 1981 ch. 782.

§56.23. Employer's Non-Liability for Unauthorized Use of Medical Information.

An employer that discloses medical information pursuant to an authorization required by this chapter shall communicate to the person or entity to which it discloses the medical information any limitations in the authorization regarding the use of the medical information. No employer that has attempted in good faith to comply with this provision shall be liable for any unauthorized use of the medical information by the person or entity to which the employer disclosed the medical information. **Leg.H.** 1981 ch. 782.

§56.24. Cancellation or Modification of Authorization.

Nothing in this part shall be construed to prevent a person who could sign the authorization pursuant to subdivision (c) of Section 56.21 from cancelling or modifying an authorization. However, the cancellation or modification shall be effective only after the employer actually receives written notice of the cancellation or modification. **Leg.H.** 1981 ch. 782.

§56.245. Confidentiality of Released Medical Information.

A recipient of medical information pursuant to an authorization as provided by this chapter may not further disclose such medical information unless in accordance with a new authorization that meets the requirements of Section 56.21, or as specifically required or permitted by other provisions of this chapter or by law. **Leg.H.** 1981 ch. 782.

CHAPTER 4
RELATIONSHIP OF CHAPTERS 2 AND 3

§56.25. Disclosure of Medical Information in Accordance With Chapters 2 and 3.

(a) An employer that is a provider of health care shall not be deemed to have violated Section 56.20 by disclosing, in accordance with Chapter 2 (commencing with Section 56.10), medical information possessed in connection with providing health care services to the provider's patients.

(b) An employer shall not be deemed to have violated Section 56.20 because a provider of health care that is an employee or agent of the employer uses or discloses, in accordance with Chapter 2 (commencing with Section 56.10), medical information possessed by the provider in connection with providing health care services to the provider's patients.

(c) A provider of health care that is an employer shall not be deemed to have violated Section 56.10 by disclosing, in accordance with Chapter 3 (commencing with Section 56.20), medical information possessed in connection with employing the provider's employees. Information maintained by a provider of health care in connection with employing the provider's employees shall not be deemed to be medical information for purposes of Chapter 3 (commencing with Section 56.20), unless it would be deemed medical information if received or maintained by an employer that is not a provider of health care. **Leg.H.** 1981 ch. 782.

CHAPTER 5
USE AND DISCLOSURE OF MEDICAL AND OTHER INFORMATION BY THIRD PARTY ADMINISTRATORS AND OTHERS

Third party administrators not to disclose information unless reasonably necessary. §56.26.
Insurance underwriters not to disclose information. §56.265.

§56.26. Third Party Administrators Not to Disclose Information Unless Reasonably Necessary.

(a) No person or entity engaged in the business of furnishing administrative services to programs that provide payment for health care services shall knowingly use, disclose, or permit its employees or agents to use or disclose medical information possessed in connection with performing administrative functions for a program, except as reasonably necessary in connection with the administration or maintenance of the program, or as required by law, or with an authorization.

(b) An authorization required by this section shall be in the same form as described in Section 56.21, except that "third party administrator" shall be substituted for "employer" wherever it appears in Section 56.21.

(c) This section shall not apply to any person or entity that is subject to the Insurance Information Privacy Act or to Chapter 2 (commencing with Section 56.10) or Chapter 3 (commencing with Section 56.20). **Leg.H.** 1981 ch. 782, 2004 ch. 183 (AB 3082).

§56.265. Insurance Underwriters Not to Disclose Information.

A person or entity that underwrites or sells annuity contracts or contracts insuring, guaranteeing, or indemnifying against loss, harm, damage, illness, disability, or death, and any affiliate of that person or entity, shall not disclose individually identifiable information concerning the health of, or the medical or genetic history of, a customer, to any affiliated or nonaffiliated depository institution, or to any other affiliated or nonaffiliated third party for use with regard to the granting of credit. **Leg.H.** 2000 ch. 278.

CHAPTER 6
RELATIONSHIP TO EXISTING LAW

Disclosure of medical information in connection with insurance transaction. §56.27.
Access to own information and disclosure pursuant to other law not affected. §56.28.
Compliance with patient authorization. §56.29.
Disclosure of medical information not subject to limitations of Part 2.6. §56.30.
Disclosure of human immunodeficiency virus. §56.31.

§56.27. Disclosure of Medical Information in Connection With Insurance Transaction.

An employer that is an insurance institution, insurance agent, or insurance support organization subject to the Insurance Information and Privacy Protection Act, Article 6.6 (commencing with Section 791) of Part 2 of Division 1 of the Insurance Code, shall not be deemed to have violated Section 56.20 by disclosing medical information gathered in connection with an insurance transaction in accordance with that act. **Leg.H.** 1981 ch. 782.

§56.28. Access to Own Information and Disclosure Pursuant to Other Law Not Affected.

Nothing in this part shall be deemed to affect existing laws relating to a patient's right of access to his or her own medical information, or relating to disclosures made pursuant to Section 1158 of the Evidence Code, or relating to privileges established under the Evidence Code. **Leg.H.** 1981 ch. 782.

§56.29. Compliance With Patient Authorization.

(a) Nothing in Chapter 1 (commencing with Section 1798) of Title 1.8 of Part 4 of Division 3 shall be construed to permit the acquisition or disclosure of medical information regarding a patient without an authorization, where the authorization is required by this part.

(b) The disclosure of medical information regarding a patient which is subject to subdivision (b) of Section 1798.24 shall be made only with an authorization which complies with the provisions of this part. Such disclosure may be made only within the time limits specified in subdivision (b) of Section 1798.24.

(c) Where the acquisition or disclosure of medical information regarding a patient is prohibited or limited by any provision of Chapter 1 (commencing with Section 1798) of Title 1.8 of Part 4 of Division 3, the prohibition or limit shall be applicable in addition to the requirements of this part. **Leg.H.** 1981 ch. 782.

§56.30. Disclosure of Medical Information Not Subject to Limitations of Part 2.6.

The disclosure and use of the following medical information shall not be subject to the limitations of this part:

(a) (Mental health and developmental disabilities) Information and records obtained in the course of providing services under Division 4 (commencing with Section 4000), Division 4.1 (commencing with Section 4400), Division 4.5 (commencing with Section 4500), Division 5 (commencing with Section 5000), Division 6 (commencing with Section 6000), or Division 7 (commencing with Section 7100) of the Welfare and Institutions Code.

(b) (Public social services) Information and records that are subject to Sections 10850, 14124.1, and 14124.2 of the Welfare and Institutions Code.

(c) (State health services, communicable diseases, developmental disabilities) Information and records maintained pursuant to former Chapter 2 (commencing with Section 200) of Part 1 of Division 1 of the Health and Safety Code and pursuant to the Communicable Disease Prevention and Control Act (subdivision (a) of Section 27 of the Health and Safety Code).

(d) (Licensing and statistics) Information and records maintained pursuant to Division 2 (commencing with Section 1200) and Part 1 (commencing with Section 102100) of Division 102 of the Health and Safety Code; pursuant to Chapter 3 (commencing with Section 1200) of Division 2 of the Business and Professions Code; and pursuant to Section 8608, 8817, or 8909 of the Family Code.

(e) (Medical survey, workers' safety) Information and records acquired and maintained or disclosed pursuant to Sections 1380 and 1382 of the Health and Safety Code and pursuant to Division 5 (commencing with Section 6300) of the Labor Code.

(f) (Industrial accidents) Information and records acquired, maintained, or disclosed pursuant to Division 1 (commencing with Section 50), Division 4 (commencing with Section 3200), Division 4.5 (commencing with Section 6100), and Division 4.7 (commencing with Section 6200) of the Labor Code.

(g) (Law enforcement) Information and records maintained by a health facility which are sought by a law enforcement agency under Chapter 3.5 (commencing with Section 1543) of Title 12 of Part 2 of the Penal Code.

(h) (Investigations of employment accident or illness) Information and records sought as part of an investigation of an on-the-job accident or illness pursuant to Division 5 (commencing with Section 6300) of the Labor Code or pursuant to Section 105200 of the Health and Safety Code.

(i) (Alcohol or drug abuse) Information and records subject to the federal alcohol and drug abuse regulations (Part 2 (commencing with Section 2.1) of subchapter A of Chapter 1 of Title 42 of the Code of Federal Regulations) or to Section 11977 of the Health and Safety Code dealing with narcotic and drug abuse.

(j) (Patient discharge data) Nothing in this part shall be construed to limit, expand, or otherwise affect the authority of the California Health Facilities Commission to collect patient discharge information from health facilities.

(k) Medical information and records disclosed to, and their use by, the Insurance Commissioner, the Director of the Department of Managed Health Care, the Division of Industrial Accidents, the Workers' Compensation Appeals Board, the Department of Insurance, or the Department of Managed Health Care. **Leg.H.** 1981 ch. 782, 1990 ch. 1363, operative July 1, 1991, 1992 ch. 163, operative January 1, 1994, 1993 ch. 1004, 1996 ch. 1023, effective September 29, 1996, 1999 ch. 526, 2000 ch. 1067.

§56.31. Disclosure of Human Immunodeficiency Virus.

Notwithstanding any other provision of law, nothing in subdivision (f) of Section 56.30 shall permit the disclosure or use of medical information regarding whether a patient is infected with or exposed to the human immunodeficiency virus without the prior authorization from the patient unless the patient is an injured worker claiming to be infected with or exposed to the human immunodeficiency virus through an exposure incident arising out of and in the course of employment. **Leg.H.** 1999 ch. 766.

1999 Note: The addition of Section 56.31 to the Civil Code by Chapter 766 is not intended either to abrogate the holdings in *Allison v. Workers' Comp. Appeals Bd.* (1999) 72 Cal.App.4th 654, or to prohibit a redaction decision by a workers' compensation judge from being appealed to the Workers' Compensation Appeals Board. Stats. 1999 ch. 766 §3.

CHAPTER 7
VIOLATIONS

Recovery of compensatory and punitive damages. §56.35.
Violation as misdemeanor; damages; administrative fines and civil penalties. §56.36.
Requiring patient to permit disclosure of medical information prohibited; waivers as unenforceable. §56.37.

§56.35. Recovery of Compensatory and Punitive Damages.

In addition to any other remedies available at law, a patient whose medical information has been used or disclosed in violation of Section 56.10 or 56.104 or 56.20 or subdivision (a) of Section 56.26 and who has sustained economic loss or personal injury therefrom may recover compensatory damages, punitive damages not to exceed three thousand dollars ($3,000), attorneys' fees not to exceed one thousand dollars ($1,000), and the costs of litigation. **Leg.H.** 1981 ch. 782, 1999 ch. 527.

§56.36. Violation as Misdemeanor; Damages; Administrative Fines and Civil Penalties.

(a) Any violation of the provisions of this part that results in economic loss or personal injury to a patient is punishable as a misdemeanor.

(b) In addition to any other remedies available at law, any individual may bring an action against any person or entity who has negligently released confidential information or records concerning him or her in violation of this part, for either or both of the following:

(1) Nominal damages of one thousand dollars ($1,000). In order to recover under this paragraph, it shall not be necessary that the plaintiff suffered or was threatened with actual damages.

(2) The amount of actual damages, if any, sustained by the patient.

(c) (1) In addition, any person or entity that negligently discloses medical information in violation of the provisions of this part shall also be liable, irrespective of the amount of damages suffered by the patient as a result of that violation, for an administrative fine or civil penalty not to exceed two thousand five hundred dollars ($2,500) per violation.

(2) (A) Any person or entity, other than a licensed health care professional, who knowingly and willfully obtains, discloses, or uses medical information in violation of this part shall be liable for an administrative fine or civil penalty not to exceed twenty-five thousand dollars ($25,000) per violation.

(B) Any licensed health care professional, who knowingly and willfully obtains, discloses, or uses medical information in violation of this part shall be liable on a first violation, for an administrative fine or civil penalty not to exceed two thousand five hundred dollars ($2,500) per violation, or on a second violation for an administrative fine or civil penalty not to exceed ten thousand dollars ($10,000) per violation, or on a third and subsequent violation for an administrative fine or civil penalty not to exceed twenty-five thousand dollars ($25,000) per violation. Nothing in this subdivision shall be construed to limit the liability of a health care service plan, a contractor, or a provider of health care that is not a licensed health care professional for any violation of this part.

(3) (A) Any person or entity, other than a licensed health care professional, who knowingly or willfully obtains or uses medical information in violation of this part for the purpose of financial gain shall be liable for an administrative fine or civil penalty not to exceed two hundred fifty thousand dollars ($250,000) per violation and shall also be subject to disgorgement of any proceeds or other consideration obtained as a result of the violation.

(B) Any licensed health care professional, who knowingly and willfully obtains, discloses, or uses medical information in violation of this part for financial gain shall be liable on a first violation, for an administrative fine or civil penalty not to exceed five thousand dollars ($5,000) per violation, or on a second violation for an administrative fine or civil penalty not to exceed twenty-five thousand dollars ($25,000) per violation, or on a third and subsequent violation for an administrative fine or civil penalty not to exceed two hundred fifty thousand dollars ($250,000) per violation and shall also be subject to disgorgement of any proceeds or other consideration obtained as a result of the violation. Nothing in this subdivision shall be construed to limit the liability of a health care service plan, a contractor, or a provider of health care that is not a licensed health care professional for any violation of this part.

(4) Nothing in this subdivision shall be construed as authorizing an administrative fine or civil penalty under both paragraphs (2) and (3) for the same violation.

(5) Any person or entity who is not permitted to receive medical information pursuant to this part and who knowingly and willfully obtains, discloses, or uses medical information without written authorization from the patient shall be liable for a civil penalty not to exceed two hundred fifty thousand dollars ($250,000) per violation.

(d) In assessing the amount of an administrative fine or civil penalty pursuant to subdivision (c), the licensing agency or certifying board or court shall consider any one or more of the relevant circumstances presented by any of the parties to the case including, but not limited to, the following:

(1) Whether the defendant has made a reasonable, good faith attempt to comply with this part.

(2) The nature and seriousness of the misconduct.

(3) The harm to the patient, enrollee, or subscriber.

(4) The number of violations.

(5) The persistence of the misconduct.

(6) The length of time over which the misconduct occurred.

(7) The willfulness of the defendant's misconduct.

(8) The defendant's assets, liabilities, and net worth.

(e) (1) The civil penalty pursuant to subdivision (c) shall be assessed and recovered in a civil action brought in the name of the people of the State of California in any court of competent jurisdiction by any of the following:

(A) The Attorney General.

(B) Any district attorney.

(C) Any county counsel authorized by agreement with the district attorney in actions involving violation of a county ordinance.

(D) Any city attorney of a city.

(E) Any city attorney of a city and county having a population in excess of 750,000, with the consent of the district attorney.

(F) A city prosecutor in any city having a full-time city prosecutor or, with the consent of the district attorney, by a city attorney in any city and county.

(2) If the action is brought by the Attorney General, one-half of the penalty collected shall be paid to the treasurer of the county in which the judgment was entered, and one-half to the General Fund. If the action is brought by a district attorney or county counsel, the penalty collected shall be paid to the treasurer of the county in which the judgment was entered. Except as provided in paragraph (3), if the action is brought by a city attorney or city prosecutor, one-half of the penalty collected shall be paid to the treasurer of the city in which the judgment was entered and one-half to the treasurer of the county in which the judgment was entered.

(3) If the action is brought by a city attorney of a city and county, the entire amount of the penalty collected shall be paid to the treasurer of the city and county in which the judgment was entered.

(4) Nothing in this section shall be construed as authorizing both an administrative fine and civil penalty for the same violation.

(5) Imposition of a fine or penalty provided for in this section shall not preclude imposition of any other sanctions or remedies authorized by law.

Sec. 56.37 CIVIL CODE 42

(f) For purposes of this section, "knowing" and "willful" shall have the same meanings as in Section 7 of the Penal Code.

(g) No person who discloses protected medical information in accordance with the provisions of this part shall be subject to the penalty provisions of this part. **Leg.H.** 1981 ch. 782, 1999 ch. 526.

§56.37. Requiring Patient to Permit Disclosure of Medical Information Prohibited; Waivers as Unenforceable.

(a) No provider of health care, health care service plan, or contractor may require a patient, as a condition of receiving health care services, to sign an authorization, release, consent, or waiver that would permit the disclosure of medical information that otherwise may not be disclosed under Section 56.10 or any other provision of law. However, a health care service plan or disability insurer may require relevant enrollee or subscriber medical information as a condition of the medical underwriting process, provided that Sections 1374.7 and 1389.1 of the Health and Safety Code are strictly observed.

(b) Any waiver by a patient of the provisions of this part, except as authorized by Section 56.11 or 56.21 or subdivision (b) of Section 56.26, shall be deemed contrary to public policy and shall be unenforceable. **Leg.H.** 1981 ch. 782, 1999 ch. 526.

PART 2.9
California Fair Dealership Law

Title of law. §80.
Definitions. §81.
Purposes and policies. §82.
Discrimination prohibited when granting dealership. §83.
Discrimination prohibited when terminating, canceling, or renewing dealership agreement. §84.
Discrimination prohibited when assigning, selling, transferring, bequeathing, or to the intestate succession to, dealership. §85.
Recovery of reasonable attorney's fees and taxable court costs. §86.

§80. Title of Law.

This part may be cited as the California Fair Dealership Law. **Leg.H.** 1980 ch. 914.

Ref.: Cal. Fms Pl. & Pr., Ch. 515, "Securities and Franchise Regulation."

§81. Definitions.

As used in this part:

(a) "Person" means a natural person, partnership, joint venture, corporation, limited liability company, or other entity.

(b) "Dealership" means a contract or agreement, either express or implied, whether oral or written, between two or more persons, by which a person is granted the right to sell or distribute goods or services, or to use a trade name, trademark, service mark, logotype, or advertising or other commercial symbol, in which there is a community of interest in the business of offering, selling, or distributing goods or services at wholesale, or at retail, by lease, agreement, or otherwise.

(c) "Grantor" means a person who sells, leases, or otherwise transfers a dealership.

(d) "Community of interest" means a continuing financial interest between the grantor and grantee in either the operation of the dealership or the marketing of goods or services.

(e) "Dealer" means a person who is a grantee of a dealership situated in this state.

(f) "Grant" means a sale, lease, or transfer of any kind. **Leg.H.** 1980 ch. 914, 1994 ch. 1010.

§82. Purposes and Policies.

This part shall be liberally construed and applied to promote its underlying purposes and policies, which are as follows:

(a) The prohibition of discrimination based upon race, color, religion, national origin, ancestry, or sex in the granting, sale, transfer, bequest, termination, and nonrenewal of dealerships; and,

The requirements of this part shall not be varied by contract or agreement and any portion of a contract or agreement purporting to do so is void and unenforceable. **Leg.H.** 1980 ch. 914.

§83. Discrimination Prohibited When Granting Dealership.

On or after January 1, 1981, no grantor, directly or indirectly, shall refuse to grant a dealership to any person because of the race, color, religion, national origin, ancestry, or sex of such person. **Leg.H.** 1980 ch. 914.

Ref.: Cal. Fms Pl. & Pr., Ch. 515, "Securities and Franchise Regulation."

§84. Discrimination Prohibited When Terminating, Canceling, or Renewing Dealership Agreement.

On or after January 1, 1981, no grantor, directly or indirectly, may terminate, cancel, or refuse to renew a dealership agreement because of the race, color, religion, national origin, ancestry, or sex of the dealer. **Leg.H.** 1980 ch. 914.

Ref.: Cal. Fms Pl. & Pr., Ch. 515, "Securities and Franchise Regulation."

§85. Discrimination Prohibited When Assigning, Selling, Transferring, Bequeathing, or to the Intestate Succession to, Dealership.

On or after January 1, 1981, no grantor or dealer, directly or indirectly, shall refuse to make or to consent to an assignment, sale, transfer, or bequest of a dealership to any person, or to the intestate succession to the dealership by any person, because of the race, color, religion, national origin, ancestry, or sex of such person. This section shall not be construed to create any right in a dealer to assign, sell, transfer, or bequeath a dealership where the right did not exist prior to January 1, 1981. **Leg.H.** 1980 ch. 914.

Ref.: Cal. Fms Pl. & Pr., Ch. 515, "Securities and Franchise Regulation."

§86. Recovery of Reasonable Attorney's Fees and Taxable Court Costs.

The prevailing party in any action based on a violation of the provisions of this part shall be entitled to recover reasonable attorney's fees and taxable court costs. **Leg.H.** 1980 ch. 914.

Ref.: Cal. Fms Pl. & Pr., Ch. 515, "Securities and Franchise Regulation."

DIVISION 2
PROPERTY

Part 1—Property in General. §§654-749.
Part 2—Real or Immovable Property. §§755-945.6.
Part 3—Personal or Movable Property. §§946-998.
Part 4—Acquisition of Property. §§1000-1422.

PART 1
Property in General

TITLE I. Nature of Property. §§654-663.
TITLE II. Ownership. §§669-742.
TITLE III. General Definitions. §§748, 749.

TITLE I
NATURE OF PROPERTY

Ownership defined. §654.
Things subject to ownership. §655.
Wild animals. §656.
Kinds of property. §657.
Real or immovable. §658.
Land. §659.
Fixtures. §660.
Appurtenances. §662.
Personalty. §663.

§654. Ownership Defined.

The ownership of a thing is the right of one or more persons to possess and use it to the exclusion of others. In this code, the thing of which there may [be] ownership is called property. **Leg.H.** 1872.

Ref.: Miller & Starr, Cal. Real Estate 3rd 11:95, 17:1, 17:2.

§655. Things Subject to Ownership.

There may be ownership of all inanimate things which are capable of appropriation or of manual delivery; of all domestic animals; of all obligations; of such products of labor or skill as the composition of an author, the goodwill of a business, trademarks and signs, and of rights created or granted by statute. **Leg.H.** 1872.

Ref.: Cal. Fms Pl. & Pr., Ch. 23, "Animals: Civil Liability"; Miller & Starr, Cal. Real Estate 3rd 17:1.

§656. Wild Animals.

Animals wild by nature are the subjects of ownership, while living, only when on the land of the person claiming them, or when tamed, or taken and held in possession, or disabled and immediately pursued. **Leg.H.** 1872.

Ref.: Cal. Fms Pl. & Pr., Ch. 23, "Animals: Civil Liability."

§657. Kinds of Property.

Property is either:
1. Real or immovable; or,
2. Personal or movable. **Leg.H.** 1872.

Ref.: Cal. Fms Pl. & Pr., Ch. 355, "Lost and Unclaimed Property"; Miller & Starr, Cal. Real Estate 3rd 10:38, 17:37.

§658. Real or Immovable.

Real or immovable property consists of:
1. Land;
2. That which is affixed to land;
3. That which is incidental or appurtenant to land;
4. That which is immovable by law; except that for the purposes of sale, emblements, industrial growing crops and things attached to or forming part of the land, which are agreed to be severed before sale or under the contract of sale, shall be treated as goods and be governed by the provisions of the title of this code regulating the sales of goods. **Leg.H.** 1872, 1931 ch. 1070.

Ref.: Cal. Fms Pl. & Pr., Ch. 369, "Mobilehomes and Mobilehome Parks," Ch. 503, "Sales: Secured Transactions"; Miller & Starr, Cal. Real Estate 3rd 17:3, 17:6, 17:19, 17:30-17:32, 17:37.

§659. Land.

Land is the material of the earth, whatever may be the ingredients of which it is composed, whether soil, rock, or other substance, and includes free or occupied space for an indefinite distance upwards as well as downwards, subject to limitations upon the use of airspace imposed, and rights in the use of airspace granted, by law. **Leg.H.** 1872, 1963 ch. 860.

Ref.: Miller & Starr, Cal. Real Estate 3rd 17:3, 17:21, 17:28.

§660. Fixtures.

A thing is deemed to be affixed to land when it is attached to it by roots, as in the case of trees, vines, or shrubs; or imbedded in it, as in the case of walls; or permanently resting upon it, as in the case of buildings; or permanently attached to what is thus permanent, as by means of cement, plaster, nails, bolts, or screws; except that for the purposes of sale, emblements, industrial growing crops and things attached to or forming part of the land, which are agreed to be severed before sale or under the contract of sale, shall be treated as goods and be governed by the provisions of the title of this code regulating the sales of goods. **Leg.H.** 1872, 1931 ch. 1070.

Ref.: Cal. Fms Pl. & Pr., Ch. 361, "Mechanics' Liens"; Miller & Starr, Cal. Real Estate 3rd 17:3, 17:6, 17:19, 17:30-17:32, 17:38, 17:40.

§662. Appurtenances.

A thing is deemed to be incidental or appurtenant to land when it is by right used with the land for its benefit, as in the case of a way, or watercourse, or of a passage for light, air, or heat from or across the land of another. **Leg.H.** 1872.

Ref.: Miller & Starr, Cal. Real Estate 3rd 15:6, 15:10, 17:25.

§663. Personalty.

Every kind of property that is not real is personal. **Leg.H.** 1872.

Ref.: Miller & Starr, Cal. Real Estate 3rd 10:38, 17:3.

TITLE II
OWNERSHIP

Chap. 1. Owners. §§669-671.
Chap. 2. Modifications of Ownership. §§678-726.
Chap. 2.6. Legal Estates Principal and Income Law. §§731-731.15.
Chap. 3. Rights of Owners. §§732, 733.
Chap. 4. Termination of Ownership. §§739-742.

CHAPTER 1
OWNERS

Seisin or ownership. §669.
Lands owned by state. §670.
Capacity to own. §671.

§669. Seisin or Ownership.

All property has an owner, whether that owner is the state, and the property public, or the owner an individual, and the property private. The state may also hold property as a private proprietor. **Leg.H.** 1872.

§670. Lands Owned by State.

The state is the owner of all land below tide-water, and below ordinary high-water mark, bordering upon tide-water within the state; of all land below the water of a navigable lake or stream; of all property lawfully appropriated by it to its own use; of all property dedicated to the state; and of all property of which there is no other owner. **Leg.H.** 1872, 1874 p. 217.

Ref.: Cal. Fms Pl. & Pr., Ch. 482, "Quieting Title"; Miller & Starr, Cal. Real Estate 3rd 8:48.

§671. Capacity to Own.

Any person, whether citizen or alien, may take, hold, and dispose of property, real or personal, within this state. **Leg.H.** 1872, 1874 p. 219.

Ref.: Miller & Starr, Cal. Real Estate 3rd 17:2.

CHAPTER 2
MODIFICATIONS OF OWNERSHIP

Art. 1. Interests in Property. §§678-703.
Art. 2. Conditions of Ownership. §§707-714.5.
Art. 3. Duration of Leases. §§715-719.
Art. 4. Accumulations and Income. §§722-726.

ARTICLE 1
Interests in Property

Absolute or qualified. §678.
Absolute ownership defined. §679.
Qualified or base ownership defined. §680.
Sole or several ownership. §681.
Joint, common, or community ownership. §682.
Community property of husband and wife. §682.1.
Joint interest defined. §683.
Interest in contents of safe-deposit box. §683.1.
Severance of joint tenant's interest without consent; severance by written declaration. §683.2.
Partnership interest defined. §684.
Common interest defined. §685.
Common interest created by mode of acquisition. §686.
Community property defined. §687.
Present or future, perpetual or limited interest. §688.
Present interest defined. §689.
Future interest defined. §690.
Perpetual interest. §691.
Limited interest. §692.
Alternative future interests. §696.
Improbability of contingency of future interest. §697.
Rights of posthumous child in interest to vest in child. §698.
Transfer of future interests. §699.
Mere possibility is no interest. §700.
Interest means estate. §701.
Applicability of statute to personalty. §702.
Future interest limited to those defined. §703.

§678. Absolute or Qualified.

The ownership of property is either:
1. Absolute; or,
2. Qualified. **Leg.H.** 1872.

Ref.: Miller & Starr, Cal. Real Estate 3rd 9:2.

§679. Absolute Ownership Defined.

The ownership of property is absolute when a single person has the absolute dominion over it, and may use it or dispose of it according to his pleasure, subject only to general laws. **Leg.H.** 1872.

Ref.: Miller & Starr, Cal. Real Estate 3rd 9:2, 11:95, 17:2.

§680. Qualified or Base Ownership Defined.

The ownership of property is qualified:
1. When it is shared with one or more persons;
2. When the time of enjoyment is deferred or limited;
3. When the use is restricted. **Leg.H.** 1872.

Ref.: Miller & Starr, Cal. Real Estate 3rd 9:2.

§681. Sole or Several Ownership.

The ownership of property by a single person is designated as a sole or several ownership. **Leg.H.** 1872.

Ref.: Miller & Starr, Cal. Real Estate 3rd 9:2, 12:1, 12:23.

§682. Joint, Common, or Community Ownership.

The ownership of property by several persons is either:
1. Of joint interests;
2. Of partnership interests;
3. Of interests in common;
4. Of community interest of husband and wife. **Leg.H.** 1872.

Ref.: Cal. Fms Pl. & Pr., Ch. 316, "Joint Tenancy and Tenancy in Common"; W. Cal. Sum., "Real Property" §§255 et seq.; Miller & Starr, Cal. Real Estate 3rd 12:1.

§682.1. Community Property of Husband and Wife.

(a) Community property of a husband and wife, when expressly declared in the transfer document to be community property with right of survivorship, and which may be accepted in writing on the face of the document by a statement signed or initialed by the grantees, shall, upon the death of one of the spouses, pass to the survivor, without administration, pursuant to the terms of the instrument, subject to the same procedures, as property held in joint tenancy. Prior to the death of either spouse, the right of survivorship may be terminated pursuant to the same procedures by which a joint tenancy may be severed. Part I (commencing with Section 5000) of Division 5 of the Probate Code and Chapter 2 (commencing with Section 13540), Chapter 3 (commencing with Section 13550) and Chapter 3.5 (commencing with Section 13560) of Part 2 of Division 8 of the Probate Code apply to this property.

(b) This section does not apply to a joint account in a financial institution to which Part 2 (commencing with Section 5100) of Division 5 of the Probate Code applies.

(c) This section shall become operative on July 1, 2001, and shall apply to instruments created on or after that date. **Leg.H.** 2000 ch. 645.

Ref.: Cal. Fms Pl. & Pr., Ch. 122, "Community Property," Ch. 316, "Joint Tenancy and Tenancy in Common"; W. Cal. Sum., "Community Property" §128A, "Wills" §26.

§683. Joint Interest Defined.

(a) A joint interest is one owned by two or more persons in equal shares, by a title created by a single will or transfer, when expressly declared in the will or transfer to be a joint tenancy, or by transfer from a sole owner to himself or herself and others, or from tenants in common or joint tenants to themselves or some of them, or to themselves or any of them and others, or from a husband and wife, when holding title as community property or otherwise to themselves or to themselves and others or to one of them and to another or others, when expressly declared in the transfer to be a joint tenancy, or when granted or devised to executors or trustees as joint tenants. A joint tenancy in personal property may be created by a written transfer, instrument, or agreement.

(b) Provisions of this section do not apply to a joint account in a financial institution if Part 2 (commencing with Section 5100) of Division 5 of the Probate Code applies to such account. **Leg.H.** 1872, 1931 ch. 1051, 1935 ch. 234, 1955 ch. 178, 1983 ch. 92, operative July 1, 1984, 1989 ch. 397, operative July 1, 1990, 1990 ch. 79, operative July 1, 1991.

Ref.: Cal. Fms Pl. & Pr., Ch. 122, "Community Property," Ch. 316, "Joint Tenancy and Tenancy in Common"; Miller & Starr, Cal. Real Estate 3rd 1:65, 12:22, 12:42.

§683.1. Interest in Contents of Safe-Deposit Box.

No contract or other arrangement made after the effective date of this section between any person, firm, or corporation engaged in the business of renting safe-deposit boxes and the renter or renters of a safe-deposit box, shall create a joint tenancy in or otherwise establish ownership in any of the contents of such safe-deposit box. Any such contract or other arrangement purporting so to do shall be to such extent void and of no effect. **Leg.H.** 1949 ch. 1597.

Ref.: Cal. Fms Pl. & Pr., Ch. 316, "Joint Tenancy and Tenancy in Common."

§683.2. Severance of Joint Tenant's Interest Without Consent; Severance by Written Declaration.

(a) Subject to the limitations and requirements of this section, in addition to any other means by which a joint tenancy may be severed, a joint tenant may sever a joint tenancy in real property as to the joint tenant's interest without the joinder or consent of the other joint tenants by any of the following means:

(1) Execution and delivery of a deed that conveys legal title to the joint tenant's interest to a third person, whether or not pursuant to an agreement that requires the third person to reconvey legal title to the joint tenant.

(2) Execution of a written instrument that evidences the intent to sever the joint tenancy, including a deed that names the joint tenant as transferee, or of a written declaration that, as to the interest of the joint tenant, the joint tenancy is severed.

(b) Nothing in this section authorizes severance of a joint tenancy contrary to a written agreement of the joint tenants, but a severance contrary to a written agreement does not defeat the rights of a purchaser or encumbrancer for value in good faith and without knowledge of the written agreement.

(c) Severance of a joint tenancy of record by deed, written declaration, or other written instrument pursuant to subdivision (a) is not effective to terminate the right of survivorship of the other joint tenants as to the severing joint tenant's interest unless one of the following requirements is satisfied:

(1) Before the death of the severing joint tenant, the deed, written declaration, or other written instrument effecting the severance is recorded in the county where the real property is located.

(2) The deed, written declaration, or other written instrument effecting the severance is executed and acknowledged before a notary public by the severing joint tenant not earlier than three days before the death of that joint tenant and is recorded in the county where the real property is located not later than seven days after the death of the severing joint tenant.

(d) Nothing in subdivision (c) limits the manner or effect of:

(1) A written instrument executed by all the joint tenants that severs the joint tenancy.

(2) A severance made by or pursuant to a written agreement of all the joint tenants.

(3) A deed from a joint tenant to another joint tenant.

(e) Subdivisions (a) and (b) apply to all joint tenancies in real property, whether the joint tenancy was created before, on, or after January 1, 1985, except that in the case of the death of a joint tenant before January 1, 1985, the validity of a severance under subdivisions (a) and (b) is determined by the law in effect at the time of death. Subdivisions (c) and (d) do not apply to or affect a severance made before January 1, 1986, of a joint tenancy. **Leg.H.** 1984 ch. 519, 1985 ch. 157.

Ref.: Cal. Fms Pl. & Pr., Ch. 316, "Joint Tenancy and Tenancy in Common"; W. Cal. Sum., "Personal Property" §22A; Miller & Starr, Cal. Real Estate 3rd 10:2, 12:29, 12:30.

§684. Partnership Interest Defined.

A partnership interest is one owned by several persons, in partnership, for partnership purposes. **Leg.H.** 1872.

Ref.: Cal. Fms Pl. & Pr., Ch. 316, "Joint Tenancy and Tenancy in Common."

§685. Common Interest Defined.

An interest in common is one owned by several persons, not in joint ownership or partnership. **Leg.H.** 1872.

Ref.: Cal. Fms Pl. & Pr., Ch. 316, "Joint Tenancy and Tenancy in Common"; Miller & Starr, Cal. Real Estate 3rd 12:33.

§686. Common Interest Created by Mode of Acquisition.

Every interest created in favor of several persons in their own right is an interest in common, unless acquired by them in partnership, for partnership purposes, or unless declared in its creation to be a joint interest, as provided in section six hundred and eighty-three, or unless acquired as community property. **Leg.H.** 1872.

Ref.: Cal. Fms Pl. & Pr., Ch. 316, "Joint Tenancy and Tenancy in Common"; Miller & Starr, Cal. Real Estate 3rd 12:33.

§687. Community Property Defined.

Community property is property that is community property under Part 2 (commencing with Section 760) of Division 4 of the Family Code. **Leg.H.** 1872, 1992 ch. 163, operative January 1, 1994.

Ref.: Cal. Fms Pl. & Pr., Ch. 122, "Community Property," Ch. 316, "Joint Tenancy and Tenancy in Common"; Miller & Starr, Cal. Real Estate 3rd 12:33.

§688. Present or Future, Perpetual or Limited Interest.

In respect to the time of enjoyment, an interest in property is either:

1. Present or future; and,
2. Perpetual or limited. **Leg.H.** 1872.

Ref.: Miller & Starr, Cal. Real Estate 3rd 9:2.

§689. Present Interest Defined.

A present interest entitles the owner to the immediate possession of the property. **Leg.H.** 1872.

Ref.: Cal. Fms Pl. & Pr., Ch. 482, "Quieting Title"; Miller & Starr, Cal. Real Estate 3rd 9:2.

§690. Future Interest Defined.

A future interest entitles the owner to the possession of the property only at a future period. **Leg.H.** 1872.

Ref.: W. Cal. Sum., "Real Property" §§330 et seq.; Miller & Starr, Cal. Real Estate 3rd 9:2, 9:26.

§691. Perpetual Interest.

A perpetual interest has a duration equal to that of the property. **Leg.H.** 1872.

Ref.: Miller & Starr, Cal. Real Estate 3rd 9:2.

§692. Limited Interest.

A limited interest has a duration less than that of the property. **Leg.H.** 1872.

Ref.: Miller & Starr, Cal. Real Estate 3rd 9:2.

§696. Alternative Future Interests.

Two or more future interests may be created to take effect in the alternative, so that if the first in order fails to vest, the next in succession shall be substituted for it, and take effect accordingly. **Leg.H.** 1872.

§697. Improbability of Contingency of Future Interest.

A future interest is not void merely because of the improbability of the contingency on which it is limited to take effect. **Leg.H.** 1872.

§698. Rights of Posthumous Child in Interest to Vest in Child.

When a future interest is limited to successors, heirs, issue, or children, posthumous children are entitled to take in the same manner as if living at the death of their parents. **Leg.H.** 1872.

Ref.: Miller & Starr, Cal. Real Estate 3rd 11:95.

§699. Transfer of Future Interests.

Future interests pass by succession, will, and transfer, in the same manner as present interests. **Leg.H.** 1872.

Ref.: Miller & Starr, Cal. Real Estate 3rd 8:45, 9:25, 9:30.

§700. Mere Possibility Is No Interest.

A mere possibility, such as the expectancy of an heir apparent, is not to be deemed an interest of any kind. **Leg.H.** 1872.

Ref.: Miller & Starr, Cal. Real Estate 3rd 9:25.

§701. Interest Means Estate.

In respect to real or immovable property, the interests mentioned in this chapter are denominated estates, and are specially named and classified in part two of this division. **Leg.H.** 1872.

Ref.: Miller & Starr, Cal. Real Estate 3rd 9:1, 19:2.

§702. Applicability of Statute to Personalty.

The names and classification of interests in real property have only such application to interest in personal property as is in this division of the code expressly provided. **Leg.H.** 1872.

§703. Future Interest Limited to Those Defined.

No future interest in property is recognized by the law, except such as is defined in this division of the code. **Leg.H.** 1872.

ARTICLE 2
Conditions of Ownership

As to time of enjoyment. §707.
Precedent and subsequent. §708.
Illegal conditions. §709.
Restraining marriage. §710.
Restraining alienation. §711.
Loan assumptions. §711.5.
Real estate sales—Prohibitions of signs void—Permissible displays. §712.
Display of signs. §713.
Voidability of covenants restricting solar energy systems; application for approval; penalties. §714.
Restrictions by common interest development on installation of solar energy systems in common areas. §714.1.
Covenants restricting use of structures constructed in offsite facility are void. §714.5.

§707. As to Time of Enjoyment.

The time when the enjoyment of property is to begin or end may be determined by computation, or be made to depend on events. In the latter case, the enjoyment is said to be upon condition. **Leg.H.** 1872.

§708. Precedent and Subsequent.

Conditions are precedent or subsequent. The former fix the beginning, the latter the ending, of the right. **Leg.H.** 1872.

§709. Illegal Conditions.

If a condition precedent requires the performance of an act wrong of itself, the instrument containing it is so far void, and the right cannot exist. If it requires the performance of an act not wrong of itself, but otherwise unlawful, the instrument takes effect and the condition is void. **Leg.H.** 1872.

§710. Restraining Marriage.

Conditions imposing restraints upon marriage, except upon the marriage of a minor, are void; but this does not affect limitations where the intent was not to forbid marriage, but only to give the use until marriage. **Leg.H.** 1872, 1874 p. 218.

Ref.: Cal. Fms Pl. & Pr., Ch. 359, "Marriage."

§711. Restraining Alienation.

Conditions restraining alienation, when repugnant to the interest created, are void. **Leg.H.** 1872.

Ref.: W. Cal. Sum., "Real Property" §§405 et seq.; Miller & Starr, Cal. Real Estate 3rd 2:16, 9:37, 9:38, 19:70-19:76, 31:24.

§711.5. Loan Assumptions.

(a) Notwithstanding the provisions of Sections 711 and 1916.5, a state or local public entity directly or indirectly providing housing purchase or rehabilitation loans shall have the authority to deny assumptions, or require the denial of assumptions, by a subsequent ineligible purchaser or transferee of the prior borrower of the obligation of any such loan made for the purpose of rehabilitating or providing affordable housing. If such a subsequent purchaser or transferee does not meet such an entity's eligibility requirements, that entity may accelerate or may require the acceleration of the principal balance of the loan to be all due and payable upon the sale or transfer of the property.

(b) As a condition of authorizing assumption of a loan pursuant to this section, the entity may recast the repayment schedule for the remainder of the term of the loan by increasing the interest to the current market rate at the time of assumption, or to such lower rate of interest as is the maximum allowed by an entity that provided any insurance or other assistance which results in an assumption being permitted. Any additional increment of interest produced by increasing the rate of interest upon a loan pursuant to this subdivision shall be transmitted or forwarded to the entity for deposit in the specified fund from which the loan was made, or, if no such fund exists, or the public entity has directed otherwise, then to the general fund of such entity.

(c) The state or local public entity providing assistance as specified in this section may implement appropriate measures to assure compliance with this section. **Leg.H.** 1979 ch. 971, effective September 22, 1979.

Ref.: Miller & Starr, Cal. Real Estate 3rd 10:108.

§712. Real Estate Sales—Prohibitions of Signs Void—Permissible Displays.

(a) Every provision contained in or otherwise affecting a grant of a fee interest in, or purchase money security instrument upon, real property in this state heretofore or hereafter made, which purports to prohibit or restrict the right of the property owner or his or her agent to display or have displayed on the real property, or on real property owned by others with their consent, or both, signs which are reasonably located, in plain view of the public, are of reasonable dimensions and design, and do not adversely affect public safety, including traffic safety, and which advertise the property for sale, lease, or exchange, or advertise directions to the property, by the property owner or his or her agent is void as an unreasonable restraint upon the power of alienation.

(b) This section shall operate retrospectively, as well as prospectively, to the full extent that it may constitutionally operate retrospectively.

(c) A sign that conforms to the ordinance adopted in conformity with Section 713 shall be deemed to be of reasonable dimension and design pursuant to this section. **Leg.H.** 1965 ch. 1591, 1975 ch. 147, 1983 ch. 51, 1990 ch. 1282, 1992 ch. 773, 1993 ch. 589.

Ref.: Cal. Fms Pl. & Pr., Ch. 14, "Advertising"; Miller & Starr, Cal. Real Estate 3rd 9:41.

§713. Display of Signs.

(a) Notwithstanding any provision of any ordinance, an owner of real property or his or her agent may display or have displayed on the owner's real property, and on real property owned by others with their consent, signs which are reasonably located, in plain view of the public, are of reasonable dimensions and design, and do not adversely affect public safety, including traffic safety, as determined by the city, county, or city and county, advertising the following:

(1) That the property is for sale, lease, or exchange by the owner or his or her agent.

(2) Directions to the property.

(3) The owner's or agent's name.

(4) The owner's or agent's address and telephone number.

(b) Nothing in this section limits any authority which a person or local governmental entity may have to limit or regulate the display or placement of a sign on a private or public right-of-way. **Leg.H.** 1975 ch. 147, 1983 ch. 51, 1990 ch. 1282, 1992 ch. 773.

Ref.: Cal. Fms Pl. & Pr., Ch. 14, "Advertising"; Miller & Starr, Cal. Real Estate 3rd 9:41.

§714. Voidability of Covenants Restricting Solar Energy Systems; Application for Approval; Penalties.

(a) Any covenant, restriction, or condition contained in any deed, contract, security instrument, or other instrument affecting the transfer or sale of, or any interest in, real property that effectively prohibits or restricts the installation or use of a solar energy system is void and unenforceable.

(b) This section does not apply to provisions that impose reasonable restrictions on solar energy systems. However, it is the policy of the state to promote and encourage the use of solar energy systems and to remove obstacles thereto. Accordingly, reasonable restrictions on a solar energy system are those restrictions that do not significantly increase the cost of the system or significantly decrease its efficiency or specified performance, or that allow for an alternative system of comparable cost, efficiency, and energy conservation benefits.

(c) (1) A solar energy system shall meet applicable health and safety standards and requirements imposed by state and local permitting authorities.

(2) A solar energy system for heating water shall be certified by the Solar Rating Certification Corporation (SRCC) or other nationally recognized certification agencies. SRCC is a nonprofit third party supported by the United States Department of Energy. The certification shall be for the entire solar energy system and installation.

(3) A solar energy system for producing electricity shall also meet all applicable safety and performance standards established by the National Electrical Code, the Institute of Electrical and Electronics Engineers, and accredited testing laboratories such as Underwriters Laboratories and, where applicable, rules of the Public Utilities Commission regarding safety and reliability.

(d) For the purposes of this section:

(1) (A) For solar domestic water heating systems or solar swimming pool heating systems that comply with state and federal law, "significantly" means an amount exceeding 20 percent of the cost of the system or decreasing the efficiency of the solar energy system by an amount exceeding 20 percent, as originally specified and proposed.

(B) For photovoltaic systems that comply with state and federal law, "significantly" means an amount not to exceed two thousand dollars ($2,000) over the system cost as originally specified and proposed, or a decrease in system efficiency of an amount exceeding 20 percent as originally specified and proposed.

(2) "Solar energy system" has the same meaning as defined in paragraphs (1) and (2) of subdivision (a) of Section 801.5.

(e) Whenever approval is required for the installation or use of a solar energy system, the application for approval shall be processed and approved by the appropriate approving entity in the same manner as an application for approval of an architectural modification to the property, and shall not be willfully avoided or delayed.

(f) Any entity, other than a public entity, that willfully violates this section shall be liable to the applicant or other party for actual damages occasioned thereby, and shall pay a civil penalty to the applicant or other party in an amount not to exceed one thousand dollars ($1,000).

(g) In any action to enforce compliance with this section, the prevailing party shall be awarded reasonable attorney's fees.

(h) (1) A public entity that fails to comply with this section may not receive funds from a state-sponsored grant or loan program for solar energy. A public entity shall certify its compliance with the requirements of this section when applying for funds from a state-sponsored grant or loan program.

(2) A local public entity may not exempt residents in its jurisdiction from the requirements of this section. **Leg.H.** 1978 ch. 1154, 1990 ch. 1517, operative July 1, 1991, 1992 ch. 1222, 1994 ch. 382, 1995 ch. 91, 2002 ch. 570 (SB 1534), 2003 ch. 290 (AB 1407), 2004 ch. 789 (AB 2473).

Ref.: Miller & Starr, Cal. Real Estate 3rd 15:11, 24:5.

§714.1. Restrictions by Common Interest Development on Installation of Solar Energy Systems in Common Areas.

Notwithstanding Section 714, any association, as defined in Section 1351, may impose reasonable provisions which:

(a) Restrict the installation of solar energy systems installed in common areas, as defined in Section 1351, to those systems approved by the association.

(b) Require the owner of a separate interest, as defined in Section 1351, to obtain the approval of the association for the installation of a solar energy system in a separate interest owned by another.

(c) Provide for the maintenance, repair, or replacement of roofs or other building components.

(d) Require installers of solar energy systems to indemnify or reimburse the association or its members for loss or damage caused by the installation, maintenance, or use of the solar energy system. **Leg.H.** 1992 ch. 1222.

§714.5. Covenants Restricting Use of Structures Constructed in Offsite Facility Are Void.

The covenants, conditions, and restrictions or other management documents shall not prohibit the sale, lease, rent, or use of real property on the basis that the structure intended for occupancy on the real property is constructed in an offsite facility or factory, and subsequently moved or transported in sections or modules to the real property. Nothing herein shall preclude the governing instruments from being uniformly applied to all structures subject to the covenants, conditions, and restrictions or other management documents.

This section shall apply to covenants, conditions, and restrictions or other management documents adopted on and after the effective date of this section. **Leg.H.** 1987 ch. 1339.

Ref.: Miller & Starr, Cal. Real Estate 3rd 25:116.

ARTICLE 3
Duration of Leases

Invalidity of lease if possession does not commence within 30 years of execution. §715.
Agricultural lease limited to 51 years. §717.
Leases of municipal property. §718.
99-year oil and gas leases. §718f.
Lease of property by cities. §719.

§715. Invalidity of Lease If Possession Does Not Commence Within 30 Years of Execution.

A lease to commence at a time certain or upon the happening of a future event becomes invalid if its term does not actually commence in possession within 30 years after its execution. **Leg.H.** 1991 ch. 156 §3.

§717. Agricultural Lease Limited to 51 Years.

No lease or grant of land for agricultural or horticultural purposes for a longer period than 51 years, in which shall be reserved any rent or service of any kind, shall be valid.

Leg.H. 1872, 1895 p. 75, 1909 p. 1000, 1915 p. 349, 1963 ch. 1906.

Ref.: Miller & Starr, Cal. Real Estate 3rd 19:33.

§718. Leases of Municipal Property.

No lease or grant of any town or city lot, which reserves any rent or service of any kind, and which provides for a leasing or granting period in excess of 99 years, shall be valid. The property owned by, or that held by, or under the management and control of, any municipality, or any department or board thereof, may be leased for a period not to exceed 55 years. The property of any municipality not acquired for park purposes may, for the purpose of producing, or effecting the production of minerals, oil, gas or other hydrocarbon substances, be leased for a period not to exceed 35 years. Any tidelands or submerged lands, granted to any city by the State of California, may be leased for a period not to exceed 66 years unless the grant from the state of the use thereof provides specifically the term for which said lands may be leased. Tidelands and submerged lands owned or controlled by any city, together with the wharves, docks, piers and other structures or improvements thereon, and so much of the uplands abutting thereon as, in the judgment of the city council, or other governing body, of said city, may be necessary for the proper development and use of its water front and harbor facilities, may be leased for a period not to exceed 66 years. Said tidelands, submerged lands and uplands may be so leased only for industrial uses, the improvement and development of any harbor, or harbors, of said city, the construction and maintenance of wharves, docks, piers or bulkhead piers, or any other public use or purpose consistent with the requirements of commerce or navigation at, or in any, such harbor or harbors. **Leg.H.** 1872, 1903 p. 247, 1911 p. 1391, 1915 p. 349, 1917 p. 798, 1927 ch. 689, 1929 ch. 110, 1935 ch. 695, 1941 ch. 492, 1961 ch. 2010, 1967 ch. 228.

Ref.: Miller & Starr, Cal. Real Estate 3rd 19:33, 19:40.

§718f. 99-Year Oil and Gas Leases.

A lease of land for the purpose of effecting the production of minerals, oil, gas, or other hydrocarbon substances from other lands may be made for a period certain or determinable by any future event prescribed by the parties but no such lease shall be enforceable after 99 years from the commencement of the term thereof. **Leg.H.** 1953 ch. 1344.

Ref.: Miller & Starr, Cal. Real Estate 3rd 17:23.

§719. Lease of Property by Cities.

Notwithstanding the 55-year limitation imposed by Section 718, property owned by, or held by, or under the management and control of, any city, or any department or board thereof, may be leased for a period which exceeds 55 years but does not exceed 99 years, if all of the following conditions are met:

(a) The lease shall be subject to periodic review by the city and shall take into consideration the then current market conditions. The local legislative body may, prior to final execution of the lease, establish the lease provisions which will periodically be reviewed, and determine when those provisions are to be reviewed.

(b) Any lease entered into by any city pursuant to this section shall be authorized by an ordinance adopted by the legislative body. The ordinance shall be subject to referendum in the manner prescribed by law for ordinances of cities.

(c) Prior to adopting an ordinance authorizing a lease, the legislative body shall hold a public hearing. Notice of the time and place of the hearing shall be published pursuant to Section 6066 of the Government Code, in one or more newspapers of general circulation within the city and shall be mailed to any person requesting special notice, to any present tenant of the public property, and to all owners of land adjoining the property.

(d) Any lease shall be awarded to the bidder which, in the determination of the legislative body, offers the greatest economic return to the city, after competitive bidding conducted in the manner determined by the legislative body. Notice inviting bids shall be published pursuant to Section 6066 in one or more newspapers of general circulation within the city.

(e) The provisions of subdivisions (b), (c), and (d) of this section do not apply to any charter city, which may utilize a procedure as specified by charter or adopted by ordinance in accordance with its charter.

(f) This section shall not apply to leases of property acquired for park purposes; to leases for the purpose of producing mineral, oil, gas, or other hydrocarbon substances; nor to leases of tidelands or submerged lands or improvements thereon. **Leg.H.** 1983 ch. 720.

Ref.: Miller & Starr, Cal. Real Estate 3rd 19:22, 19:33.

ARTICLE 4
Accumulations and Income

Future interests. §722.
Restrictions upon. §723.
Permissible accumulations. §724.
Prohibited accumulations. §725.
Acceleration. §726.

§722. Future Interests.

Dispositions of the income of property to accrue and to be received at any time subsequent to the execution of the instrument creating such disposition are governed by the rules relating to future interests. **Leg.H.** 1872, 1991 ch. 156.

§723. Restrictions Upon.

All directions for the accumulation of the income of property, except such as are allowed by this title, are void. **Leg.H.** 1872.

§724. Permissible Accumulations.

(a) An accumulation of the income of property may be directed by any will, trust or transfer in writing sufficient to pass the property or create the trust out of which the fund is to arise, for the benefit of one or more persons, objects or purposes, but may not extend beyond the time permitted for the vesting of future interests.

(b) Notwithstanding subdivision (a), the income arising from real or personal property held in a trust forming part of a profit-sharing plan of an employer for the exclusive benefit of its employees or their beneficiaries or forming part of a retirement plan formed primarily for the purpose of providing benefits for employees on or after retirement may be permitted to accumulate until the fund is sufficient, in the opinion of the trustee or trustees, to accomplish the purposes of the trust. **Leg.H.** 1929 p. 276 ch. 143, 1959 ch. 470, 1991 ch. 156.

§725. Prohibited Accumulations.

If the direction for an accumulation of the income of property is for a longer term than is limited in the last section, the direction only, whether separable or not from the other provisions of the instrument, is void as respects the time beyond the limit prescribed in said last section, and no other part of such instrument is affected by the void portion of such direction. **Leg.H.** 1929 p. 276 ch. 143.

§726. Acceleration.

When one or more persons for whose benefit an accumulation of income has been directed is or are destitute of other sufficient means of support or education, the proper court, upon application, may direct a suitable sum to be applied thereto out of the fund directed to be accumulated for the benefit of such person or persons. **Leg.H.** 1929 p. 276 ch. 143.

Ref.: Cal. Fms Pl. & Pr., Ch. 560, "Trusts"; Miller & Starr, Cal. Real Estate 3rd 10:191, 10:222, 10:223.

CHAPTER 2.6
LEGAL ESTATES PRINCIPAL AND INCOME LAW

Title cited. §731.
Saving clause. §731.01.
Applicability of chapter. §731.02.
Definitions. §731.03.
Governing provisions. §731.04.
Income and principal construed. §731.05.
Termination of tenant's right to income. §731.06.
Disbursement of corporate assets. §731.07.
Bonds or obligations for payment of money. §731.08.
Use of principal to continue business. §731.09.
Animals. §731.10.
Natural resources. §731.11.
Property subject to depletion. §731.12.
Delayed income. §731.13.
Mortgages and acquisition of property. §731.14.
Administration and management expenses. §731.15.

§731. Title Cited.

This chapter may be cited as the Legal Estates Principal and Income Law. **Leg.H.** 1968 ch. 193, effective July 1, 1968.

Ref.: Miller & Starr, Cal. Real Estate 3rd 22:28.

§731.01. Saving Clause.

Nothing in this chapter shall affect the provisions of the Personal Income Tax Law and the Bank and Corporation Tax Law. **Leg.H.** 1968 ch. 193, effective July 1, 1968.

§731.02. Applicability of Chapter.

This chapter shall apply to all transactions by which a principal was established without the interposition of a trust on or after September 13, 1941, or is hereafter so established. Transactions by which a principal is held in trust are governed by Chapter 3 (commencing with Section 16300) of Part 4 of Division 9 of the Probate Code. **Leg.H.** 1968 ch. 193, effective July 1, 1968, 1986 ch. 820, operative July 1, 1987.

Ref.: Miller & Starr, Cal. Real Estate 3rd 9:33.

§731.03. Definitions.

(a) "Principal" as used in this chapter means any realty or personalty which has been so set aside or limited by the owner thereof or a person thereto legally empowered that it and any substitutions for it are eventually to be conveyed, delivered, or paid to a person, while the return therefrom or use thereof or any part of such return or use is in the meantime to be taken or received by or held for accumulation for the same or another person;

(b) "Income" as used in this chapter means the return derived from principal;

(c) "Tenant" as used in this chapter means the person to whom income is presently or currently payable, or for whom it is accumulated or who is entitled to the beneficial use of the principal presently and for a time prior to its distribution;

(d) "Remainderman" as used in this chapter means the person ultimately entitled to the principal, whether named or designated by the terms of the transaction by which the principal was established or determined by operation of law. **Leg.H.** 1968 ch. 193, effective July 1, 1968.

§731.04. Governing Provisions.

This chapter shall govern the ascertainment of income and principal and the apportionment of receipts and expenses between tenants and remaindermen in all cases where a principal has been established without the interposition of a trust, except that in the establishment of the principal, provision may be made touching all matters covered by this chapter, and the person establishing the principal may himself direct the manner of ascertainment of income and principal and the apportionment of receipts and expenses or grant discretion to the tenant or other person to do so, and such provision and direction, where not otherwise contrary to law shall control notwithstanding this chapter. The exercise by the tenant or other designated person, of such discretionary power if in good faith and according to his best judgment, shall be conclusive, irrespective of whether it may be in accordance with the determination which the court having jurisdiction would have made. **Leg.H.** 1968 ch. 193, effective July 1, 1968.

Ref.: Miller & Starr, Cal. Real Estate 3rd 9:33.

§731.05. Income and Principal Construed.

(a) All receipts of money or other property paid or delivered as rent of realty or hire of personalty, or interest on money loaned, or interest on or the rental or use value of property wrongfully withheld or tortiously damaged or otherwise in return for the use of principal, shall be deemed income unless otherwise expressly provided in this chapter. Dividends on corporate shares, payable in stock or otherwise, shall be deemed income except as provided in Section 731.07.

(b) All receipts of money or other property paid or delivered as the consideration for the sale or other transfer, not a leasing or letting, of property forming a part of principal, or as a repayment of loans, or in liquidation of the assets of a corporation, or as the proceeds of property taken on eminent domain proceedings where separate awards to tenant and remainderman are not made, or as proceeds of insurance upon property forming a part of the principal except where such insurance has been issued for the benefit of either tenant or remainderman alone, or otherwise as a refund or replacement or change in form of principal, shall be deemed principal unless otherwise expressly provided in this chapter. Any profit or loss resulting upon any change in form of principal shall inure to or fall upon principal, except in the case of property referred to and defined by Section 731.14, in which case the provisions of Section 731.14 shall govern.

(c) All income, after payment of expenses properly chargeable to it, shall be paid and delivered to the tenant or retained by him if already in his possession or held for accumulation where legally so directed by the terms of the transaction by which the principal was established; while the principal shall be held for ultimate distribution as determined by the terms of the transaction by which it was established or by law, except in the case of property referred to and defined by Section 731.14, in which case the provisions of Section 731.14 shall govern. **Leg.H.** 1968 ch. 193, effective July 1, 1968.

§731.06. Termination of Tenant's Right to Income.

Whenever a tenant's right to income shall cease by death, or in any other manner, all payments theretofore actually paid to the tenant shall belong to the tenant or to his personal representative; all income actually received after such termination shall be paid to the person next entitled to income by the terms of the transaction by which the principal was established. **Leg.H.** 1968 ch. 193, effective July 1, 1968.

Ref.: Miller & Starr, Cal. Real Estate 3rd 9:33.

§731.07. Disbursement of Corporate Assets.

(a) All dividends on shares of a corporation forming a part of the principal which are payable

(1) In shares of the declaring corporation of the same kind and rank as the shares on which such dividend is paid; and

(2) In shares of the declaring corporation of a different kind or rank to the extent that they represent a capitalization of surplus not derived from earnings, shall be deemed principal.

Subject to the provisions of this section, all dividends, other than those awarded to principal under (1) and (2) above, including ordinary and extraordinary dividends and dividends payable in shares or other securities or obligations of corporations other than the declaring corporation, shall be deemed income.

Where the tenant shall have the option of receiving a dividend either in cash or in the shares of the declaring corporation, it shall be considered as a cash dividend and deemed income, irrespective of the choice made by the tenant except as provided in subdivision (f) of this section.

(b) All rights to subscribe to the shares or other securities or obligations of a corporation accruing on account of the ownership of shares or other securities in such corporation, and the proceeds of any sale of such rights, shall be deemed principal. All rights to subscribe to the shares or other securities or obligations of a corporation accruing on account of the ownership of shares or other securities in another corporation, and the proceeds of any sale of such rights shall be deemed income.

(c) Where the assets of a corporation are liquidated, amounts paid upon corporate shares as cash dividends declared before such liquidation occurred or as arrears of preferred or guaranteed dividends shall be deemed income; all other amounts paid upon corporate shares on disbursement of the corporate assets to the stockholders shall be deemed principal. All disbursements of corporate assets to the stockholders, whenever made, which are designated by the corporation as a return of capital or division of corporate property shall be deemed principal.

(d) Where a corporation succeeds another by merger, consolidation, or reorganization or otherwise acquires its assets, and the corporate shares of the succeeding corporation are issued to the shareholders of the original corporation in like proportion to, or in substitution for, their shares of the original corporation, the two corporations shall be considered a single corporation in applying the provisions of this section. But, two corporations shall not be considered a single corporation under this section merely because one owns corporate shares of or otherwise controls or directs the other.

(e) In applying this section the date when a dividend accrues to the person who is entitled to it shall be held to be the date specified by the corporation as the one on which the stockholders entitled thereto are determined, or in default thereof the date of declaration of the dividend.

(f) Distributions made from ordinary income by a regulated investment company or by a trust qualifying and electing to be taxed under federal law as a real estate investment trust are income. All other distributions made by the company or trust, including distributions from capital gains, depreciation, or depletion, whether in the form of cash or an option to take new stock or cash or an option to purchase additional shares, are principal.

(g) The tenant may rely upon the statement of the paying corporation as to whether dividends are paid from profits or earnings or are a return of capital or division of corporate property, and as to any other fact, relevant under any provision of this chapter, concerning the source or character of dividends or disbursements of corporate assets. **Leg.H.** 1968 ch. 193, effective July 1, 1968.

§731.08. Bonds or Obligations for Payment of Money.

Where any part of the principal consists of bonds or other obligations for the payment of money, they shall be deemed principal at their inventory value as fixed by the appraiser or appraisers regularly appointed by the court, or, in default thereof, at their market value at the time the principal was established, or at their cost where purchased later, regardless of their par or maturity value; and upon their respective maturities or upon their sale or other disposition any loss or gain realized thereon shall fall upon or inure to the principal, except in the case of property referred to and defined by Section 731.14, in which case the provisions of Section 731.14 shall govern. Where any part of the principal consists of a bond or other obligation for the payment of money, bearing no stated interest but redeemable at maturity or a future time at an amount in excess of the amount in consideration of which it was issued, such accretion, as when realized, shall inure to income. **Leg.H.** 1968 ch. 193, effective July 1, 1968.

§731.09. Use of Principal to Continue Business.

(a) Whenever a tenant is authorized by the terms of the transaction by which the principal was established or by law, to use any part of the principal in the continuance of a business which the original owner of the property comprising the principal had been carrying on, the net profits of such business attributable to such principal shall be deemed income.

(b) Where such business consists of buying and selling property, the net profits for any period shall be ascertained by deducting from the gross returns during, and the inventory value of the property at the end of, such period, the expenses during, and the inventory value of the property at the beginning of, such period.

(c) Where such business does not consist of buying and selling property, the net income shall be computed in accordance with the customary practice of such business, but not in such way as to decrease the principal.

(d) Any increase in the value of the principal used in such business shall be deemed principal, and all losses in any one calendar year, after the income from such business for that year has been exhausted, shall fall upon principal. **Leg.H.** 1968 ch. 193, effective July 1, 1968.

§731.10. Animals.

Where any part of the principal consists of animals employed in business, the provisions of Section 731.09 shall apply; and in other cases where the animals are held as a part of the principal partly or wholly because of the offspring or increase which they are expected to produce, all offspring or increase shall be deemed principal to the extent necessary to maintain the original number of such animals and the remainder shall be deemed income; and in all other cases such offspring or increase shall be deemed income. **Leg.H.** 1968 ch. 193, effective July 1, 1968.

§731.11. Natural Resources.

(a) Where any part of the principal consists of property in lands from which may be taken timber, minerals, oils, gas, or other natural resources, and the tenant in possession is not under a duty to change the form of the investment of the principal, or (the duty to change the form of the investment being absent) is authorized by law or by the terms of the transaction by which the principal was established, to lease or otherwise develop such natural resources, and no provision is made for the disposition of the net proceeds thereof after the payment of expenses and carrying charges on such property, such proceeds shall be deemed income, whether received as rent or bonus on a lease or as a consideration, by way of royalties or otherwise for the permanent severance of such natural resources from the lands. A duty to change the form of the investment shall be negatived, and authority to develop such natural resources shall be deemed to exist (not excluding other cases where appropriate intent is manifested) where: (1) the resources or the right to exploit them is specifically devised or granted, or (2) where development or exploitation of the resources had begun prior to the transaction by which the principal was established, or (3) where by the terms of that transaction a general authority to lease or otherwise develop is conferred, or (4) where the lands are directed to be retained. The fact that such property received upon creation of the principal does not fall within the category of investments which the tenant or a trustee would be authorized to make under the law or the terms of the particular instrument by which the principal is established, nor the conferring of a mere authority, as distinguished from a direction, to sell such property, shall not be deemed to evidence an intent that the form of the investment shall be changed.

(b) Where any part of the principal consists of property in lands containing such natural resources, and the conditions under which the proceeds thereof become income shall not exist, then in the absence of the expression of contrary intent in the terms of the transaction by which the principal was established, all such proceeds from such resources, not in excess of 5 percent per annum of the inventory value of such resources as fixed by the appraiser or appraisers regularly appointed by the court, or in default thereof their fair market value at the time the principal was established, or their cost if acquired later, shall be deemed income and the remainder principal.

(c) Nothing in this section shall be construed to abrogate or extend any right which may otherwise have accrued by law to a tenant to develop or work such natural resources for his own benefit. **Leg.H.** 1968 ch. 193, effective July 1, 1968.

§731.12. Property Subject to Depletion.

Where any part of the principal consists of property subject to depletion, such as leaseholds, patents, copyrights, and royalty rights, and the tenant in possession is not under a duty to change the form of the investment of the principal, the full amount of rents, royalties, or income from the property shall be income to the tenant; but where the tenant is under a duty to change the form of the investment, either at once or as soon as a reasonable price, not representing an undue sacrifice of value, may be obtained, then the rents, royalties or income from such property not in excess of 5 percent per annum of its inventory value as fixed by the appraiser or appraisers regularly appointed by the court, or in default thereof its market value at the time the principal was established or at its cost where purchased later, shall be deemed income and the remainder principal. **Leg.H.** 1968 ch. 193, effective July 1, 1968.

§731.13. Delayed Income.

(a) Where any part of a principal in the possession of a tenant consists of realty or personalty which for more than a year and until disposed of as hereinafter stated has not produced an average net income of at least 1 percent per annum of its inventory value as fixed by the appraiser or appraisers regularly appointed by the court, or in default thereof its market value at the time the principal was established or of its cost where purchased or otherwise acquired later, and the tenant is under a duty to change the form of the investment as soon as a reasonable price, not representing an undue sacrifice of value, may be obtained and such change is delayed, but is made before the principal is finally distributed, then the tenant shall be entitled to share in the net proceeds received from the property as delayed income to the extent hereinafter stated.

(b) Such income shall be the difference between the net proceeds received from the property and the amount which, had it been placed at simple interest at the rate of 5 percent per annum for the period during which the change was delayed, would have produced the net proceeds at the time of change, but in no event shall such income be more than the amount by which the net proceeds exceed the inventory value of the property as fixed by the appraiser or appraisers regularly appointed by the court, or in default thereof its market value at the time the principal was established or its cost where purchased later. The net proceeds shall consist of the gross proceeds received from the property less any expenses incurred in disposing of it and less all carrying charges which had been paid out of principal during the period while it has been unproductive.

(c) The change shall be taken to have been delayed from the time when the duty to make it first arose, which shall be presumed in the absence of evidence to the contrary, to be one year after the tenant first received the property if then unproductive, otherwise one year after it became unproductive.

(d) If the tenant has received any income from the property or has had any beneficial use thereof during the period while the change has been delayed, his share of the delayed income shall be reduced by the amount of such income received or the value of the use had.

(e) As between successive tenants, or a tenant and a remainderman, delayed income shall be apportioned in the same manner as provided for income by Section 731.06. **Leg.H.** 1968 ch. 193, effective July 1, 1968.

§731.14. Mortgages and Acquisition of Property.

(a) Where any part of the principal in possession of the tenant consists of an obligation for the payment of money secured by a mortgage or other hypothecation of real or personal property, and by reason of the enforcement of such obligation or by agreement in lieu of enforcement the tenant acquires any property, real or personal, of whatsoever kind, including a money judgment, such property shall be treated as a single substituted asset, and thereafter all income therefrom, expenses incident thereto and proceeds received upon sale, satisfaction, or transfer thereof, not a leasing or letting, excepting gain or profit on such sale, satisfaction or transfer, shall be apportioned in the same manner as provided by this chapter for property of like character acquired by purchase or held as a part of the estate at the time the principal was established.

Gain or profit realized on sale, satisfaction, or transfer, not a leasing or a letting, of property referred to in this section shall be credited to the income in an amount up to, but not exceeding, the accrued unpaid interest on the original obligation secured by such property as of the date of its acquisition by enforcement of the obligation or agreement in lieu thereof, and the balance shall be credited to principal. Such credit to income on account of accrued interest shall be in addition to any and all other credits due income by the terms of any other section of this chapter. Should any portion of such credit to income on account of accrued interest be in a form other than cash, then, and in that event, the full amount of such credit to income shall be paid first out of any sums received from the conversion of such asset into cash whether by payment, sale, or transfer before any sums so received shall be paid to principal.

As between successive tenants or a tenant and a remainderman, all sums paid hereunder on account of accrued interest shall be apportioned in the same manner as provided for income by Section 731.06.

The cost price of the property shall be the unpaid balance of the principal sum of the debt secured by such property, plus all sums whenever paid on any of the following items:

(1) All costs, charges, and expenses incident to the acquisition of such property;

(2) All taxes, bonds, and assessments, or any of them, which were payable at the date of the acquisition of such property by the tenant, excepting, however, interest accruing thereon from the date of the acquisition of such property by the tenant; and all such sums shall be a charge against the principal.

(b) Upon the sale, surrender, or other disposition of a bond, debenture, note, or other evidence of an indebtedness, voluntarily created, or of a certificate of deposit evidencing the deposit of any such instrument with a protective or reorganization committee, or of stock or other security received through participation in the enforcement of such obligation or the foreclosure of the security therefor, upon which bond or other obligation there is overdue unpaid interest which accrued after the establishment of the principal, the proceeds realized upon such sale, surrender, or other disposition, after repayment (1) of expenses incurred in connection therewith and (2) of any sums paid to protect or preserve such security, shall be divided pro rata between income and principal, computing interest at the rate specified in such obligation. The amount allocable to income shall in no case exceed the interest accrued and unpaid on the original obligation up to the time of such sale or other disposition or, where another security has been received in lieu of the original obligation, the income which would have accrued on the latter up to such time, less income received from the original or the substituted security. The terms sale, surrender, or other disposition, as above used, shall include compromise, settlement, accord and satisfaction, and similar arrangements. **Leg.H.** 1968 ch. 193, effective July 1, 1968.

§731.15. Administration and Management Expenses.

(a) All ordinary expenses incurred in connection with the principal or with its administration and management, including regularly recurring taxes assessed against any portion of the principal, water rates, premiums on insurance taken upon the estates of both tenant and remainderman, interest on mortgages on the principal, ordinary repairs, compensation of assistants and court costs on regular accountings, except attorneys' fees, shall be paid out of income. But such expenses where incurred in disposing of, or as carrying charges on, unproductive property as defined in Section 731.13, shall be paid out of principal, subject to the provisions of subdivision (b) of Section 731.13. Attorneys' fees for ordinary or current services shall be paid one-half out of income; one-half out of principal or in such other proportion as the court may direct.

(b) Attorneys' fees and other costs incurred in maintaining or defending any action to protect the property or assure the title thereof, unless due to the fault or cause of the tenant, costs of, or assessments for, improvements to property forming part of the principal, brokers' commissions, title charges, and other costs incurred in connection with purchasing, selling, or leasing property, or investing or reinvesting principal, and all other expenses, except as specified in subdivision (a) of this section, shall be paid out of principal. Any tax levied by any authority, federal, state, or foreign, upon profit or gain defined under the terms of subdivision (b) of Section 731.05 shall be paid out of principal, notwithstanding such tax may be denominated a tax upon income by the taxing authority. **Leg.H.** 1968 ch. 193, effective July 1, 1968.

CHAPTER 3
RIGHTS OF OWNERS

Right to accessions and increase. §732.
Right to income pending suspension of alienation. §733.

§732. Right to Accessions and Increase.

The owner of a thing owns also all its products and accessions. **Leg.H.** 1872.

Ref.: Miller & Starr, Cal. Real Estate 3rd 17:38, 19:122.

§733. Right to Income Pending Suspension of Alienation.

When, in consequence of a valid limitation of a future interest, there is a suspension of the power of alienation or of the ownership during the continuation of which the income is undisposed of, and no valid direction for its accumulation is given, such income belongs to the persons presumptively entitled to the next eventual interest. **Leg.H.** 1872.

CHAPTER 4
TERMINATION OF OWNERSHIP

By birth of posthumous child. §739.
By happening of contingency. §740.
By act of intermediate holder or by forfeiture. §741.
By determination of precedent estate. §742.

§739. By Birth of Posthumous Child.

A future interest, depending on the contingency of the death of any person without successors, heirs, issue, or children, is defeated by the birth of a posthumous child of such person, capable of taking by succession. **Leg.H.** 1872.

§740. By Happening of Contingency.

A future interest may be defeated in any manner or by any act or means which the party creating such interest provided for or authorized in the creation thereof; nor is a future interest, thus liable to be defeated, to be on that ground adjudged void in its creation. **Leg.H.** 1872.

Ref.: Miller & Starr, Cal. Real Estate 3rd 9:31.

§741. By Act of Intermediate Holder or by Forfeiture.

No future interest can be defeated or barred by any alienation or other act of the owner of the intermediate or precedent interest, nor by any destruction of such precedent interest by forfeiture, surrender, merger, or otherwise, except as provided by the next section, or where a forfeiture is imposed by statute as a penalty for the violation thereof. **Leg.H.** 1872.

Ref.: Cal. Fms Pl. & Pr., Ch. 13, "Adverse Possession"; Miller & Starr, Cal. Real Estate 3rd 9:31, 9:32.

§742. By Determination of Precedent Estate.

No future interest, valid in its creation, is defeated by the determination of the precedent interest before the happening of the contingency on which the future interest is limited to take effect; but should such contingency afterwards happen, the future interest takes effect in the same manner and to the same extent as if the precedent interest had continued to the same period. **Leg.H.** 1872.

Ref.: Miller & Starr, Cal. Real Estate 3rd 9:31.

TITLE III
GENERAL DEFINITIONS

Income defined. §748.
Time of delivery of title or grant based upon condition. §749.

§748. Income Defined.

The income of property, as the term is used in this part of the code, includes the rents and profits of real property, the interest of money, dividends upon stock, and other produce of personal property. **Leg.H.** 1872.

§749. Time of Delivery of Title or Grant Based Upon Condition.

The delivery of the grant, where a limitation, condition, or future interest is created by grant, and the death of the testator, where it is created by will, is to be deemed the time of the creation of the limitation, condition, or interest, within the meaning of this part of the code. **Leg.H.** 1872.

Ref.: Miller & Starr, Cal. Real Estate 3rd 9:20, 9:29.

PART 2
Real or Immovable Property

TITLE I. General Provisions. §755.
TITLE II. Estates in Real Property. §§761-816.
TITLE III. Rights and Obligations of Owners. §§818-855.
TITLE 5. Marketable Record Title. §§880.020-887.090.
TITLE 6. Rent Skimming. §§890-894.
TITLE 7. Requirements for Actions for Construction Defects. §§895-945.5.
TITLE 8. Reconstruction of Homes Lost in Cedar Fire, October 2003. §945.6.

TITLE I
GENERAL PROVISIONS

§755. Law Governing.
Real property within this State is governed by the law of this State, except where the title is in the United States. **Leg.H.** 1872, 1874 p. 218.

Ref.: Miller & Starr, Cal. Real Estate 3rd 17:4.

TITLE II
ESTATES IN REAL PROPERTY

Chap. 1. Estates in General. §§761-784.
Chap. 2. Termination of Estates. §§789-793.
Chap. 2.5. Mobilehome Residency Law. §§798-799.10.
Chap. 2.6. Recreational Vehicle Park Occupancy Law. §§799.20-799.79.
Chap. 2.7. Floating Home Residency Law. §§800-800.306.
Chap. 3. Servitudes or Easements. §§801-813.
Chap. 4. Conservation Easements. §§815-816.

CHAPTER 1
ESTATES IN GENERAL

Kinds of estates. §761.
Fee simple. §762.
Estates tail—Abolition. §763.
Estates as conditional limitation. §764.
Freeholds, chattels real, and chattel interests. §765.
Life estate is freehold. §766.
Future estates—Legal conditions. §767.
Reversion defined. §768.
Remainder defined. §769.
Freeholds to commence in future—Life estate in term of years with remainder over—Fee limited on fee. §773.
Conditional limitations. §778.
Heirs of life tenant take by purchase. §779.
Remainder based on life estate vests on death of tenant. §780.
Special power of appointment as limitation. §781.
Racial, national, and ethnic restrictions in deeds void. §782.
Omission of restrictions as to race or color in deeds or written instruments. §782.5.
Condominium defined. §783.
Stock cooperative defined. §783.1.
Definition of restrictions on real property. §784.

§761. Kinds of Estates.
Estates in real property, in respect to the duration of their enjoyment, are either:
1. Estates of inheritance or perpetual estates;
2. Estates for life;
3. Estates for years; or,
4. Estates at Will. **Leg.H.** 1872.

Ref.: W. Cal. Sum., "Real Property" §231; Miller & Starr, Cal. Real Estate 3rd 9:2, 19:2.

§762. Fee Simple.
Every estate of inheritance is a fee, and every such estate, when not defeasible or conditional, is a fee-simple or an absolute fee. **Leg.H.** 1872, 1874 p. 218.

Ref.: Miller & Starr, Cal. Real Estate 3rd 9:3, 11:95.

§763. Estates Tail—Abolition.
Estates tail are abolished, and every estate which would be at common law adjudged to be a fee-tail is a fee-simple; and if no valid remainder is limited thereon, is a fee-simple absolute. **Leg.H.** 1872.

Ref.: Miller & Starr, Cal. Real Estate 3rd 9:3.

§764. Estates as Conditional Limitation.
Where a remainder in fee is limited upon any estate, which would by the common law be adjudged a fee-tail, such remainder is valid as a contingent limitation upon a fee, and vests in possession on the death of the first taker, without issue living at the time of his death. **Leg.H.** 1872.

§765. Freeholds, Chattels Real, and Chattel Interests.
Estates of inheritance and for life are called estates of freehold; estates for years are chattels real; and estates at will are chattel interests, but are not subject to enforcement of a money judgment. **Leg.H.** 1872, 1982 ch. 497, operative July 1, 1983.

Ref.: Miller & Starr, Cal. Real Estate 3rd 9:2, 9:25, 19:2.

§766. Life Estate Is Freehold.
An estate during the life of a third person, whether limited to heirs or otherwise, is a freehold. **Leg.H.** 1872, 1874 p. 218.

Ref.: Miller & Starr, Cal. Real Estate 3rd 9:25.

§767. Future Estates—Legal Conditions.
A future estate may be limited by the act of the party to commence in possession at a future day, either without the intervention of a precedent estate, or on the termination, by lapse of time or otherwise, of a precedent estate created at the same time. **Leg.H.** 1872.

§768. Reversion Defined.
A reversion is the residue of an estate left by operation of law in the grantor or his successors, or in the successors of a testator, commencing in possession on the determination of a particular estate granted or devised. **Leg.H.** 1872.

Ref.: W. Cal. Sum., "Real Property" §§331 et seq.; Miller & Starr, Cal. Real Estate 3rd 9:26.

§769. Remainder Defined.

When a future estate, other than a reversion, is dependent on a precedent estate, it may be called a remainder, and may be created and transferred by that name. **Leg.H.** 1872.

Ref.: W. Cal. Sum., "Real Property" §§334 et seq.; Miller & Starr, Cal. Real Estate 3rd 9:29.

§773. Freeholds to Commence in Future—Life Estate in Term of Years With Remainder Over—Fee Limited on Fee.

Subject to the rules of this title, and of part 1 of this division, a freehold estate, as well as a chattel real, may be created to commence at a future day; an estate for life may be created in a term of years, and a remainder limited thereon; a remainder of a freehold or chattel real, either contingent or vested, may be created, expectant on the determination of a term of years; and a fee may be limited on a fee, upon a contingency, which, if it should occur, must happen within the period prescribed by the statutory rule against perpetuities in Article 2 (commencing with Section 21205) of Chapter 1 of Part 2 of Division 11 of the Probate Code. **Leg.H.** 1872, 1951 ch. 1463, 1991 ch. 156.

§778. Conditional Limitations.

A remainder may be limited on a contingency which, in case it should happen, will operate to abridge or determine the precedent estate; and every such remainder is to be deemed a conditional limitation. **Leg.H.** 1872.

§779. Heirs of Life Tenant Take by Purchase.

When a remainder is limited to the heirs, or heirs of the body, of a person to whom a life estate in the same property is given, the persons who, on the termination of the life estate, are the successors or heirs of the body of the owner for life, are entitled to take by virtue of the remainder so limited to them, and not as mere successors of the owner for life. **Leg.H.** 1872.

§780. Remainder Based on Life Estate Vests on Death of Tenant.

When a remainder on an estate for life or for years is not limited on a contingency defeating or avoiding such precedent estate, it is to be deemed intended to take effect only on the death of the first taker, or the expiration, by lapse of time, of such term of years. **Leg.H.** 1872.

Ref.: Miller & Starr, Cal. Real Estate 3rd 9:29.

§781. Special Power of Appointment as Limitation.

A general or special power of appointment does not prevent the vesting of a future estate limited to take effect in case such power is not executed. **Leg.H.** 1872.

Ref.: Miller & Starr, Cal. Real Estate 3rd 9:30.

§782. Racial, National, and Ethnic Restrictions in Deeds Void.

Any provision in any deed of real property in California, whether executed before or after the effective date of this section, which purports to restrict the right of any persons to sell, lease, rent, use or occupy the property to persons of a particular racial, national or ethnic group, by providing for payment of a penalty, forfeiture, reverter, or otherwise, is void. **Leg.H.** 1961 ch. 1078, 1965 ch. 283.

Ref.: Miller & Starr, Cal. Real Estate 3rd 8:58, 9:42, 24:21.

§782.5. Omission of Restrictions as to Race or Color in Deeds or Written Instruments.

(a) Any deed or other written instrument which relates to title to real property, or any written covenant, condition, or restriction annexed or made a part of, by reference or otherwise, any such deed or instrument, which contains any provision which purports to forbid, restrict, or condition the right of any person or persons to sell, buy, lease, rent, use, or occupy the property because of the race or color of the person or persons, shall be deemed to be revised to omit that provision.

(b) This section shall not be construed to limit or expand the powers of a court to reform a deed or other written instrument. **Leg.H.** 1987 ch. 500.

Ref.: Miller & Starr, Cal. Real Estate 3rd 9:42, 24:21.

§783. Condominium Defined.

A condominium is an estate in real property described in subdivision (f) of Section 1351. A condominium may, with respect to the duration of its enjoyment, be either (1) an estate of inheritance or perpetual estate, (2) an estate for life, (3) an estate for years, such as a leasehold or a subleasehold, or (4) any combination of the foregoing. **Leg.H.** 1985 ch. 874 §9.

Ref.: Miller & Starr, Cal. Real Estate 3rd 25:7.

§783.1. Stock Cooperative Defined.

In a stock cooperative, as defined in subdivision (m) of Section 1351, both the separate interest, as defined in paragraph (4) of subdivision (*l*) of Section 1351, and the correlative interest in the stock cooperative corporation, however designated, are interests in real property. **Leg.H.** 1985 ch. 874.

Ref.: Miller & Starr, Cal. Real Estate 3rd 25:14.

§784. Definition of Restrictions on Real Property.

"Restriction," when used in a statute that incorporates this section by reference, means a limitation on, or provision affecting, the use of real property in a deed, declaration, or other instrument, whether in the form of a covenant, equitable servitude, condition subsequent, negative easement, or other form of restriction. **Leg.H.** 1998 ch. 14.

Ref.: Cal. Fms Pl. & Pr., Ch. 184, "Deeds."

CHAPTER 2
TERMINATION OF ESTATES

Estates at will. §789.
Landlord not to willfully interrupt or terminate service furnished tenant—Liability of landlo
Time right of re-entry accrues. §790.
Three-day notice prerequisite to right given
Forcible entry and unlawful detainer. §792.
No notice prerequisite to suit when lease o
right of re-entry. §793.

§789. Estates at Will.

A tenancy or other estate at will, however created, may be terminated by the landlord's giving notice in writing to the tenant, in the manner prescribed by Section 1162 of the Code of Civil Procedure, to remove from the premises within a period of not less than 30 days, to be specified in the notice. **Leg.H.** 1872, 1911 p. 61, 2002 ch. 664 (AB 3034).

Ref.: Cal. Fms Pl. & Pr., Ch. 332, "Landlord and Tenant: The Tenancy"; Miller & Starr, Cal. Real Estate 3rd 19:31, 19:183, 19:187; MB Prac. Guide: Landlord-Tenant, Ch. 4.

§789.3. Landlord Not to Willfully Interrupt or Terminate Any Utility Service Furnished Tenant—Liability of Landlord.

(a) A landlord shall not with intent to terminate the occupancy under any lease or other tenancy or estate at will, however created, of property used by a tenant as his residence willfully cause, directly or indirectly, the interruption or termination of any utility service furnished the tenant, including, but not limited to, water, heat, light, electricity, gas, telephone, elevator, or refrigeration, whether or not the utility service is under the control of the landlord.

(b) In addition, a landlord shall not, with intent to terminate the occupancy under any lease or other tenancy or estate at will, however created, of property used by a tenant as his or her residence, willfully:

(1) Prevent the tenant from gaining reasonable access to the property by changing the locks or using a bootlock or by any other similar method or device;

(2) Remove outside doors or windows; or

(3) Remove from the premises the tenant's personal property, the furnishings, or any other items without the prior written consent of the tenant, except when done pursuant to the procedure set forth in Chapter 5 (commencing with Section 1980) of Title 5 of Part 4 of Division 3.

Nothing in this subdivision shall be construed to prevent the lawful eviction of a tenant by appropriate legal authorities, nor shall anything in this subdivision apply to occupancies defined by subdivision (b) of Section 1940.

(c) Any landlord who violates this section shall be liable to the tenant in a civil action for all of the following:

(1) Actual damages of the tenant.

(2) An amount not to exceed one hundred dollars ($100) for each day or part thereof the landlord remains in violation of this section. In determining the amount of such award, the court shall consider proof of such matters as justice may require; however, in no event shall less than two hundred fifty dollars ($250) be awarded for each separate cause of action. Subsequent or repeated violations, which are not committed contemporaneously with the initial violation, shall be treated as separate causes of action and shall be subject to a separate award of damages.

(d) In any action under subdivision (c) the court shall award reasonable attorney's fees to the prevailing party.

In any such action the tenant may seek appropriate injunctive relief to prevent continuing or further violation of the provisions of this section during the pendency of the action. The remedy provided by this section is not exclusive and shall not preclude the tenant from pursuing any other remedy which the tenant may have under any other provision of law. **Leg.H.** 1971 ch. 1275, 1979 ch. 333.

Ref.: Cal. Fms Pl. & Pr., Ch. 333, "Landlord and Tenant: Eviction Actions," Ch. 334, "Landlord and Tenant: Claims For Damages"; W. Cal. Sum., "Torts" 1332; Miller & Starr, Cal. Real Estate 3rd 19:153, 34:88; MB Prac. Guide: Landlord-Tenant, Ch. 4.

§790. Time Right of Re-Entry Accrues.

After such notice has been served, and the period specified by such notice has expired, but not before, the landlord may re-enter, or proceed according to law to recover possession. **Leg.H.** 1872.

Ref.: Miller & Starr, Cal. Real Estate 3rd 19:183; MB Prac. Guide: Landlord-Tenant, Ch. 4.

§791. Three-Day Notice Prerequisite to Right Given in Lease.

Whenever the right of re-entry is given to a grantor or a lessor in any grant or lease or otherwise, such re-entry may be made at any time after the right has accrued, upon three days' notice, as provided in sections 1161 and 1162, Code of Civil Procedure; provided, however, that the said three days' notice shall not be required in cases where the hiring of real property is for a term not specified by the parties and where such hiring was terminated under and in accordance with the provisions of section 1946 of the Civil Code. **Leg.H.** 1872, 1931 ch. 1033.

Ref.: Miller & Starr, Cal. Real Estate 3rd 19:33, 19:183, 19:196, 19:197; MB Prac. Guide: Landlord-Tenant, Ch. 4.

§792. Forcible Entry and Unlawful Detainer.

Summary proceedings for obtaining possession of real property forcibly entered, or forcibly and unlawfully detained, are provided for in sections eleven hundred and fifty-nine to eleven hundred and seventy-five, both inclusive, of the Code of Civil Procedure. **Leg.H.** 1872.

Ref.: MB Prac. Guide: Landlord-Tenant, Ch. 4.

§793. No Notice Prerequisite to Suit When Lease or Grant Contains Right of Re-Entry.

An action for the possession of real property leased or granted, with a right of re-entry, may be maintained at any time, after the right to re-enter has accrued, without the notice prescribed in section seven hundred and ninety-one. **Leg.H.** 1872, 1905 p. 199.

Ref.: Cal. Fms Pl. & Pr., Ch. 241, "Ejectment"; Miller & Starr, Cal. Real Estate 3rd 19:207; MB Prac. Guide: Landlord-Tenant, Ch. 4.

CHAPTER 2.5
MOBILEHOME RESIDENCY LAW

Art. 1. General. §§798-798.14.
Art. 2. Rental Agreement. §§798.15-798.22.
Art. 3. Rules and Regulations. §§798.23-798.29.5.
Art. 4. Fees and Charges. §§798.30-798.44.
Art. 4.5. Rent Control. §§798.45, 798.49.
Art. 5. Homeowner Communications and Meetings. §§798.50-798.52.
Art. 5.5. Homeowners Meetings With Management. §798.53.
Art. 6. Termination of Tenancy. §§798.55-798.61.
Art. 7. Transfer of Mobilehome or Mobilehome Park. §§798.70-798.83.

Art. 8. Actions, Proceedings, and Penalties. §§798.84-798.88.
Art. 9. Subdivisions, Cooperatives, and Condominiums. §§799-799.10.

ARTICLE 1
General

Title of chapter. §798.
Definitions in §§798.2 et seq. govern construction. §798.1.
"Management" defined. §798.2.
"Mobilehome" defined. §798.3.
"Mobilehome park" defined. §798.4.
"Park" defined. §798.6.
"New construction" defined. §798.7.
"Rental agreement" defined. §798.8.
"Homeowner" defined. §798.9.
"Change of use" defined. §798.10.
"Resident" defined. §798.11.
"Tenancy" defined. §798.12.
State employee housing. §798.13.
Manner of giving notice. §798.14.

§798. Title of Chapter.

This chapter shall be known and may be cited as the "Mobilehome Residency Law." **Leg.H.** 1978 chs. 1033, 1035, 1992 ch. 958, effective September 28, 1992.

§798.1. Definitions in §§798.2 Et Seq. Govern Construction.

Unless the provisions or context otherwise requires, the following definitions shall govern the construction of this chapter. **Leg.H.** 1978 ch. 1031.

§798.2. "Management" Defined.

"Management" means the owner of a mobilehome park or an agent or representative authorized to act on his behalf in connection with matters relating to a tenancy in the park. **Leg.H.** 1978 ch. 1031.

Ref.: Cal. Fms Pl. & Pr., Ch. 369, "Mobilehomes and Mobilehome Parks"; Miller & Starr, Cal. Real Estate 3rd 31:24.

§798.3. "Mobilehome" Defined.

(a) "Mobilehome" is a structure designed for human habitation and for being moved on a street or highway under permit pursuant to Section 35790 of the Vehicle Code. Mobilehome includes a manufactured home, as defined in Section 18007 of the Health and Safety Code, and a mobilehome, as defined in Section 18008 of the Health and Safety Code, but, except as provided in subdivision (b), does not include a recreational vehicle, as defined in Section 799.29 of this code and Section 18010 of the Health and Safety Code or a commercial coach as defined in Section 18001.8 of the Health and Safety Code.

(b) "Mobilehome," for purposes of this chapter, other than Section 798.73, also includes trailers and other recreational vehicles of all types defined in Section 18010 of the Health and Safety Code, other than motor homes, truck campers, and camping trailers, which are used for human habitation if the occupancy criteria of either paragraph (1) or (2), as follows, are met:

(1) The trailer or other recreational vehicle occupies a mobilehome site in the park, on November 15, 1992, under a rental agreement with a term of one month or longer, and the trailer or other recreational vehicle occupied a mobilehome site in the park prior to January 1, 1991.

(2) The trailer or other recreational vehicle occupies a mobilehome site in the park for nine or more continuous months commencing on or after November 15, 1992.

"Mobilehome" does not include a trailer or other recreational vehicle located in a recreational vehicle park subject to Chapter 2.6 (commencing with Section 799.20) [1]. **Leg.H.** 1978 ch. 1033, 1980 ch. 502, 1982 ch. 419, 1983 ch. 1124, operative July 1, 1984, 1992 ch. 958, effective September 28, 1992, 1993 ch. 666, 2005 ch. 595 (SB 253) §1.

§798.3. 2005 Deletes. [1] , except as otherwise provided in subdivision (b) of Section 799.45

Ref.: Cal. Fms Pl. & Pr., Ch. 369, "Mobilehomes and Mobilehome Parks"; Miller & Starr, Cal. Real Estate 3rd 31:15, 31:34.

§798.4. "Mobilehome Park" Defined.

"Mobilehome park" is an area of land where two or more mobilehome sites are rented, or held out for rent, to accommodate mobilehomes used for human habitation. **Leg.H.** 1978 ch. 1031.

Ref.: Cal. Fms Pl. & Pr., Ch. 369, "Mobilehomes and Mobilehome Parks."

§798.6. "Park" Defined.

"Park" is a manufactured housing community as defined in Section 18801 of the Health and Safety Code, or a mobilehome park. **Leg.H.** 1978 ch. 1031, 1980 ch. 502, 1993 ch. 858.

§798.7. "New Construction" Defined.

"New Construction" means any newly constructed spaces initially held out for rent after January 1, 1990. **Leg.H.** 1989 ch. 412.

§798.8. "Rental Agreement" Defined.

"Rental agreement" is an agreement between the management and the homeowner establishing the terms and conditions of a park tenancy. A lease is a rental agreement. **Leg. H.** 1978 ch. 1031, 1980 ch. 502, 1982 ch. 1397.

Ref.: Cal. Fms Pl. & Pr, Ch. 369, "Mobilehomes and Mobilehome Parks"; Miller & Starr, Cal. Real Estate 3rd 31:31.

§798.9. "Homeowner" Defined.

"Homeowner" is a person who has a tenancy in a mobilehome park under a rental agreement. **Leg.H.** 1978 ch. 1031, 1982 ch. 1397.

Ref.: Miller & Starr, Cal. Real Estate 3rd 31:31.

§798.10. "Change of Use" Defined.

"Change of use" means a use of the park for a purpose other than the rental, or the holding out for rent, of two or more mobilehome sites to accommodate mobilehomes used for human habitation, and does not mean the adoption, amendment, or repeal of a park rule or regulation. A change of use may affect an entire park or any portion thereof. "Change of use" includes, but is not limited to, a change of the park or any portion thereof to a condominium, stock cooperative, planned unit development, or any form of ownership wherein spaces within the park are to be sold. **Leg.H.** 1979 ch. 945, 1980 ch. 137.

Ref.: Cal. Fms Pl. & Pr., Ch. 369, "Mobilehomes and Mobilehome Parks"; Miller & Starr, Cal. Real Estate 3rd 31:31.

§798.11. "Resident" Defined.

"Resident" is a homeowner or other person who lawfully occupies a mobilehome. **Leg.H.** 1978 ch. 1031, 1980 ch. 502, 1981 ch. 714, 1982 ch. 1397.

§798.12. "Tenancy" Defined.

"Tenancy" is the right of a homeowner to the use of a site within a mobilehome park on which to locate, maintain, and occupy a mobilehome, site improvements, and accessory structures for human habitation, including the use of the services and facilities of the park. **Leg.H.** 1978 chs. 1031, 1033, 1980 ch. 502, 1982 ch. 1397.

Ref.: Cal. Fms Pl. & Pr., Ch. 369, "Mobilehomes and Mobilehome Parks."

§798.13. State Employee Housing.

(a) This chapter does not apply to any area owned, operated, or maintained by the state for the purpose of providing employee housing or space for a mobilehome owned or occupied by an employee of the state.

(b) Notwithstanding subdivision (a), a state employer shall provide the occupant of a privately owned mobilehome that is situated in an employee housing area owned, operated, or maintained by the state, and that is occupied by a state employee by agreement with his or her state employer and subject to the terms and conditions of that state employment, with a minimum of 60-days' notice prior to terminating the tenancy for any reason. **Leg.H.** 2000 ch. 471.

Ref.: Cal. Fms Pl. & Pr., Ch. 369, "Mobilehomes and Mobilehome Parks."

§798.14. Manner of Giving Notice.

Unless otherwise provided, all notices required by this chapter shall be either delivered personally to the homeowner or deposited in the United States mail, postage prepaid, addressed to the homeowner at his or her site within the mobilehome park. **Leg.H.** 1988 ch. 301.

ARTICLE 2
Rental Agreement

Written rental agreement to be furnished to prospective homeowner—Required provisions. §798.15.
Provisions permitted by law. §798.16.
Rental agreements exempt from rent control ordinances. §798.17.
Rental agreement for 12 or more or less months. §798.18.
Waiver of chapter prohibited. §798.19.
Rental agreement not to grant management right of first refusal to purchase mobilehome; separate agreement not precluded. §798.19.5.
Membership in restricted club as condition for tenancy prohibited. §798.20.
Mobilehome space exempt from rent control if not principal residence of homeowner or rented by homeowner to other party; notice by management prior to modification of rent. §798.21.
Rental of mobilehome spaces for recreational vehicles as prohibited unless separate area provided. §798.22.

§798.15. Written Rental Agreement to Be Furnished to Prospective Homeowner—Required Provisions.

The rental agreement shall be in writing and shall contain, in addition to the provisions otherwise required by law to be included, all of the following:

(a) The term of the tenancy and the rent therefor.

(b) The rules and regulations of the park.

(c) A copy of the text of this chapter shall be attached as an exhibit and shall be incorporated into the rental agreement by reference. Management shall provide all homeowners with a copy of this chapter prior to February 1 of each year, if a significant change was made in the chapter by legislation enacted in the prior year.

(d) A provision specifying that (1) it is the responsibility of the management to provide and maintain physical improvements in the common facilities in good working order and condition and (2) with respect to a sudden or unforeseeable breakdown or deterioration of these improvements, the management shall have a reasonable period of time to repair the sudden or unforeseeable breakdown or deterioration and bring the improvements into good working order and condition after management knows or should have known of the breakdown or deterioration. For purposes of this subdivision, a reasonable period of time to repair a sudden or unforeseeable breakdown or deterioration shall be as soon as possible in situations affecting a health or safety condition, and shall not exceed 30 days in any other case except where exigent circumstances justify a delay.

(e) A description of the physical improvements to be provided the homeowner during his or her tenancy.

(f) A provision listing those services which will be provided at the time the rental agreement is executed and will continue to be offered for the term of tenancy and the fees, if any, to be charged for those services.

(g) A provision stating that management may charge a reasonable fee for services relating to the maintenance of the land and premises upon which a mobilehome is situated in the event the homeowner fails to maintain the land or premises in accordance with the rules and regulations of the park after written notification to the homeowner and the failure of the homeowner to comply within 14 days. The written notice shall state the specific condition to be corrected and an estimate of the charges to be imposed by management if the services are performed by management or its agent.

(h) All other provisions governing the tenancy. **Leg.H.** 1978 chs. 1031, 1033, 1980 ch. 137, 1981 ch. 667, 1982 ch. 1397, 1983 ch. 519, 1987 ch. 126, 1993 ch. 666.

Ref.: Cal. Fms Pl. & Pr., Ch. 369, "Mobilehomes and Mobilehome Parks"; Miller & Starr, Cal. Real Estate 3rd 31:17, 31:24.

§798.16. Provisions Permitted by Law.

(a) The rental agreement may include other provisions permitted by law, but need not include specific language contained in state or local laws not a part of this chapter.

(b) Management shall return an executed copy of the rental agreement to the homeowner within 15 business days after management has received the rental agreement signed by the homeowner. **Leg.H.** 1978 chs. 1031, 1033, 1981 ch. 667, 2004 ch. 302 (AB 2351).

Ref.: Cal. Fms Pl. & Pr., Ch. 369, "Mobilehomes and Mobilehome Parks"; Miller & Starr, Cal. Real Estate 3rd 31:24.

§798.17. Rental Agreements Exempt From Rent Control Ordinances.

(a) (1) Rental agreements meeting the criteria of subdivision (b) shall be exempt from any ordinance, rule, regulation, or initiative measure adopted by any local governmental entity which establishes a maximum amount that a landlord may charge a tenant for rent. The terms of a rental agreement meeting the criteria of subdivision (b) shall prevail over conflicting provisions of an ordinance, rule, regulation, or initiative measure limiting or restricting rents in mobilehome parks, only during the term of the rental agreement or one or more uninterrupted, continuous extensions thereof. If the rental agreement is not extended and no new rental agreement in excess of 12 months' duration is entered into, then the last rental rate charged for the space under the previous rental agreement shall be the base rent for purposes of applicable provisions of law concerning rent regulation, if any.

(2) In the first sentence of the first paragraph of a rental agreement entered into on or after January 1, 1993, pursuant to this section, there shall be set forth a provision in at least 12-point boldface type if the rental agreement is printed, or in capital letters if the rental agreement is typed, giving notice to the homeowner that the rental agreement will be exempt from any ordinance, rule, regulation, or initiative measure adopted by any local governmental entity which establishes a maximum amount that a landlord may charge a tenant for rent.

(b) Rental agreements subject to this section shall meet all of the following criteria:

(1) The rental agreement shall be in excess of 12 months' duration.

(2) The rental agreement shall be entered into between the management and a homeowner for the personal and actual residence of the homeowner.

(3) The homeowner shall have at least 30 days from the date the rental agreement is first offered to the homeowner to accept or reject the rental agreement.

(4) The homeowner who executes a rental agreement offered pursuant to this section may void the rental agreement by notifying management in writing within 72 hours of the homeowner's execution of the rental agreement.

(c) If, pursuant to paragraph (3) or (4) of subdivision (b), the homeowner rejects the offered rental agreement or rescinds a signed rental agreement, the homeowner shall be entitled to instead accept, pursuant to Section 798.18, a rental agreement for a term of 12 months or less from the date the offered rental agreement was to have begun. In the event the homeowner elects to have a rental agreement for a term of 12 months or less, including a month-to-month rental agreement, the rental agreement shall contain the same rental charges, terms, and conditions as the rental agreement offered pursuant to subdivision (b), during the first 12 months, except for options, if any, contained in the offered rental agreement to extend or renew the rental agreement.

(d) Nothing in subdivision (c) shall be construed to prohibit the management from offering gifts of value, other than rental rate reductions, to homeowners who execute a rental agreement pursuant to this section.

(e) With respect to any space in a mobilehome park that is exempt under subdivision (a) from any ordinance, rule, regulation, or initiative measure adopted by any local governmental entity that establishes a maximum amount that a landlord may charge a homeowner for rent, and notwithstanding any ordinance, rule, regulation, or initiative measure, a mobilehome park shall not be assessed any fee or other exaction for a park space that is exempt under subdivision (a) imposed pursuant to any ordinance, rule, regulation, or initiative measure. No other fee or other exaction shall be imposed for a park space that is exempt under subdivision (a) for the purpose of defraying the cost of administration thereof.

(f) At the time the rental agreement is first offered to the homeowner, the management shall provide written notice to the homeowner of the homeowner's right (1) to have at least 30 days to inspect the rental agreement, and (2) to void the rental agreement by notifying management in writing within 72 hours of the acceptance of a rental agreement. The failure of the management to provide the written notice shall make the rental agreement voidable at the homeowner's option upon the homeowner's discovery of the failure. The receipt of any written notice provided pursuant to this subdivision shall be acknowledged in writing by the homeowner.

(g) No rental agreement subject to subdivision (a) that is first entered into on or after January 1, 1993, shall have a provision which authorizes automatic extension or renewal of, or automatically extends or renews, the rental agreement for a period beyond the initial stated term at the sole option of either the management or the homeowner.

(h) This section does not apply to or supersede other provisions of this part or other state law. **Leg.H.** 1985 ch. 1084, 1986 ch. 1416, 1990 chs. 1013, 1046 §2, 1991 ch. 24, effective May 6, 1991, operative May 10, 1991, ch. 170, 1992 chs. 289, 427 (ch. 289 prevails; ch. 427 not effective), 1993 ch. 9, effective April 29, 1993.

Ref.: Cal. Fms Pl. & Pr., Ch. 369, "Mobilehomes and Mobilehome Parks"; Miller & Starr, Cal. Real Estate 3rd 19:89, 31:24, 31:37.

§798.18. Rental Agreement for 12 or More or Less Months.

(a) A homeowner shall be offered a rental agreement for (1) a term of 12 months, or (2) a lesser period as the homeowner may request, or (3) a longer period as mutually agreed upon by both the homeowner and management.

(b) No rental agreement shall contain any terms or conditions with respect to charges for rent, utilities, or incidental reasonable service charges that would be different during the first 12 months of the rental agreement from the corresponding terms or conditions that would be offered to the homeowners on a month-to-month basis.

(c) No rental agreement for a term of 12 months or less shall include any provision which authorizes automatic extension or renewal of, or automatically extends or renews, the rental agreement beyond the initial term for a term longer than 12 months at the sole option of either the management or the homeowner. **Leg.H.** 1978 chs. 1031, 1032, 1033 §7.5, 1980 ch. 206, 1981 ch. 667, 1982 ch. 1397, 1992 ch. 289.

Ref.: Cal. Fms Pl. & Pr., Ch. 369, "Mobilehomes and Mobilehome Parks"; Miller & Starr, Cal. Real Estate 3rd 31:24.

§798.19. Waiver of Chapter Prohibited.

No rental agreement for a mobilehome shall contain a provision by which the homeowner waives his or her rights under the provisions of Articles 1 to 8, inclusive, of this chapter. Any such waiver shall be deemed contrary to public policy and void. **Leg.H.** 1978 chs. 1031, 1033, 1982 ch. 1397.

Ref.: Cal. Fms Pl. & Pr., Ch. 369, "Mobilehomes and Mobilehome Parks"; Miller & Starr, Cal. Real Estate 3rd 31:24.

§798.19.5. Rental Agreement Not to Grant Management Right of First Refusal to Purchase Mobilehome; Separate Agreement Not Precluded.

A rental agreement entered into or renewed on and after January 1, 2006, shall not include a clause, rule, regulation, or any other provision that grants to management the right of first refusal to purchase a homeowner's mobilehome that is in the park and offered for sale to a third party pursuant to Article 7 (commencing with Section 798.70). This section does not preclude a separate agreement for separate consideration granting the park owner or management a right of first refusal to purchase the homeowner's mobilehome that is in the park and offered for sale. **Leg.H.** 2005 ch. 35 (SB 237) §1.

§798.20. Membership in Restricted Club as Condition for Tenancy Prohibited.

Membership in any private club or organization which is a condition for tenancy in a park shall not be denied on the basis of race, color, religion, sex, national origin, ancestry, or marital status. **Leg.H.** 1978 ch. 1031.

Ref.: Cal. Fms Pl. & Pr., Ch. 369, "Mobilehomes and Mobilehome Parks"; Miller & Starr, Cal. Real Estate 3rd 31:24.

§798.21. Mobilehome Space Exempt From Rent Control If Not Principal Residence of Homeowner or Rented by Homeowner to Other Party; Notice by Management Prior to Modification of Rent.

(a) Notwithstanding Section 798.17, if a mobilehome space within a mobilehome park is not the principal residence of the homeowner and the homeowner has not rented the mobilehome to another party, it shall be exempt from any ordinance, rule, regulation, or initiative measure adopted by any city, county, or city and county, which establishes a maximum amount that the landlord may charge a tenant for rent.

(b) Nothing in this section is intended to require any homeowner to disclose information concerning his or her personal finances. Nothing in this section shall be construed to authorize management to gain access to any records which would otherwise be confidential or privileged.

(c) For purposes of this section, a mobilehome shall be deemed to be the principal residence of the homeowner, unless a review of state or county records demonstrates that the homeowner is receiving a homeowner's exemption for another property or mobilehome in this state, or unless a review of public records reasonably demonstrates that the principal residence of the homeowner is out of state.

(d) Before modifying the rent or other terms of tenancy as a result of a review of records, as described in subdivision (c), the management shall notify the homeowner, in writing, of the proposed changes and provide the homeowner with a copy of the documents upon which management relied.

(e) The homeowner shall have 90 days from the date the notice described in subdivision (d) is mailed to review and respond to the notice. Management may not modify the rent or other terms of tenancy prior to the expiration of the 90-day period or prior to responding, in writing, to information provided by the homeowner. Management may not modify the rent or other terms of tenancy if the homeowner provides documentation reasonably establishing that the information provided by management is incorrect or that the homeowner is not the same person identified in the documents. However, nothing in this subdivision shall be construed to authorize the homeowner to change the homeowner's exemption status of the other property or mobilehome owned by the homeowner.

(f) This section does not apply under any of the following conditions:

(1) The homeowner is unable to rent or lease the mobilehome because the owner or management of the mobilehome park in which the mobilehome is located does not permit, or the rental agreement limits or prohibits, the assignment of the mobilehome or the subletting of the park space.

(2) The mobilehome is being actively held available for sale by the homeowner, or pursuant to a listing agreement with a real estate broker licensed pursuant to Chapter 3 (commencing with Section 10130) of Part 1 of Division 4 of the Business and Professions Code, or a mobilehome dealer, as defined in Section 18002.6 of the Health and Safety Code. A homeowner, real estate broker, or mobilehome dealer attempting to sell a mobilehome shall actively market and advertise the mobilehome for sale in good faith to bona fide purchasers for value in order to remain exempt pursuant to this subdivision.

(3) The legal owner has taken possession or ownership, or both, of the mobilehome from a registered owner through either a surrender of ownership interest by the registered owner or a foreclosure proceeding. **Leg.H.** 1996 ch. 392, 2003 ch. 132 (AB 1173).

Ref.: Cal. Fms Pl. & Pr., Ch. 369, "Mobilehomes and Mobilehome Parks."

§798.22. Rental of Mobilehome Spaces for Recreational Vehicles as Prohibited Unless Separate Area Provided.

(a) In any new mobilehome park that is developed after January 1, 1982, mobilehome spaces shall not be rented for the accommodation of recreational vehicles as defined by Section 799.29 unless the mobilehome park has a specifically designated area within the park for recreational vehicles, which is separate and apart from the area designated for mobilehomes. Recreational vehicles may be located only in the specifically designated area.

(b) Any new mobilehome park that is developed after January 1, 1982, is not subject to the provisions of this section until 75 percent of the spaces have been rented for the first time. **Leg.H.** 1982 ch. 1146, 1993 ch. 666.

ARTICLE 3
Rules and Regulations

Rules and regulations applicable to owners and employees to same extent as residents and guests; exceptions. §798.23.

Circumstances where homeowner may rent or sublet primary residence; approval of prospective renter or sublessee; limitations on amount of rent charged. §798.23.5.
Hours of common area facility. §798.24.
Proposed amendment to rules or regulations—Notice, consultation, implementation, requirements for notice; new fees not in rental agreement prohibited. §798.25.
Conditions under which rules and regulations are void and unenforceable. §798.25.5.
No right of entry to mobilehome without prior written consent of resident. §798.26.
Written notice to homeowners of mobilehome park matters. §798.27.
Disclosure of mobilehome park owner's name, business address, and business telephone number. §798.28.
Removal of vehicle other than mobilehome from mobilehome park. §798.28.5.
Mobilehome ombudsman sign. §798.29.
Written advance notice of interruption in utility service. §798.29.5.

§798.23. Rules and Regulations Applicable to Owners and Employees to Same Extent as Residents and Guests; Exceptions.

(a) The owner of the park, and any person employed by the park, shall be subject to, and comply with, all park rules and regulations, to the same extent as residents and their guests.

(b) Subdivision (a) of this section does not apply to either of the following:

(1) Any rule or regulation that governs the age of any resident or guest.

(2) Acts of a park owner or park employee which are undertaken to fulfill a park owner's maintenance, management, and business operation responsibilities. **Leg.H.** 1993 ch. 520, 1994 ch. 340, 2002 ch. 672 (SB 1410).

§798.23.5. Circumstances Where Homeowner May Rent or Sublet Primary Residence; Approval of Prospective Renter or Sublessee; Limitations on Amount of Rent Charged.

(a) (1) Management shall permit a homeowner to rent his or her home that serves as the homeowner's primary residence or sublet his or her space, under the circumstances described in paragraph (2) and subject to the requirements of this section.

(2) A homeowner shall be permitted to rent or sublet pursuant to paragraph (1) if a medical emergency or medical treatment requires the homeowner to be absent from his or her home and this is confirmed in writing by an attending physician.

(b) The following provisions shall apply to a rental or sublease pursuant to this section:

(1) The minimum term of the rental or sublease shall be six months, unless the management approves a shorter term, but no greater than 12 months, unless management approves a longer term.

(2) The management may require approval of a prospective renter or sublessee, subject to the process and restrictions provided by subdivision (a) of Section 798.74 for prospective purchasers of mobilehomes. A prospective sublessee shall comply with any rule or regulation limiting residency based on age requirements, pursuant to Section 798.76. The management may charge a prospective sublessee a credit screening fee for the actual cost of any personal reference check or consumer credit report that is provided by a consumer credit reporting agency, as defined in Section 1785.3, if the management or his or her agent requires that personal reference check or consumer credit report.

(3) The renter or sublessee shall comply with all rules and regulations of the park. The failure of a renter or sublessee to comply with the rules and regulations of the park may result in the termination of the homeowner's tenancy in the mobilehome park, in accordance with Section 798.56. A homeowner's tenancy may not be terminated under this paragraph if the homeowner completes an action for unlawful detainer or executes a judgement for possession, pursuant to Chapter 4 (commencing with Section 1159) of Title 3 of Part 3 of the Code of Civil Procedure within 60 days of the homeowner receiving notice of termination of tenancy.

(4) The homeowner shall remain liable for the mobilehome park rent and other park charges.

(5) The management may require the homeowner to reside in the mobilehome park for a term of one year before management permits the renting or subletting of a mobilehome or mobilehome space.

(6) Notwithstanding subdivision (a) of Section 798.39, if a security deposit has been refunded to the homeowner pursuant to subdivision (b) or (c) of Section 798.39, the management may require the homeowner to resubmit a security deposit in an amount or value not to exceed two months' rent in addition to the first month's rent. Management may retain this security deposit for the duration of the term of the rental or sublease.

(7) The homeowner shall keep his or her current address and telephone number on file with the management during the term of rental or sublease. If applicable, the homeowner may provide the name, address, and telephone number of his or her legal representative.

(c) A homeowner may not charge a renter or sublessee more than an amount necessary to cover the cost of space rent, utilities, and scheduled loan payments on the mobilehome, if any. **Leg.H.** 2002 ch. 672 (SB 1410).

§798.24. Hours of Common Area Facility.

Each common area facility shall be open or available to residents at all reasonable hours and the hours of the common area facility shall be posted at the facility. **Leg.H.** 1983 ch. 503, 1994 ch. 380, 2001 ch. 83.

Ref.: Cal. Fms Pl. & Pr., Ch. 369, "Mobilehomes and Mobilehome Parks"; Miller & Starr, Cal. Real Estate 3rd 31:24.

§798.25. Proposed Amendment to Rules or Regulations—Notice, Consultation, Implementation, Requirements for Notice; New Fees Not in Rental Agreement Prohibited.

(a) Except as provided in subdivision (d), when the management proposes an amendment to the park's rules and regulations, the management shall meet and consult with the homeowners in the park, their representatives, or both, after written notice has been given to all the homeowners in the park 10 days or more before the meeting. The notice shall set forth the proposed amendment to the [1] **park's** rules and regulations and shall state the date, time, and location of the meeting.

(b) Except as provided in subdivision (d) following the meeting and consultation with the homeowners, the noticed amendment to the [2] **park's** rules and regulations may be implemented, as to any homeowner, with the consent of that homeowner, or without the homeowner's consent upon written notice of not less than six months, except for regulations applicable to recreational facilities, which may be amended without homeowner consent upon written notice of not less than 60 days.

(c) Written notice to a homeowner whose tenancy commences within the required period of notice of a proposed amendment to the park's rules and regulations under subdivision (b) or (d) shall constitute compliance with this section where the written notice is given before the inception of the tenancy.

(d) When the management proposes an amendment to the park's rules and regulations mandated by a change in the law, including, but not limited to, a change in a statute, ordinance, or governmental regulation, the management may implement the amendment to the [3] **park's** rules and regulations, as to any homeowner, with the consent of that homeowner or without the homeowner's consent upon written notice of not less than 60 days. For purposes of this subdivision, the management shall specify in the notice [4] **the** citation to the statute, ordinance, or regulation, including the section number, that necessitates the proposed amendment to the park's rules and regulations.

(e) Any amendment to the park's rules and regulations that creates a new fee payable by the homeowner and that has not been expressly agreed upon by the homeowner and management in the written rental agreement or lease, shall be void and unenforceable. **Leg.H.** 1978 chs. 1031, 1033, 1982 ch. 1397, 1983 ch. 519, 1993 ch. 102, 1999 ch. 323, 2004 ch. 622 (SB 1176), 2005 ch. 22 (SB 1108) §11.

§798.25. **2005 Deletes.** [1] park [2] park [3] park [4] a

1999 Note: The Legislature finds and declares that this act is intended to prohibit park owners from amending park rules and regulations to impose new fees on park residents. The act is not intended to limit the provisions of Article 4 (commencing with Section 798.30) of Chapter 2.5 of Title 2 of Part 2 of Division 2 of the Civil Code with respect to the imposition of fees. Stats. 1999 ch. 323 §2.

Ref.: Cal. Fms Pl. & Pr., Ch. 369, "Mobilehomes and Mobilehome Parks"; W. Cal. Sum., "Real Property" §533A; Miller & Starr, Cal. Real Estate 3rd 31:24.

§798.25.5. Conditions Under Which Rules and Regulations Are Void and Unenforceable.

Any rule or regulation of a mobilehome park that (a) is unilaterally adopted by the management, (b) is implemented without the consent of the homeowners, and (c) by its terms purports to deny homeowners their right to a trial by jury or which would mandate binding arbitration of any dispute between the management and homeowners shall be void and unenforceable. **Leg.H.** 1993 ch. 889.

§798.26. No Right of Entry to Mobilehome Without Prior Written Consent of Resident.

(a) Except as provided in subdivision (b), the ownership or management of a park shall have no right of entry to a mobilehome without the prior written consent of the resident. The consent may be revoked in writing by the resident at any time. The ownership or management shall have a right of entry upon the land upon which a mobilehome is situated for maintenance of utilities, trees, and driveways, for maintenance of the premises in accordance with the rules and regulations of the park when the homeowner or resident fails to so maintain the premises, and protection of the mobilehome park at any reasonable time, but not in a manner or at a time that would interfere with the resident's quiet enjoyment.

(b) The ownership or management of a park may enter a mobilehome without the prior written consent of the resident in case of an emergency or when the resident has abandoned the mobilehome. **Leg.H.** 1978 chs. 396, 1033, 1981 ch. 667, 1982 ch. 1397, 1983 ch. 519, 2000 ch. 423, 2004 ch. 302 (AB 2351).

Ref.: Cal. Fms Pl. & Pr., Ch. 369, "Mobilehomes and Mobilehome Parks"; Miller & Starr, Cal. Real Estate 3rd 31:24.

§798.27. Written Notice to Homeowners of Mobilehome Park Matters.

(a) The management shall give written notice to all homeowners and prospective homeowners concerning the following matters: (1) the nature of the zoning or use permit under which the mobilehome park operates. If the mobilehome park is operating pursuant to a permit subject to a renewal or expiration date, the relevant information and dates shall be included in the notice. (2) The duration of any lease of the mobilehome park, or any portion thereof, in which the management is a lessee.

(b) If a change occurs concerning the zoning or use permit under which the park operates or a lease in which the management is a lessee, all homeowners shall be given written notice within 30 days of that change. Notification regarding the change of use of the park, or any portion thereof, shall be governed by subdivision (g) of Section 798.56. A prospective homeowner shall be notified prior to the inception of the tenancy. **Leg.H.** 1980 ch. 864, 1981 ch. 667, 1982 ch. 1397, 1991 ch. 190.

Ref.: Miller & Starr, Cal. Real Estate 3rd 31:24.

§798.28. Disclosure of Mobilehome Park Owner's Name, Business Address, and Business Telephone Number.

The management of a mobilehome park shall disclose, in writing, the name, business address, and business telephone number of the mobilehome park owner upon the request of a homeowner. **Leg.H.** 1981 ch. 505, 1982 ch. 1397, 1991 ch. 62.

Ref.: Miller & Starr, Cal. Real Estate 3rd 31:24.

§798.285. Renumbered to §798.28.5 by Stats. 2004 ch. 302 (AB 2351).

§798.28.5. Removal of Vehicle Other Than Mobilehome From Mobilehome Park.

(a) Except as otherwise provided in this section, the management may cause the removal, pursuant to Section 22658 of the Vehicle Code, of a vehicle other than a mobilehome that is parked in the park when there is displayed a sign at each entrance to the park as provided in paragraph (1) of subdivision (a) of Section 22658 of the Vehicle Code.

(b) (1) Management may not cause the removal of a vehicle from a homeowner's or resident's driveway or a homeowner's or resident's designated parking space except if management has first posted on the windshield of the vehicle a notice stating management's intent to remove the vehicle in seven days and stating the specific park rule that the vehicle has violated that justifies its removal. After the expiration of seven days following the posting of the notice, management may remove a vehicle that remains in violation of a rule for which notice has been posted upon the vehicle. If a vehicle rule violation is corrected within seven days after the rule violation notice is posted on the vehicle, the vehicle may not be removed. If a vehicle upon which a rule violation notice has been posted is removed from the park by a homeowner or resident and subsequently is returned to the park still in violation of the rule stated in the notice, management is not required to post any additional notice on the vehicle, and the vehicle may be removed after the expiration of the seven-day period following the original notice posting.

(2) If a vehicle poses a significant danger to the health or safety of a park resident or guest, or if a homeowner or resident requests to have a vehicle removed from his or her driveway or designated parking space, the requirements of paragraph (1) do not apply, and management may remove the vehicle pursuant to Section 22658 of the Vehicle Code. **Leg.H.** 1993 ch. 32, 2004 ch. 302 (AB 2351) (amended and renumbered from §798.285).

§798.29. Mobilehome Ombudsman Sign.

The management shall post a mobilehome ombudsman sign provided by the Department of Housing and Community Development, as required by Section 18253.5 of the Health and Safety Code. **Leg.H.** 1988 ch. 333, 1996 ch. 402.

Ref.: Miller & Starr, Cal. Real Estate 3rd 31:15.

§798.29.5. Advance Written Notice of Interruption in Utility Service.

The management shall provide, by posting notice on the mobilehomes of all affected homeowners and residents, at least 72 hours' written advance notice of an interruption in utility service of more than two hours for the maintenance, repair, or replacement of facilities of utility systems over which the management has control within the park, provided that the interruption is not due to an emergency. The management shall be liable only for actual damages sustained by a homeowner or resident for violation of this section.

"Emergency," for purposes of this section, means the interruption of utility service resulting from an accident or act of nature, or cessation of service caused by other than the management's regular or planned maintenance, repair, or replacement of utility facilities. **Leg.H.** 1992 ch. 317.

ARTICLE 4
Fees and Charges

90-day notice of rent increase required. §798.30.
Fees other than rent, utilities, and incidental charges. §798.31.
60-day notice of charges not in rental agreement; charges noted separately in periodic billing. §798.32.
Homeowners allowed 1 pet; fees for pets prohibited—Exception. §798.33.
Exclusion of fees for guests or person providing live-in health care. §798.34.
Fees not to be based on number of family members. §798.35.
Fees for enforcement of rules prohibited—Exceptions. §798.36.
Fees for hookup and landscaping. §798.37.
Park management responsible for maintenance and related costs of trees and management-installed driveways. §798.37.5.
Charges for utilities—Posting of rate schedule; disclosure of third-party billing agent or company. §798.38.
Security deposits. §798.39.
Lien or security interest. §798.40.
Separate billing for utility service fees and charges. §798.41.
Fees or rent increases reflecting cost of court assessment or award prohibited. §798.42.
Utility charges—Disclosure to homeowner regarding measurement of usage for common area facilities and equipment. §798.43.
Duties of master-meter park management for California Alternate Rates for Energy (CARE) program. §798.43.1.
Cost of liquefied petroleum gas sold by park management to mobilehome owners or park tenants. §798.44.

§798.30. 90-Day Notice of Rent Increase Required.

The management shall give a homeowner written notice of any increase in his or her rent at least 90 days before the date of the increase. **Leg.H.** 1978 ch. 1031, 1982 ch. 1397, 1993 ch. 448.

Ref.: Miller & Starr, Cal. Real Estate 3rd 31:17.

§798.31. Fees Other Than Rent, Utilities, and Incidental Charges.

A homeowner shall not be charged a fee for other than rent, utilities, and incidental reasonable charges for services actually rendered.

A homeowner shall not be charged a fee for obtaining a lease on a mobilehome lot for (1) a term of 12 months, or (2) a lesser period as the homeowner may request. A fee may be charged for a lease of more than one year if the fee is mutually agreed upon by both the homeowner and management. **Leg.H.** 1978 ch. 1031, 1982 ch. 1397, 1984 ch. 624.

Ref.: Cal. Fms Pl. & Pr., Ch. 369, "Mobilehomes and Mobilehome Parks"; Miller & Starr, Cal. Real Estate 3rd 31:17.

§798.32. 60-Day Notice of Charges Not in Rental Agreement; Charges Noted Separately in Periodic Billing.

(a) A homeowner shall not be charged a fee for services actually rendered which are not listed in the rental agreement unless he or she has been given written notice thereof by the management, at least 60 days before imposition of the charge.

(b) Those fees and charges specified in subdivision (a) shall be separately stated on any monthly or other periodic billing to the homeowner. If the fee or charge has a limited duration or is amortized for a specified period, the expiration date shall be stated on the initial notice and each subsequent billing to the homeowner while the fee or charge is billed to the homeowner. **Leg.H.** 1978 ch. 1031, 1982 ch. 1397, 1992 ch. 338.

Ref.: Cal. Fms Pl. & Pr., Ch. 369, "Mobilehomes and Mobilehome Parks"; Miller & Starr, Cal. Real Estate 3rd 31:17.

§798.33. Homeowners Allowed 1 Pet; Fees for Pets Prohibited—Exception.

(a) No lease agreement entered into, modified, or renewed on or after January 1, 2001, shall prohibit a homeowner from keeping at least one pet within the park, subject to reasonable rules and regulations of the park.

This section may not be construed to affect any other rights provided by law to a homeowner to keep a pet within the park.

(b) A homeowner shall not be charged a fee for keeping a pet in the park unless the management actually provides special facilities or services for pets. If special pet facilities are maintained by the management, the fee charged shall reasonably relate to the cost of maintenance of the facilities or services and the number of pets kept in the park.

(c) For purposes of this section, "pet" means any domesticated bird, cat, dog, aquatic animal kept within an aquarium, or other animal as agreed to between the management and the homeowner. **Leg.H.** 1978 chs. 1031, 1033, 1982 ch. 1397, 1989 ch. 42, 2000 ch. 551.

Ref.: Cal. Fms Pl. & Pr., Ch. 369, "Mobilehomes and Mobilehome Parks"; Miller & Starr, Cal. Real Estate 3rd 31:17.

§798.34. Exclusion of Fees for Guests or Person Providing Live-In Health Care.

(a) A homeowner shall not be charged a fee for a guest who does not stay with him or her for more than a total of 20 consecutive days or a total of 30 days in a calendar year. A person who is a guest, as described in this subdivision, shall not be required to register with the management.

(b) A homeowner who is living alone and who wishes to share his or her mobilehome with one person may do so, and a fee shall not be imposed by management for that person. The person shall be considered a guest of the homeowner and any agreement between the homeowner and the person shall not change the terms and conditions of the rental agreement between management and the homeowner. The guest shall comply with the provisions of the rules and regulations of the mobilehome park.

(c) A senior homeowner may share his or her mobilehome with any person over 18 years of age if that person is providing live-in health care or live-in supportive care to the homeowner pursuant to a written treatment plan prepared by the homeowner's physician. A fee shall not be charged by management for that person. That person shall have no rights of tenancy in the park, and any agreement between the homeowner and the person shall not change the terms and conditions of the rental agreement between management and the homeowner. That person shall comply with the rules and regulations of the mobilehome park. As used in this subdivision, "senior homeowner" means a homeowner who is 55 years of age or older.

(d) A senior homeowner who resides in a mobilehome park that has implemented rules or regulations limiting residency based on age requirements for housing for older persons, pursuant to Section 798.76, may share his or her mobilehome with any person over 18 years of age if this person is a parent, sibling, child, or grandchild of the senior homeowner and requires live-in health care, live-in supportive care, or supervision pursuant to a written treatment plan prepared by a physician and surgeon. Management may not charge a fee for this person. Any agreement between the senior homeowner and this person shall not change the terms and conditions of the rental agreement between management and the senior homeowner. Unless otherwise agreed upon, park management shall not be required to manage, supervise, or provide for this person's care during his or her stay in the mobilehome park. This person shall have no rights of tenancy in the park, but shall comply with the rules and regulations of the mobilehome park. A violation of the mobilehome park rules and regulations by this person shall be deemed a violation of the rules and regulations by the homeowner pursuant to subdivision (d) of Section 798.56. As used in this subdivision, "senior homeowner" means a homeowner who is 55 years of age or older. **Leg.H.** 1978 ch. 1031, 1981 ch. 240, 1982 ch. 1397, 1983 ch. 128, 1990 ch. 881, 1992 ch. 337, 1996 ch. 157.

Ref.: Cal. Fms Pl. & Pr., Ch. 369, "Mobilehomes and Mobilehome Parks"; Miller & Starr, Cal. Real Estate 3rd 31:17.

§798.35. Fees Not to Be Based on Number of Family Members.

A homeowner shall not be charged a fee based on the number of members in his or her immediate family. As used in this section, the "immediate family" shall be limited to the homeowner, his or her spouse, their parents, their children, and their grandchildren under 18 years of age. **Leg.H.** 1978 ch. 1031, 1980 ch. 845, 1982 ch. 1397, 1995 ch. 24.

Ref.: Cal. Fms Pl. & Pr., Ch. 369, "Mobilehomes and Mobilehome Parks"; Miller & Starr, Cal. Real Estate 3rd 31:17.

§798.36. Fees for Enforcement of Rules Prohibited—Exceptions.

(a) A homeowner shall not be charged a fee for the enforcement of any of the rules and regulations of the park, except [1] **a** reasonable fee may be charged by management for the maintenance **or cleanup, as described in subdivision (b),** of the land and premises upon which the mobilehome is situated in the event the homeowner fails to do so in accordance with the rules and regulations of the park after written notification to the homeowner and the failure of the homeowner to comply within 14 days. The written notice shall state the specific condition to be corrected and an estimate of the charges to be imposed by management if the services are performed by management or its agent.

(b) (1) If management determines, in good faith, that the removal of a homeowner's or resident's personal property from the land and premises upon which the mobilehome is situated is necessary to bring the premises into compliance with the reasonable rules and regulations of the park or the provisions of the Mobilehome Parks Act (Part 2.1 (commencing with Section 18200) of Division 13 of the Health and Safety Code) or Title 25 of the California Code of Regulations, management may remove the property to a reasonably secure storage facility. Management shall provide written notice of at least 14 days of its intent to remove the personal property, including a description of the property to be removed. The notice shall include the rule, regulation, or code justifying the removal and shall provide an estimate of the charges to be imposed by management. The property to be removed shall not include the mobilehome or its appurtenances or accessory structures.

(2) The homeowner or resident shall be responsible for reimbursing to management the actual, reasonable costs, if any, of removing and storing the property.

These costs incurred by management in correcting the rules violation associated with the removal and storage of the property, are deemed reasonable incidental service charges and may be collected pursuant to subdivision (e) of Section 798.56 if a notice of nonpayment of the removal and storage fees, as described in paragraph (3), is personally served on the homeowner.

(3) Within seven days from the date the property is removed to a storage area, management shall provide the homeowner or resident a written notice that includes an inventory of the property removed, the location where the property may be claimed, and notice that the cost of removal and storage shall be paid by the resident or homeowner. If, within 60 days, the homeowner or resident does not claim the property, the property shall be deemed to be abandoned, and management may dispose of the property in any manner. The homeowner's or resident's liability for storage charges shall not exceed 60 days. If the homeowner or resident claims the property, but has not reimbursed management for storage costs, management may bill those costs in a monthly statement which shall constitute notice of nonpayment, and the costs shall become the obligation of the homeowner or resident. If a resident or homeowner communicates in writing his or her intent to abandon the property before 60 days has expired, management may dispose of the property immediately and no further storage charges shall accrue.

(4) If management elects to dispose of the property by way of sale or auction, and the funds received from the sale or auction exceed the amount owed to management, management shall refund the difference to the homeowner or resident within 15 days from the date of management's receipt of the funds from the sale or auction. The refund shall be delivered to the homeowner or resident by first-class mail postage prepaid to his or her address in the park, or by personal delivery, and shall include an accounting specifying the costs of removal and storage of the property incurred by management in correcting the rules violation and the amount of proceeds realized from any sale or auction. If a sale or auction of the property yields less than the costs incurred by management, the homeowner or resident shall be responsible for the difference, and this amount shall be deemed a reasonable incidental service charge and may be collected pursuant to subdivision (e) of Section 798.56 if a notice of nonpayment of the removal and storage fees, as described in paragraph (3), is personally served on the homeowner. If management elects to proceed under this section, it may not also terminate the tenancy pursuant to subdivision (d) of Section 798.56 based upon the specific violations relied upon to proceed under this section. In any proceeding under this section, management shall bear the burden of proof that enforcement was undertaken in a nondiscriminatory, nonselective fashion. **Leg.H.** 1978 ch. 1031, 1982 ch. 1397, 1983 ch. 519, 2005 ch. 24 (SB 125) §1.

§798.36. 2005 Deletes. [1] as

Ref.: Cal. Fms Pl. & Pr., Ch. 369, "Mobilehomes and Mobilehome Parks"; Miller & Starr, Cal. Real Estate 3rd 31:17.

§798.37. Fees for Hookup and Landscaping.

A homeowner may not be charged a fee for the entry, installation, hookup, or landscaping as a condition of tenancy except for an actual fee or cost imposed by a local governmental ordinance or requirement directly related to the occupancy of the specific site upon which the mobilehome is located and not incurred as a portion of the development of the mobilehome park as a whole. However, reasonable landscaping and maintenance requirements may be included in the park rules and regulations. The management may not require a homeowner or prospective homeowner to purchase, rent, or lease goods or services for landscaping, remodeling, or maintenance from any person, company, or corporation. **Leg.H.** 1978 ch. 1031, 1980 ch. 845, 1982 ch. 1397, 1983 ch. 519, 2004 ch. 302 (AB 2351).

Ref.: Cal. Fms Pl. & Pr., Ch. 369, "Mobilehomes and Mobilehome Parks"; Miller & Starr, Cal. Real Estate 3rd 31:17.

§798.37.5. Park Management Responsible for Maintenance and Related Costs of Trees and Management-Installed Driveways.

(a) With respect to trees on rental spaces in a mobilehome park, park management shall be solely responsible for the trimming, pruning, or removal of any tree, and the costs thereof, upon written notice by a homeowner or a determination by park management that the tree poses a specific hazard or health and safety violation. In the case of a dispute over that assertion, the park management or a homeowner may request an inspection by the Department of Housing and Community Development or a local agency responsible for the enforcement of the Mobilehome Parks Act (Part 2.1 (commencing with Section 18200) of Division 3 of the Health and Safety Code) in order to determine whether a violation of that act exists.

(b) With respect to trees in the common areas of a mobilehome park, park management shall be solely responsible for the trimming, pruning, or removal of any tree, and the costs thereof.

(c) Park management shall be solely responsible for the maintenance, repair, replacement, paving, sealing, and the expenses related to the maintenance of all driveways installed by park management including, but not limited to, repair of root damage to driveways and foundation systems and removal. Homeowners shall be responsible for the maintenance, repair, replacement, paving, sealing, and the expenses related to the maintenance of a homeowner installed driveway. A homeowner may be charged for the cost of any damage to the driveway caused by an act of the homeowner or a breach of the homeowner's responsibilities under the rules and regulations so long as those rules and regulations are not inconsistent with the provisions of this section.

(d) No homeowner may plant a tree within the mobilehome park without first obtaining written permission from the management.

(e) This section shall not apply to alter the terms of any rental agreement in effect prior to January 1, 2001, between the park management and the homeowner regarding the responsibility for the maintenance of trees and driveways within the mobilehome park, except that upon any renewal or extension, the rental agreement shall be subject to this section. This section is not intended to abrogate the content of any existing rental agreement or other written agreements regarding trees or driveways that are in effect prior to January 1, 2001.

(f) This section shall only apply to rental agreements entered into, renewed, or extended on or after January 1, 2001.

(g) Any mobilehome park rule or regulation shall be in compliance with this section. **Leg.H.** 2000 ch. 423.

Ref.: W. Cal. Sum., "Real Property" §533.

§798.38. Charges for Utilities—Posting of Rate Schedule; Disclosure of Third-Party Billing Agent or Company.

(a) Where the management provides both master-meter and submeter service of utilities to a homeowner, for each billing period the cost of the charges for the period shall be separately stated along with the opening and closing readings for his or her meter. The management shall post in a conspicuous place, the prevailing residential utilities rate schedule as published by the serving utility.

(b) If a third-party billing agent or company prepares utility billing for the park, the management shall disclose on each resident's billing, the name, address, and telephone number of the billing agent or company. **Leg.H.** 1978 ch. 1031, 1981 ch. 714, 1982 ch. 1397, 2004 ch. 728 (SB 1163).

Ref.: Cal. Fms Pl. & Pr., Ch. 369, "Mobilehomes and Mobilehome Parks"; Miller & Starr, Cal. Real Estate 3rd 31:17.

§798.39. Security Deposits.

(a) The management may only demand a security deposit on or before initial occupancy and the security deposit may not be in an amount or value in excess of an amount equal to two months' rent that is charged at the inception of the occupancy, in addition to any rent for the first month. In no event shall additional security deposits be demanded of a homeowner following the initial occupancy.

(b) As to all security deposits collected on or after January 1, 1989, after the homeowner has promptly paid to the management, within five days of the date the amount is due, all of the rent, utilities, and reasonable service charges for any 12-consecutive-month period subsequent to the collection of the security deposit by the management, or upon resale of the mobilehome, whichever occurs earlier, the management shall, upon the receipt of a written request from the homeowner, refund to the homeowner the amount of the security deposit within 30 days following the end of the 12-consecutive-month period of the prompt payment or the date of the resale of the mobilehome.

(c) As to all security deposits collected prior to January 1, 1989, upon the extension or renewal of the rental agreement or lease between the homeowner and the management, and upon the receipt of a written request from the homeowner, if the homeowner has promptly paid to the management, within five days of the date the amount is due, all of the rent, utilities, and reasonable service charges for the 12-consecutive-month period preceding the receipt of the written request, the management shall refund to the homeowner the amount of the security deposit within 60 days.

(d) As to all security deposits collected prior to January 1, 1989, and not disbursed pursuant to subdivision (c), in the event that the mobilehome park is sold or transferred to any other party or entity, the selling park owner shall deposit in escrow an amount equal to all security deposits that the park owner holds. The seller's escrow instructions shall direct that, upon close of escrow, the security deposits therein that were held by the selling park owner (including the period in escrow) for 12 months or more, shall be disbursed to the persons who paid the deposits to the selling park owner and promptly paid, within five days of the date the amount is due, all rent, utilities, and reasonable service charges for the 12-month period preceding the close of escrow.

(e) Any and all security deposits in escrow that were held by the selling park owner that are not required to be disbursed pursuant to subdivision (b), (c), or (d) shall be disbursed to the successors in interest to the selling or transferring park owner, who shall have the same obligations of the park's management and ownership specified in this section with respect to security deposits. The disbursal may be made in escrow by a debit against the selling park owner and a credit to the successors in interest to the selling park owner.

(f) The management shall not be required to place any security deposit collected in an interest-bearing account or to provide a homeowner with any interest on the security deposit collected.

(g) Nothing in this section shall affect the validity of title to real property transferred in violation of this section. **Leg.H.** 1988 ch. 59, 1994 ch. 119, 2001 ch. 151.

Ref.: Miller & Starr, Cal. Real Estate 3rd 31:17.

§798.40. Lien or Security Interest.

The management shall not acquire a lien or security interest, other than an interest arising by reason of process issued to enforce a judgment of any court, in a mobilehome located in the park unless it is mutually agreed upon by both the homeowner and management. Any billing and payment upon the obligation shall be kept separate from current rent. **Leg.H.** 1986 ch. 390.

Ref.: Miller & Starr, Cal. Real Estate 3rd 31:17.

§798.41. Separate Billing for Utility Service Fees and Charges.

(a) Where a rental agreement, including a rental agreement specified in Section 798.17, does not specifically provide otherwise, the park management may elect to bill a homeowner separately for utility service fees and charges assessed by the utility for services provided to or for spaces in the park. Any separately billed utility fees and charges shall not be deemed to be included in the rent charged for those spaces under the rental agreement, and shall not be deemed to be rent or a rent increase for purposes of any ordinance, rule, regulation, or initiative measure adopted or enforced by any local governmental entity which establishes a maximum amount that a landlord may charge a tenant for rent, provided that at the time of the initial separate billing of any utility fees and charges the rent chargeable under the rental agreement or the base rent chargeable under the terms of a local rent control provision is simultaneously reduced by an amount equal to the fees and charges separately billed. The amount of this reduction shall be equal to the average amount charged to the park management for that utility service for that space during the 12 months immediately preceding notice of the commencement of the separate billing for that utility service.

Utility services to which this section applies are natural gas or liquid propane gas, electricity, water, cable television, garbage or refuse service, and sewer service.

(b) This section does not apply to rental agreements entered into prior to January 1, 1991, until extended or renewed on or after that date.

(c) Nothing in this section shall require rental agreements to provide for separate billing to homeowners of fees and charges specified in subdivision (a).

(d) Those fees and charges specified in subdivision (a) shall be separately stated on any monthly or other periodic billing to the homeowner. If the fee or charge has a limited duration or is amortized for a specified period, the expiration date shall be stated on the initial notice and each subsequent billing to the homeowner while the fee or charge is billed to the homeowner. **Leg.H.** 1990 ch. 1013, 1992 chs. 160, 338.

§798.42. Fees or Rent Increases Reflecting Cost of Court Assessment or Award Prohibited.

(a) The management shall not charge or impose upon a homeowner any fee or increase in rent which reflects the cost to the management of any fine, forfeiture, penalty, money damages, or fee assessed or awarded by a court of law against the management for a violation of this chapter, including any attorney's fees and costs incurred by the management in connection therewith.

(b) A court shall consider the remoteness in time of the assessment or award against the management of any fine, forfeiture, penalty, money damages, or fee in determining whether the homeowner has met the burden of proof that the fee or increase in rent is in violation of this section.

(c) Any provision in a rental agreement entered into, renewed, or modified on or after January 1, 1995, that permits a fee or increase in rent that reflects the cost to the management of any money damages awarded against the management for a violation of this chapter shall be void. **Leg.H.** 1990 ch. 1374, 1994 ch. 1254.

§798.43. Utility Charges—Disclosure to Homeowner Regarding Measurement of Usage for Common Area Facilities and Equipment.

(a) Except as provided in subdivision (b), whenever a homeowner is responsible for payment of gas, water, or electric utility service, management shall disclose to the homeowner any condition by which a gas, water, or electric meter on the homeowner's site measures gas, water, or electric service for common area facilities or equipment, including lighting, provided that management has knowledge of the condition.

Management shall disclose this information prior to the inception of the tenancy or upon discovery and shall complete either of the following:

(1) Enter into a mutual written agreement with the homeowner for compensation by management for the cost of the portion of the service measured by the homeowner's meter for the common area facilities or equipment to the extent that this cost accrues on or after January 1, 1991.

(2) Discontinue using the meter on the homeowner's site for the utility service to the common area facilities and equipment.

(b) On or after January 1, 1994, if the electric meter on the homeowner's site measures electricity for lighting mandated by Section 18602 of the Health and Safety Code and this lighting provides lighting for the homeowner's site, management shall be required to comply with subdivision (a). **Leg.H.** 1990 ch. 380, 1991 ch. 1091 (amended and renumbered from §798.41), 1993 ch. 147.

§798.43.1. Duties of Master-Meter Park Management for California Alternate Rates for Energy (CARE) Program.

(a) The management of a master-meter park shall give written notice to homeowners and residents on or before February 1 of each year in their utility billing statements about assistance to low-income persons for utility costs available under the California Alternate Rates for Energy (CARE) program, established pursuant to Section 739.1 of the Public Utilities Code. The notice shall include CARE information available to master-meter customers from their serving utility, to include, at a minimum: (1) the fact that CARE offers a discount on monthly gas or electric bills for qualifying low-income residents; and (2) the telephone number of the serving utility which provides CARE information and applications. The park shall also post the notice in a conspicuous place in the clubhouse, or if there is no clubhouse, in a conspicuous public place in the park.

(b) The management of a master-meter park may accept and help process CARE program applications from homeowners and residents in the park, fill in the necessary account or other park information required by the serving utility to process the applications, and send the applications to the serving utility. The management shall not deny a homeowner or resident who chooses to submit a CARE application to the utility himself or herself any park information, including a utility account number, the serving utility requires to process a homeowner or resident CARE program application.

(c) The management of a master-meter park shall pass through the full amount of the CARE program discount in monthly utility billings to homeowners and residents who have qualified for the CARE rate schedule, as defined in the serving utility's applicable rate schedule. The management shall notice the discount on the billing statement of any homeowner or resident who has qualified for the CARE rate schedule as either the itemized amount of the discount or a notation on the statement that the homeowner or resident is receiving the CARE discount on the electric bill, the gas bill, or both the electric and gas bills.

(d) "Master-meter park" as used in this section means "master-meter customer" as used in Section 739.5 of the Public Utilities Code. **Leg.H.** 2001 ch. 437.

§798.44. Cost of Liquefied Petroleum Gas Sold by Park Management to Mobilehome Owners or Park Tenants.

(a) The management of a park that does not permit mobilehome owners or park tenants to purchase liquefied petroleum gas for use in the mobilehome park from someone other than the mobilehome park management shall not sell liquefied petroleum gas to mobilehome owners and tenants within the park at a cost which exceeds 110 percent of the actual price paid by the management of the park for liquefied petroleum gas.

(b) The management of a park shall post in a visible location the actual price paid by management for liquefied petroleum gas sold pursuant to subdivision (a).

(c) This section shall apply only to mobilehome parks regulated under the Mobilehome Residency Law. This section shall not apply to recreational vehicle parks, as defined in Section 18215 of the Health and Safety Code, which exclusively serve recreational vehicles, as defined in Section 18010 of the Health and Safety Code.

(d) Nothing in this section is intended to abrogate any rights a mobilehome park owner may have under Section 798.31 of the Civil Code.

(e) In addition to a mobilehome park described in subdivision (a), the requirements of subdivisions (a) and (b) shall apply to a mobilehome park where requirements of federal, state, or local law or regulation, including, but not limited to, requirements for setbacks between mobilehomes, prohibit homeowners or tenants from installing their own liquefied petroleum gas supply tanks, notwithstanding that the management of the mobilehome park permits mobilehome owners and park tenants to buy their own liquefied petroleum gas. **Leg.H.** 1999 ch. 326, 2000 ch. 232.

ARTICLE 4.5
Rent Control

New construction exempt from rent control. §798.45.
Pass-through of specified charges imposed by any governmental entity. §798.49.

§798.45. New Construction Exempt From Rent Control.

Notwithstanding Section 798.17, "new construction" as defined in Section 798.7, shall be exempt from any ordinance, rule, regulation, or initiative measure adopted by any city, county, or city and county, which establishes a maximum amount that a landlord may charge a tenant for rent. **Leg.H.** 1989 ch. 412.

Ref.: Cal. Fms Pl. & Pr., Ch. 369, "Mobilehomes and Mobilehome Parks."

§798.49. Pass-Through of Specified Charges Imposed by Any Governmental Entity.

(a) Except as provided in subdivision (d), the local agency of any city, including a charter city, county, or city and county, which administers an ordinance, rule, regulation, or initiative measure that establishes a maximum amount that management may charge a tenant for rent shall permit the management to separately charge a homeowner for any of the following:

(1) The amount of any fee, assessment or other charge first imposed by a city, including a charter city, a county, a city and county, the state, or the federal government on or after January 1, 1995, upon the space rented by the homeowner.

(2) The amount of any increase on or after January 1, 1995, in an existing fee, assessment or other charge imposed by any governmental entity upon the space rented by the homeowner.

(3) The amount of any fee, assessment or other charge upon the space first imposed or increased on or after January 1, 1993, pursuant to any state or locally mandated program relating to housing contained in the Health and Safety Code.

(b) If management has charged the homeowner for a fee, assessment, or other charge specified in subdivision (a) that was increased or first imposed on or after January 1, 1993, and the fee, assessment, or other charge is decreased or eliminated thereafter, the charge to the homeowner shall be decreased or eliminated accordingly.

(c) The amount of the fee, assessment or other charges authorized by subdivision (a) shall be separately stated on any billing to the homeowner. Any change in the amount of the fee, assessment, or other charges that are separately billed pursuant to subdivision (a) shall be considered when determining any rental adjustment under the local ordinance.

(d) This section shall not apply to any of the following:

(1) Those fees, assessments, or charges imposed pursuant to the Mobilehome Parks Act (Part 2.1 (commencing with Section 18200) of Division 13 of the Health and Safety Code), unless specifically authorized by Section 18502 of the Health and Safety Code.

(2) Those costs that are imposed on management by a court pursuant to Section 798.42.

(3) Any fee or other exaction imposed upon management for the specific purpose of defraying the cost of administration of any ordinance, rule, regulation, or initiative measure that establishes a maximum amount that management may charge a tenant for rent.

(4) Any tax imposed upon the property by a city, including a charter city, county, or city and county.

(e) Those fees and charges specified in subdivision (a) shall be separately stated on any monthly or other periodic billing to the homeowner. If the fee or charge has a limited duration or is amortized for a specified period, the expiration date shall be stated on the initial notice and each subsequent billing to the homeowner while the fee or charge is billed to the homeowner. **Leg.H.** 1992 ch. 338, 1994 ch. 340.

ARTICLE 5
Homeowner Communications and Meetings

Legislative intent. §798.50.
Prohibited contract provisions; cleaning deposit; liability insurance; parking or occupancy limitations or restrictions. §798.51.
Action for injunctive relief. §798.52.

§798.50. Legislative Intent.

It is the intent of the Legislature in enacting this article to ensure that homeowners and residents of mobilehome parks have the right to peacefully assemble and freely communicate with one another and with others with respect to mobilehome living or for social or educational purposes. **Leg.H.** 1989 ch. 198 §2.

Ref.: Miller & Starr, Cal. Real Estate 3rd 31:24.

§798.51. Prohibited Contract Provisions; Cleaning Deposit; Liability Insurance; Parking or Occupancy Limitations or Restrictions.

(a) No provision contained in any mobilehome park rental agreement, rule, or regulation shall deny or prohibit the right of any homeowner or resident in the park to do any of the following:

(1) Peacefully assemble or meet in the park, at reasonable hours and in a reasonable manner, for any lawful purpose. Meetings may be held in the park community or recreation hall or clubhouse when the facility is not otherwise in use, and, with the consent of the homeowner, in any mobilehome within the park.

(2) Invite public officials, candidates for public office, or representatives of mobilehome owner organizations to meet with homeowners and residents and speak upon matters of public interest, in accordance with Section 798.50.

(3) Canvass and petition homeowners and residents for noncommercial purposes relating to mobilehome living, election to public office, or the initiative, referendum, or recall processes, at reasonable hours and in a reasonable manner, including the distribution or circulation of information.

(b) A homeowner or resident may not be charged a cleaning deposit in order to use the park recreation hall or clubhouse for meetings of resident organizations for any of the purposes stated in Section 798.50 and this section, whether or not guests or visitors from outside the park are invited to attend the meeting, if a homeowner or resident of the park is hosting the meeting and all homeowners or residents of the park are allowed to attend.

(c) A homeowner or resident may not be required to obtain liability insurance in order to use common area facilities for the purposes specified in this section and Section 798.50. However, if alcoholic beverages are to be served at any meeting or private function, a liability insurance binder may be required by the park ownership or management. The ownership or management of a mobilehome park may prohibit the consumption of alcoholic beverages in the park common area facilities if the terms of the rental agreement or the rules and regulations of the park prohibit it.

(d) A homeowner, organization, or group of homeowners using a recreation hall or clubhouse pursuant to this section shall be required to adhere to any limitations or restrictions regarding vehicle parking or maximum occupancy for the clubhouse or recreation hall.

(e) A homeowner or resident may not be prohibited from displaying a political campaign sign relating to a candidate for election to public office or to the initiative, referendum, or recall process in the window or on the side of a manufactured home or mobilehome, or within the site on which the home is located or installed. The size of the face of a political sign may not exceed six square feet, and the sign may not be displayed in excess of a period of time from 90 days prior to an election to 15 days following the election, unless a local ordinance within the jurisdiction where the mobilehome park is located imposes a more restrictive period of time for the display of such a sign. **Leg.H.** 1989 ch. 198 §2, 2001 ch. 83, 2003 ch. 249 (SB 116).

Ref.: Miller & Starr, Cal. Real Estate 3rd 31:24.

§798.52. Action for Injunctive Relief.

Any homeowner or resident who is prevented by management from exercising the rights provided for in Section 798.51 may bring an action in a court of law to enjoin enforcement of any rule, regulation, or other policy which unreasonably deprives a homeowner or resident of those rights. **Leg.H.** 1989 ch. 198.

ARTICLE 5.5
Homeowners Meetings With Management

§798.53. Meetings With Management—Request, Subject Matter, Notice.

The management shall meet and consult with the homeowners, upon written request, within 30 days of the request, either individually, collectively, or with representatives of a group of homeowners who have signed a request to be so represented on the following matters:

(a) Resident concerns regarding existing park rules that are not subject to Section 798.25.

(b) Standards for maintenance of physical improvements in the park.

(c) Addition, alteration, or deletion of service, equipment, or physical improvements.

(d) Rental agreements offered pursuant to Section 798.17.

Any collective meeting shall be conducted only after notice thereof has been given to all the requesting homeowners 10 days or more before the meeting. **Leg.H.** 1989 ch. 198, 1994 ch. 340.

ARTICLE 6
Termination of Tenancy

Eviction—Manner of terminating tenancy—60-day notice. §798.55.
Permissible reasons for termination. §798.56.
Written notification to management by legal owner following notice of termination. §798.56a.
Notice of termination to specify reason. §798.57.
Termination to make site available to mobilehome purchaser or renter prohibited. §798.58.
Homeowner to give 60-day notice before vacating. §798.59.
Rights under Code of Civil Procedure not affected. §798.60.
Selling abandoned mobilehome—Requirements and procedure. §798.61.

§798.55. Eviction—Manner of Terminating Tenancy—60-Day Notice.

(a) The Legislature finds and declares that, because of the high cost of moving mobilehomes, the potential for damage resulting therefrom, the requirements relating to the installation of mobilehomes, and the cost of landscaping or lot preparation, it is necessary that the owners of mobilehomes occupied within mobilehome parks be provided with the unique protection from actual or constructive eviction afforded by the provisions of this chapter.

(b) (1) The management may not terminate or refuse to renew a tenancy, except for a reason specified in this article and upon the giving of written notice to the homeowner, in the manner prescribed by Section 1162 of the Code of Civil Procedure, to sell or remove, at the homeowner's election, the mobilehome from the park within a period of not less than 60 days, which period shall be specified in the notice. A copy of this notice shall be sent to the legal owner, as defined in Section 18005.8 of the Health and Safety Code, each junior lienholder, as defined in Section 18005.3 of the Health and Safety Code, and the registered owner of the mobilehome, if other than the homeowner, by United States mail within 10 days after notice to the homeowner. The copy may be sent by regular mail or by certified or registered mail with return receipt requested, at the option of the management.

(2) The homeowner shall pay past due rent and utilities upon the sale of a mobilehome pursuant to paragraph (1).

(c) If the homeowner has not paid the rent due within three days after notice to the homeowner, and if the first notice was not sent by certified or registered mail with return receipt requested, a copy of the notice shall again be sent to the legal owner, each junior lienholder, and the registered owner, if other than the homeowner, by certified or registered mail with return receipt requested within 10 days after notice to the homeowner. Copies of the notice shall be addressed to the legal owner, each junior lienholder, and the registered owner at their addresses, as set forth in the registration card specified in Section 18091.5 of the Health and Safety Code.

(d) **If management obtains a court judgment against a homeowner or resident, the cost incurred by management in obtaining a title search for the purpose of complying with the notice requirements of this section shall be recoverable as a cost of suit.**

(e) The resident of a mobilehome that remains in the mobilehome park after service of the notice to sell or remove the mobilehome shall continue to be subject to this chapter and the rules and regulations of the park, including rules regarding maintenance of the space.

[1] (f) No lawful act by the management to enforce this chapter or the rules and regulations of the park may be deemed or construed to waive or otherwise affect the notice to remove the mobilehome. **Leg.H.** 1978 chs. 1031, 1033, 1979 ch. 493, 1980 ch. 1149, 1982 ch. 1397, 1983 chs. 519 §7, 1124, operative July 1, 1984, 1992 ch. 835, 1993 ch. 666, 1998 ch. 542, 2003 ch. 561 (AB 682), 2005 ch. 24 (SB 125) §2.

§798.55. 2005 Deletes. [1] (e)

2003 Note: This act is not intended to affect park management's existing rights and remedies to recover unpaid rent, utility charges, or reasonable incidental charges, and may not be construed to provide for an exclusive remedy. Stats. 2003 ch. 561 (AB 682) §4.

Ref.: Cal. Fms Pl. & Pr., Ch. 369, "Mobilehomes and Mobilehome Parks"; Miller & Starr, Cal. Real Estate 3rd 31:31.

§798.56. Permissible Reasons for Termination.

A tenancy shall be terminated by the management only for one or more of the following reasons:

(a) Failure of the homeowner or resident to comply with a local ordinance or state law or regulation relating to mobilehomes within a reasonable time after the homeowner receives a notice of noncompliance from the appropriate governmental agency.

(b) Conduct by the homeowner or resident, upon the park premises, that constitutes a substantial annoyance to other homeowners or residents.

(c) (1) Conviction of the homeowner or resident for prostitution, for a violation of subdivision (d) of Section 243, paragraph (2) of subdivision (a), or subdivision (b), of Section 245, Section 288, or Section 451, of the Penal Code, or a felony controlled substance offense, if the act resulting in the conviction was committed anywhere on the premises of the mobilehome park, including, but not limited to, within the homeowner's mobilehome.

(2) However the tenancy may not be terminated for the reason specified in this subdivision if the person convicted of the offense has permanently vacated, and does not subsequently reoccupy, the mobilehome.

(d) Failure of the homeowner or resident to comply with a reasonable rule or regulation of the park that is part of the rental agreement or any amendment thereto.

No act or omission of the homeowner or resident shall constitute a failure to comply with a reasonable rule or regulation unless and until the management has given the homeowner written notice of the alleged rule or regulation violation and the homeowner or resident has failed to adhere to the rule or regulation within seven days. However, if a homeowner has been given a written notice of an alleged violation of the same rule or regulation on three or more occasions within a 12-month period after the homeowner or resident has violated that rule or regulation, no written notice shall be required for a subsequent violation of the same rule or regulation.

Nothing in this subdivision shall relieve the management from its obligation to demonstrate that a rule or regulation has in fact been violated.

(e) (1) Nonpayment of rent, utility charges, or reasonable incidental service charges; provided that the amount due has been unpaid for a period of at least five days from its due date, and provided that the homeowner shall be given a three-day written notice subsequent to that five-day period to pay the amount due or to vacate the tenancy. For purposes of this subdivision, the five-day period does not include the date the payment is due. The three-day written notice shall be given to the homeowner in the manner prescribed by Section 1162 of the Code of Civil Procedure. A copy of this notice shall be sent to the persons or entities specified in subdivision (b) of Section 798.55 within 10 days after notice is delivered to the homeowner. If the homeowner cures the default, the notice need not be sent. The notice may be given at the same time as the 60 days' notice required for termination of the tenancy. A three-day notice given pursuant to this subdivision shall contain the following provisions printed in at least 12-point boldface type at the top of the notice, with the appropriate number written in the blank:

"Warning: This notice is the (insert number) three-day notice for nonpayment of rent, utility charges, or other reasonable incidental services that has been served upon you in the last 12 months. Pursuant to Civil Code Section 798.56 (e) (5), if you have been given a three-day notice to either pay rent, utility charges, or other reasonable incidental services or to vacate your tenancy on three or more occasions within a 12-month period, management is not required to give you a further three-day period to pay rent or vacate the tenancy before your tenancy can be terminated."

(2) Payment by the homeowner prior to the expiration of the three-day notice period shall cure a default under this subdivision. If the homeowner does not pay prior to

the expiration of the three-day notice period, the homeowner shall remain liable for all payments due up until the time the tenancy is vacated.

(3) Payment by the legal owner, as defined in Section 18005.8 of the Health and Safety Code, any junior lienholder, as defined in Section 18005.3 of the Health and Safety Code, or the registered owner, as defined in Section 18009.5 of the Health and Safety Code, if other than the homeowner, on behalf of the homeowner prior to the expiration of 30 calendar days following the mailing of the notice to the legal owner, each junior lienholder, and the registered owner provided in subdivision (b) of Section 798.55, shall cure a default under this subdivision with respect to that payment.

(4) Cure of a default of rent, utility charges, or reasonable incidental service charges by the legal owner, any junior lienholder, or the registered owner, if other than the homeowner, as provided by this subdivision, may not be exercised more than twice during a 12-month period.

(5) If a homeowner has been given a three-day notice to pay the amount due or to vacate the tenancy on three or more occasions within the preceding 12-month period and each notice includes the provisions specified in paragraph (1), no written three-day notice shall be required in the case of a subsequent nonpayment of rent, utility charges, or reasonable incidental service charges.

In that event, the management shall give written notice to the homeowner in the manner prescribed by Section 1162 of the Code of Civil Procedure to remove the mobilehome from the park within a period of not less than 60 days, which period shall be specified in the notice. A copy of this notice shall be sent to the legal owner, each junior lienholder, and the registered owner of the mobilehome, if other than the homeowner, as specified in paragraph (b) of Section 798.55, by certified or registered mail, return receipt requested, within 10 days after notice is sent to the homeowner.

(6) When a copy of the 60 days' notice described in paragraph (5) is sent to the legal owner, each junior lienholder, and the registered owner of the mobilehome, if other than the homeowner, the default may be cured by any of them on behalf of the homeowner prior to the expiration of 30 calendar days following the mailing of the notice, if all of the following conditions exist:

(A) A copy of a three-day notice sent pursuant to subdivision (b) of Section 798.55 to a homeowner for the nonpayment of rent, utility charges, or reasonable incidental service charges was not sent to the legal owner, junior lienholder, or registered owner, of the mobilehome, if other than the homeowner, during the preceding 12-month period.

(B) The legal owner, junior lienholder, or registered owner of the mobilehome, if other than the homeowner, has not previously cured a default of the homeowner during the preceding 12-month period.

(C) The legal owner, junior lienholder or registered owner, if other than the homeowner, is not a financial institution or mobilehome dealer.

If the default is cured by the legal owner, junior lienholder, or registered owner within the 30-day period, the notice to remove the mobilehome from the park described in paragraph (5) shall be rescinded.

(f) Condemnation of the park.

(g) Change of use of the park or any portion thereof, provided:

(1) The management gives the homeowners at least 15 days' written notice that the management will be appearing before a local governmental board, commission, or body to request permits for a change of use of the mobilehome park.

(2) After all required permits requesting a change of use have been approved by the local governmental board, commission, or body, the management shall give the homeowners six months' or more written notice of termination of tenancy.

If the change of use requires no local governmental permits, then notice shall be given 12 months or more prior to the management's determination that a change of use will occur. The management in the notice shall disclose and describe in detail the nature of the change of use.

(3) The management gives each proposed homeowner written notice thereof prior to the inception of his or her tenancy that the management is requesting a change of use before local governmental bodies or that a change of use request has been granted.

(4) The notice requirements for termination of tenancy set forth in Sections 798.56 and 798.57 shall be followed if the proposed change actually occurs.

(5) A notice of a proposed change of use given prior to January 1, 1980, that conforms to the requirements in effect at that time shall be valid. The requirements for a notice of a proposed change of use imposed by this subdivision shall be governed by the law in effect at the time the notice was given.

(h) The report required pursuant to subdivisions (b) and (i) of Section 65863.7 of the Government Code shall be given to the homeowners or residents at the same time that notice is required pursuant to subdivision (g) of this section.

(i) For purposes of this section, "financial institution" means a state or national bank, state or federal savings and loan association or credit union, or similar organization, and mobilehome dealer as defined in Section 18002.6 of the Health and Safety Code or any other organization that, as part of its usual course of business, originates, owns, or provides loan servicing for loans secured by a mobilehome. **Leg.H.** 1978 chs. 1031, 1033, 1979 chs. 945, 1185 §1.5, 1980 ch. 1149, 1981 ch. 458, 1982 chs. 777, 1397 §25.5, 1983 chs. 519 §8, 1124, operative July 1, 1984, 1987 chs. 55, 883 §2, 1988 chs. 171, 301 §2.5, 1990 chs. 42, 1357 §1.5, 1998 ch. 427, 2003 chs. 85 (AB 805), 388 (AB 767) §1.5.

Ref.: Cal. Fms Pl. & Pr., Ch. 369, "Mobilehomes and Mobilehome Parks."

§798.56a. Written Notification to Management by Legal Owner Following Notice of Termination.

(a) Within 60 days after receipt of, or no later than 65 days after the mailing of, the notice of termination of tenancy pursuant to any reason provided in Section 798.56, the legal owner, if any, and each junior lienholder, if any, shall notify the management in writing of at least one of the following:

(1) Its offer to sell the obligation secured by the mobilehome to the management for the amount specified in its written offer. In that event, the management shall have 15 days following receipt of the offer to accept or reject the offer in writing. If the offer is rejected, the person or entity that made the offer shall have 10 days in which to exercise one of the other options contained in this section and shall notify management in writing of its choice.

(2) Its intention to foreclose on its security interest in the mobilehome.

(3) Its request that the management pursue the termination of tenancy against the homeowner and its offer to reimburse management for the reasonable attorney's fees and court costs incurred by the management in that action. If this request and offer are made, the legal owner, if any, or junior lienholder, if any, shall reimburse the management the amount of reasonable attorney's fees and court costs, as agreed upon by the management and the legal owner or junior lienholder, incurred by the management in an action to terminate the homeowner's tenancy, on or before the earlier of (A) the 60th calendar day following receipt of written notice from the management of the aggregate amount of those reasonable attorney's fees and costs or (B) the date the mobilehome is resold.

(b) A legal owner, if any, or junior lienholder, if any, may sell the mobilehome within the park to a third party and keep the mobilehome on the site within the mobilehome park until it is resold only if all of the following requirements are met:

(1) The legal owner, if any, or junior lienholder, if any, notifies management in writing of the intention to exercise either option described in paragraph (2) or (3) of subdivision (a) within 60 days following receipt of, or no later than 65 days after the mailing of, the notice of termination of tenancy and satisfies all of the responsibilities and liabilities of the homeowner owing to the management for the 90 days preceding the mailing of the notice of termination of tenancy and then continues to satisfy these responsibilities and liabilities as they accrue from the date of the mailing of that notice until the date the mobilehome is resold.

(2) Within 60 days following receipt of, or no later than 65 days after the mailing of, the notice of termination of tenancy, the legal owner or junior lienholder commences all repairs and necessary corrective actions so that the mobilehome complies with park rules and regulations in existence at the time the notice of termination of tenancy was given as well as the health and safety standards specified in Sections 18550, 18552, and 18605 of the Health and Safety Code, and completes these repairs and corrective actions within 90 calendar days of that notice, or before the date that the mobilehome is sold, whichever is earlier.

(3) The legal owner, if any, or junior lienholder, if any, complies with the requirements of Article 7 (commencing with Section 798.70) as it relates to the transfer of the mobilehome to a third party.

(c) For purposes of subdivision (b), the "homeowner's responsibilities and liabilities" means all rents, utilities, reasonable maintenance charges of the mobilehome and its premises, and reasonable maintenance of the mobilehome and its premises pursuant to existing park rules and regulations.

(d) If the homeowner files for bankruptcy, the periods set forth in this section are tolled until the mobilehome is released from bankruptcy.

(e) Notwithstanding any other provision of law, including, but not limited to, Section 18099.5 of the Health and Safety Code, if neither the legal owner nor a junior lienholder notifies the management of its decision pursuant to subdivision (a) within the period allowed, or performs as agreed within 30 days, or if a registered owner of a mobilehome, that is not encumbered by a lien held by a legal owner or a junior lienholder, fails to comply with a notice of termination and is either legally evicted or vacates the premises, the management may either remove the mobilehome from the premises and place it in storage or store it on its site. In this case, notwithstanding any other provision of law, the management shall have a warehouseman's lien in accordance with Section 7209 of the Commercial Code against the mobilehome for the costs of dismantling and moving, if appropriate, as well as storage, that shall be superior to all other liens, except the lien provided for in Section 18116.1 of the Health and Safety Code, and may enforce the lien pursuant to Section 7210 of the Commercial Code either after the date of judgment in an unlawful detainer action or after the date the mobilehome is physically vacated by the resident, whichever occurs earlier. Upon completion of any sale to enforce the warehouseman's lien in accordance with Section 7210 of the Commercial Code, the management shall provide the purchaser at the sale with evidence of the sale, as shall be specified by the Department of Housing and Community Development, that shall, upon proper request by the purchaser of the mobilehome, register title to the mobilehome to this purchaser, whether or not there existed a legal owner or junior lienholder on this title to the mobilehome.

(f) All written notices required by this section shall be sent to the other party by certified or registered mail with return receipt requested.

(g) Satisfaction, pursuant to this section, of the homeowner's accrued or accruing responsibilities and liabilities shall not cure the default of the homeowner. **Leg.H.** 1990 ch. 1357, 1992 chs. 88, 835, 1996 ch. 95, 1998 ch. 542.

§798.57. Notice of Termination to Specify Reason.

The management shall set forth in a notice of termination, the reason relied upon for the termination with specific facts to permit determination of the date, place, witnesses, and circumstances concerning that reason. Neither reference to the section number or a subdivision thereof, nor a recital of the language of this article will constitute compliance with this section. **Leg.H.** 1978 ch. 1031.

Ref.: Cal. Fms Pl. & Pr., Ch. 332, "Landlord and Tenant: The Tenancy"; Miller & Starr, Cal. Real Estate 3rd 31:31.

§798.58. Termination to Make Site Available to Mobilehome Purchaser or Renter Prohibited.

Tenancy may only be terminated for reasons contained in Section 798.56, and a tenancy may not be terminated for the purpose of making a homeowner's site available for a person who purchased or proposes to purchase, or rents or proposes to rent, a mobilehome from the owner of the park or the owner's agent. **Leg.H.** 1978 ch. 1031, 1982 ch. 1397, 2002 ch. 672 (SB 1410).

Ref.: Cal. Fms Pl. & Pr., Ch. 369, "Mobilehomes and Mobilehome Parks"; Miller & Starr, Cal. Real Estate 3rd 31:31.

§798.59. Homeowner to Give 60-Day Notice Before Vacating.

A homeowner shall give written notice to the management of not less than 60 days before vacating his or her tenancy. **Leg.H.** 1978 ch. 1031, 1982 ch. 1397.

Ref.: Cal. Fms Pl. & Pr., Ch. 369, "Mobilehomes and Mobilehome Parks"; Miller & Starr, Cal. Real Estate 3rd 31:31.

§798.60. Rights Under Code of Civil Procedure Not Affected.

The provisions of this article shall not affect any rights or proceedings set forth in Chapter 4 (commencing with Section 1159) of Title 3 of Part 3 of the Code of Civil Procedure except as otherwise provided herein. **Leg.H.** 1978 chs. 1031, 1033.

Ref.: Cal. Fms Pl. & Pr., Ch. 369, "Mobilehomes and Mobilehome Parks"; Miller & Starr, Cal. Real Estate 3rd 31:15, 31:31.

§798.61. Selling Abandoned Mobilehome— Requirements and Procedure.

(a) (1) As used in this section, "abandoned mobilehome" means a mobilehome about which all of the following are true:

(A) It is located in a mobilehome park on a site for which no rent has been paid to the management for the preceding 60 days.

(B) It is unoccupied.

(C) A reasonable person would believe it to be abandoned.

(2) For purposes of this section:

(A) "Mobilehome" shall include a trailer coach, as defined in Section 635 of the Vehicle Code, or a recreational vehicle, as defined in Section 18010 of the Health and Safety Code, if the trailer coach or recreational vehicle also satisfies the requirements of paragraph (1), including being located on any site within a mobilehome park, even if the site is in a separate designated section pursuant to Section 18215 of the Health and Safety Code.

(B) "Abandoned mobilehome" shall include a mobilehome that is uninhabitable because of its total or partial destruction that cannot be rehabilitated, if the mobilehome also satisfies the requirements of paragraph (1).

(b) After determining a mobilehome in a mobilehome park to be an abandoned mobilehome, the management shall post a notice of belief of abandonment on the mobilehome for not less than 30 days, and shall deposit copies of the notice in the United States mail, postage prepaid, addressed to the homeowner at the last known address and to any known registered owner, if different from the homeowner, and to any known holder of a security interest in the abandoned mobilehome. This notice shall be mailed by registered or certified mail with a return receipt requested.

(c) Thirty or more days following posting pursuant to subdivision (b), the management may file a petition in the superior court in the county in which the mobilehome park is located, for a judicial declaration of abandonment of the mobilehome. A proceeding under this subdivision is a limited civil case. Copies of the petition shall be served upon the homeowner, any known registered owner, and any known person having a lien or security interest of record in the mobilehome by posting a copy on the mobilehome and mailing copies to those persons at their last known addresses by registered or certified mail with a return receipt requested in the United States mail, postage prepaid.

(d) (1) Hearing on the petition shall be given precedence over other matters on the court's calendar.

(2) If, at the hearing, the petitioner shows by a preponderance of the evidence that the criteria for an abandoned mobilehome has been satisfied and no party establishes an interest therein at the hearing, the court shall enter a judgment of abandonment, determine the amount of charges to which the petitioner is entitled, and award attorney's fees and costs to the petitioner. For purposes of this subdivision, an interest in the mobilehome shall be established by evidence of a right to possession of the mobilehome or a security or ownership interest in the mobilehome.

(3) A default may be entered by the court clerk upon request of the petitioner, and a default judgment shall be thereupon entered, if no responsive pleading is filed within 15 days after service of the petition by mail.

(e) (1) Within 10 days following a judgment of abandonment, the management shall enter the abandoned mobilehome and complete an inventory of the contents and submit the inventory to the court.

(2) During this period the management shall post and mail notice of intent to sell the abandoned mobilehome and its contents under this section, and announcing the date of sale, in the same manner as provided for the notice of determination of abandonment under subdivision (b).

(3) At any time prior to the sale of a mobilehome under this section, any person having a right to possession of the mobilehome may recover and remove it from the premises upon payment to the management of all rent or other charges due, including reasonable costs of storage and other costs awarded by the court. Upon receipt of this payment and removal of the mobilehome from the premises pursuant to this paragraph, the management shall immediately file an acknowledgment of satisfaction of judgment pursuant to Section 724.030 of the Code of Civil Procedure.

(f) Following the judgment of abandonment, but not less than 10 days following the notice of sale specified in subdivision (e), the management may conduct a public sale of the abandoned mobilehome and its contents. The management may bid at the sale and shall have the right to offset its bids to the extent of the total amount due it under this section. The proceeds of the sale shall be retained by the management, but any unclaimed amount thus retained over and above the amount to which the management is entitled under this section shall be deemed abandoned property and shall be paid into the treasury of the county in which the sale took place within 30 days of the date of the sale. The former homeowner or any other owner may claim any or all of that unclaimed amount within one year from the date of payment to the county by making application to the county treasurer or other official designated by the county. If the county pays any or all of that unclaimed amount to a claimant, neither the county nor any officer or employee of the county is liable to any other claimant as to the amount paid.

(g) Within 30 days of the date of the sale, the management shall submit to the court an accounting of the moneys received from the sale and the disposition of the money and the items contained in the inventory submitted to the court pursuant to subdivision (e).

(h) The management shall provide the purchaser at the sale with a copy of the judgment of abandonment and evidence of the sale, as shall be specified by the State Department of Housing and Community Development or the Department of Motor Vehicles, which shall register title in the abandoned mobilehome to the purchaser upon presentation thereof. The sale shall pass title to the purchaser free of any prior interest, including any security interest or lien, except the lien provided for in Section 18116.1 of the Health and Safety Code, in the abandoned mobilehome. **Leg.H.** 1986 ch. 1153, 1988 ch. 301, 1991 ch. 564, 1995 ch. 446, 1998 ch. 931, effective September 28, 1998, 2003 ch. 449 (AB 1712).

Ref.: Miller & Starr, Cal. Real Estate 3rd 31:45.

ARTICLE 7
Transfer of Mobilehome or Mobilehome Park

Advertising—Contents, size, and placement of sign. §798.70.
Owner's written authorization to show or list manufactured home or mobilehome required; use of park management as agent not required. §798.71.
Transfer fee to management when homeowner sells mobilehome—When permitted. §798.72.
When management may require removal of mobilehome from park; homeowner liable for park or property damage. §798.73.
Repairs management may require when mobilehome remains in park after sale or transfer; written summary. §798.73.5.
Management's right to prior approval of mobilehome purchaser who will remain in park; fees and charges. §798.74.
Transfer or sale of manufactured home or mobilehome subject to transfer disclosure requirements. §798.74.4.
When management to provide copies of "Information for Prospective Homeowners," rules and regulations of park, and Mobilehome Residency Law. §798.74.5.
Sale or transfer of mobilehome located in park—Rental agreement; purchaser's rights of tenancy; unlawful occupant. §798.75.
Mobilehome park rental agreement disclosure form. §798.75.5.
Age requirements enforceable; condition. §798.76.
Waiver prohibited. §798.77.
Sale of mobilehome by heir, joint tenant, or personal representative of estate. §798.78.
Repossession and sale of mobilehome. §798.79.
Listing agreement between park owner and real estate broker—Notice to residents' organization. §798.80.
Sale of used mobilehome within park—Prohibited practices by park management. §798.81.
Park management disclosure—Manufactured home or mobilehome subject to school facilities fee. §798.82.
Sale or transfer of mobilehome within park—Limitation on repairs or improvements required by management. §798.83.

§798.70. Advertising—Contents, Size, and Placement of Sign.

A homeowner, an heir, joint tenant, or personal representative of the estate who gains ownership of a mobilehome in the mobilehome park through the death of the owner of the mobilehome who was a homeowner at the time of his or her death, or the agent of any such person, may advertise the sale or exchange of his or her mobilehome, or, if not prohibited by the terms of an agreement with the management, may advertise the rental of his or her mobilehome, by displaying a sign in the window of the mobilehome, or by a sign posted on the side of the mobilehome facing the street, or by a sign in front of the mobilehome facing the street, stating that the mobilehome is for sale or exchange or, if not prohibited, for rent by the owner of the mobilehome or his or her agent. Any such person also may display a sign conforming to these requirements indicating that the mobilehome is on display for an "open house," unless the park rules prohibit the display of an open house sign. The sign shall state the name, address, and telephone number of the owner of the mobilehome or his or her agent and the sign face shall not exceed 24 inches in width and 36 inches in height. Signs posted in front of a mobilehome pursuant to this section may be of an H-frame or A-frame design with the sign face perpendicular to, but not extending into, the street. Homeowners may attach to the sign or their mobilehome tubes or holders for leaflets which provide information on the mobilehome for sale, exchange, or rent. **Leg.H.** 1978 chs. 1031, 1033, 1982 ch. 1397, 1986 ch. 174, 1989 ch. 745, 1993 ch. 329.

Ref.: Cal. Fms Pl. & Pr., Ch. 369, "Mobilehomes and Mobilehome Parks"; Miller & Starr, Cal. Real Estate 3rd 9:41, 31:42.

§798.71. Owner's Written Authorization to Show or List Manufactured Home or Mobilehome Required; Use of Park Management as Agent Not Required.

(a) (1) The management may not show or list for sale a manufactured home or mobilehome without first obtaining the owner's written authorization. The authorization shall specify the terms and conditions regarding the showing or listing.

(2) Management may require that a homeowner advise management in writing that his or her manufactured home or mobilehome is for sale. If management requires that a homeowner advise management in writing that his or her manufactured home or mobilehome is for sale, failure to comply with this requirement does not invalidate a transfer.

(b) The management shall prohibit neither the listing nor the sale of a manufactured home or mobilehome within the park by the homeowner, an heir, joint tenant, or personal representative of the estate who gains ownership of a manufactured home or mobilehome in the mobilehome park through the death of the owner of the manufactured home or mobilehome who was a homeowner at the time of his or her death, or the agent of any such person other than the management.

(c) The management shall not require the selling homeowner, or an heir, joint tenant, or personal representative of the estate who gains ownership of a manufactured home or mobilehome in the mobilehome park through the death of the owner of the manufactured home or mobilehome who was a homeowner at the time of his or her death, to authorize the management or any other specified broker, dealer, or person to act as the agent in the sale of a manufactured home or mobilehome as a condition of resale of the home in the park or of management's approval of the buyer or prospective homeowner for residency in the park.

(d) Nothing in this section shall be construed as affecting the provisions of the Health and Safety Code governing the licensing of manufactured home or mobilehome salespersons or dealers. **Leg.H.** 1978 ch. 1031, 1982 ch. 1346, 1983 ch. 1076, 1988 ch. 498, 1989 ch. 745, 2003 ch. 767 (AB 1287), 2004 ch. 567 (SB 1090).

Ref.: Cal. Fms Pl. & Pr., Ch. 369, "Mobilehomes and Mobilehome Parks"; Miller & Starr, Cal. Real Estate 3rd 31:42.

§798.72. Transfer Fee to Management When Homeowner Sells Mobilehome—When Permitted.

(a) The management shall not charge a homeowner, an heir, joint tenant, or personal representative of the estate who gains ownership of a mobilehome in the mobilehome park through the death of the owner of the mobilehome who was a homeowner at the time of his or her death, or the agent of any such person a transfer or selling fee as a condition of a sale of his mobilehome within a park unless the management performs a service in the sale. The management shall not perform any such service in connection with the sale unless so requested, in writing, by the homeowner, an heir, joint tenant, or personal representative of the estate who gains ownership of a mobilehome in the mobilehome park through the death of the owner of the mobilehome who was a homeowner at the time of his or her death, or the agent of any such person.

(b) The management shall not charge a prospective homeowner or his or her agent, upon purchase of a mobilehome, a fee as a condition of approval for residency in a park unless the management performs a specific service in the sale. The management shall not impose a fee, other than for a credit check in accordance with subdivision (b) of Section 798.74, for an interview of a prospective homeowner. **Leg.H.** 1978 ch. 1031, 1982 ch. 1397, 1988 ch. 498, 1989 ch. 745.

Ref.: Cal. Fms Pl. & Pr., Ch. 369, "Mobilehomes and Mobilehome Parks"; Miller & Starr, Cal. Real Estate 3rd 31:42.

§798.73. When Management May Require Removal of Mobilehome From Park; Homeowner Liable for Park or Property Damage.

The management may not require the removal of a mobilehome from the park in the event of its sale to a third party during the term of the homeowner's rental agreement or in the 60 days following the initial notice required by paragraph (1) of subdivision (b) of Section 798.55. However, in the event of a sale to a third party, in order to upgrade the quality of the park, the management may require that a mobilehome be removed from the park where:

(a) It is not a "mobilehome" within the meaning of Section 798.3.

(b) It is more than 20 years old, or more than 25 years old if manufactured after September 15, 1971, and is 20 feet wide or more, and the mobilehome does not comply with the health and safety standards provided in Sections 18550, 18552, and 18605 of the Health and Safety Code and the regulations established thereunder, as determined following an inspection by the appropriate enforcement agency, as defined in Section 18207 of the Health and Safety Code.

(c) The mobilehome is more than 17 years old, or more than 25 years old if manufactured after September 15, 1971, and is less than 20 feet wide, and the mobilehome does not comply with the construction and safety standards under Sections 18550, 18552, and 18605 of the Health and Safety Code and the regulations established thereunder, as determined following an inspection by the appropriate enforcement agency, as defined in Section 18207 of the Health and Safety Code.

(d) It is in a significantly rundown condition or in disrepair, as determined by the general condition of the mobilehome and its acceptability to the health and safety of the occupants and to the public, exclusive of its age. The management shall use reasonable discretion in determining the general condition of the mobilehome and its accessory structures. The management shall bear the burden of demonstrating that the mobilehome is in a significantly rundown condition or in disrepair. The management of the park may not require repairs or improvements to the park space or property owned by the management, except for damage caused by the actions or negligence of the homeowner or an agent of the homeowner. **Leg.H.** 1978 chs. 1031, 1033, 1034, 1982 chs. 1392, 1397 §30.5, 1991 ch. 576, 1994 ch. 729, 1997 ch. 367, 2003 ch. 561 (AB 682).

2003 Note: This act is not intended to provide the purchaser of a mobilehome a right to a tenancy in a mobilehome park when the selling tenant has had his or her tenancy terminated pursuant to subdivision (f) or (g) of Section 798.56 of the Civil Code. Stats. 2003 ch. 561 (AB 682) §3.

Ref.: Cal. Fms Pl. & Pr., Ch. 369, "Mobilehomes and Mobilehome Parks"; Miller & Starr, Cal. Real Estate 3rd 31:42.

§798.73.5. Repairs Management May Require When Mobilehome Remains in Park After Sale or Transfer; Written Summary.

(a) In the case of a sale or transfer of a mobilehome that will remain in the park, the management may only require repairs or improvements to the mobilehome, its appurtenances, or an accessory structure that meet all of the following conditions:

(1) Except as provided by Section 798.83, the repair or improvement is to the mobilehome, its appurtenances, or an accessory structure that is not owned and installed by the management.

(2) The repair or improvement is based upon or is required by a local ordinance or state statute or regulation relating to mobilehomes, or a rule or regulation of the mobilehome park that implements or enforces a local ordinance or a state statute or regulation relating to mobilehomes.

(3) The repair or improvement relates to the exterior of the mobilehome, its appurtenances, or an accessory

structure that is not owned and installed by the management.

(b) The management, in the case of sale or transfer of a mobilehome that will remain in the park, shall provide a homeowner with a written summary of repairs or improvements that management requires to the mobilehome, its appurtenances, or an accessory structure that is not owned and installed by the management no later than 10 business days following the receipt of a request for this information, as part of the notice required by Section 798.59. This summary shall include specific references to park rules and regulations, local ordinances, and state statutes and regulations relating to mobilehomes upon which the request for repair or improvement is based.

(c) The provisions of this section enacted at the 1999–2000 Regular Session of the Legislature are declarative of existing law as they pertain to allowing park management to enforce park rules and regulations; these provisions specifically limit repairs and improvements that can be required of a homeowner by park management at the time of sale or transfer to the same repairs and improvements that can be required during any other time of a residency. **Leg.H.** 2000 ch. 554.

Ref.: W. Cal. Sum., "Real Property" §536.

§798.74. Management's Right to Prior Approval of Mobilehome Purchaser Who Will Remain in Park; Fees and Charges.

(a) The management may require the right of prior approval of a purchaser of a mobilehome that will remain in the park and that the selling homeowner or his or her agent give notice of the sale to the management before the close of the sale. Approval cannot be withheld if the purchaser has the financial ability to pay the rent and charges of the park unless the management reasonably determines that, based on the purchaser's prior tenancies, he or she will not comply with the rules and regulations of the park. In determining whether the purchaser has the financial ability to pay the rent and charges of the park, the management shall not require the purchaser to submit copies of any personal income tax returns in order to obtain approval for residency in the park. However, management may require the purchaser to document the amount and source of his or her gross monthly income or means of financial support.

Upon request of any prospective homeowner who proposes to purchase a mobilehome that will remain in the park, management shall inform that person of the information management will require in order to determine if the person will be acceptable as a homeowner in the park.

Within 15 business days of receiving all of the information requested from the prospective homeowner, the management shall notify the seller and the prospective homeowner, in writing, of either acceptance or rejection of the application, and the reason if rejected. During this 15-day period the prospective homeowner shall comply with the management's request, if any, for a personal interview. If the approval of a prospective homeowner is withheld for any reason other than those stated in this article, the management or owner may be held liable for all damages proximately resulting therefrom.

(b) If the management collects a fee or charge from a prospective purchaser of a mobilehome in order to obtain a financial report or credit rating, the full amount of the fee or charge shall be credited toward payment of the first month's rent for that mobilehome purchaser. If, for whatever reason, the prospective purchaser is rejected by the management, the management shall refund to the prospective purchaser the full amount of that fee or charge within 30 days from the date of rejection. If the prospective purchaser is approved by the management, but, for whatever reason, the prospective purchaser elects not to purchase the mobilehome, the management may retain the fee, or a portion thereof, to defray its administrative costs under this section. **Leg.H.** 1978 chs. 541, 1031 §18, 1982 ch. 1397, 1985 ch. 76, 1987 ch. 830, 1988 ch. 522, 1990 ch. 645.

Ref.: Cal. Fms Pl. & Pr., Ch. 369, "Mobilehomes and Mobilehome Parks"; Miller & Starr, Cal. Real Estate 3rd 31:42.

§798.74.4. Transfer or Sale of Manufactured Home or Mobilehome Subject to Transfer Disclosure Requirements.

The transfer or sale of a manufactured home or mobilehome in a mobilehome park is subject to the transfer disclosure requirements and provisions set forth in Article 1.5 (commencing with Section 1102) of Chapter 2 of Title 4 of Part 4 of the Civil Code. The requirements include, but are not limited to, the use of the Manufactured Home and Mobilehome Transfer Disclosure Statement set forth in Section 1102.6d of the Civil Code. **Leg.H.** 2003 ch. 249 (SB 116).

§798.74.5. When Management to Provide Copies of "Information for Prospective Homeowners," Rules and Regulations of Park, and Mobilehome Residency Law.

(a) Within two business days of receiving a request from a prospective homeowner for an application for residency for a specific space within a mobilehome park, if the management has been advised that the mobilehome occupying that space is for sale, the management shall give the prospective homeowner a separate document in at least 12-point type entitled "INFORMATION FOR PROSPECTIVE HOMEOWNERS," which includes the following statements:

"As a prospective homeowner you are being provided with certain information you should know prior to applying for tenancy in a mobilehome park. This is not meant to be a complete list of information.

Owning a home in a mobilehome park incorporates the dual role of "homeowner" (the owner of the home) and park resident or tenant (also called a "homeowner" in the Mobilehome Residency Law). As a homeowner under the Mobilehome Residency Law, you will be responsible for paying the amount necessary to rent the space for your home, in addition to other fees and charges described below. You must also follow certain rules and regulations to reside in the park.

If you are approved for tenancy, and your tenancy commences within the next 30 days, your beginning monthly rent will be $_____ (must be completed by the management) for space number _____ (must be completed by the management). Additional information regarding future rent or fee increases may also be provided.

In addition to the monthly rent, you will be obligated to pay to the park the following additional fees and charges listed below. Other fees or charges may apply depending upon your specific requests. Metered utility charges are based on use.

_____

(Management shall describe the fee or charge and a good faith estimate of each fee or charge.)

Some spaces are governed by an ordinance, rule, regulation, or initiative measure that limits or restricts rents in mobilehome parks. Long-term leases specify rent increases during the term of the lease. By signing a rental agreement or lease for a term of more than one year, you may be removing your rental space from a local rent control ordinance during the term, or any extension, of the lease if a local rent control ordinance is in effect for the area in which the space is located.

A fully executed lease or rental agreement, or a statement signed by the park's management and by you stating that you and the management have agreed to the terms and conditions of a rental agreement, is required to complete the sale or escrow process of the home. You have no rights to tenancy without a properly executed lease or agreement or that statement. (Civil Code Section 798.75)

If the management collects a fee or charge from you in order to obtain a financial report or credit rating, the full amount of the fee or charge will be either credited toward your first month's rent or, if you are rejected for any reason, refunded to you. However, if you are approved by management, but, for whatever reason, you elect not to purchase the mobilehome, the management may retain the fee to defray its administrative costs. (Civil Code Section 798.74)

We encourage you to request from management a copy of the lease or rental agreement, the park's rules and regulations, and a copy of the Mobilehome Residency Law. Upon request, park management will provide you a copy of each document. We urge you to read these documents before making the decision that you want to become a mobilehome park resident.

Dated: _____

Signature of Park Manager: _____

Acknowledge Receipt by Prospective Homeowner: _____ "

(b) Management shall provide a prospective homeowner, upon his or her request, with a copy of the rules and regulations of the park and with a copy of this chapter.

(c) This section shall become operative on October 1, 2004. **Leg.H.** 2003 ch. 767 (AB 1287).

§798.75. Sale or Transfer of Mobilehome Located in Park—Rental Agreement; Purchaser's Rights of Tenancy; Unlawful Occupant.

(a) An escrow, sale, or transfer agreement involving a mobilehome located in a park at the time of the sale, where the mobilehome is to remain in the park, shall contain a copy of either a fully executed rental agreement or a statement signed by the park's management and the prospective homeowner that the parties have agreed to the terms and conditions of a rental agreement.

(b) In the event the purchaser fails to execute the rental agreement, the purchaser shall not have any rights of tenancy.

(c) In the event that an occupant of a mobilehome has no rights of tenancy and is not otherwise entitled to occupy the mobilehome pursuant to this chapter, the occupant is considered an unlawful occupant if, after a demand is made for the surrender of the mobilehome park site, for a period of five days, the occupant refuses to surrender the site to the mobilehome park management. In the event the unlawful occupant fails to comply with the demand, the unlawful occupant shall be subject to the proceedings set forth in Chapter 4 (commencing with Section 1159) of Title 3 of Part 3 of the Code of Civil Procedure.

(d) The occupant of the mobilehome shall not be considered an unlawful occupant and shall not be subject to the provisions of subdivision (c) if all of the following conditions are present:

(1) The occupant is the registered owner of the mobilehome.

(2) The management has determined that the occupant has the financial ability to pay the rent and charges of the park; will comply with the rules and regulations of the park, based on the occupant's prior tenancies; and will comply with this article.

(3) The management failed or refused to offer the occupant a rental agreement. **Leg.H.** 1978 ch. 1031, 1981 ch. 667, 1983 ch. 519, 1987 ch. 323, 1989 ch. 119, 1990 ch. 645.

Ref.: Cal. Fms Pl. & Pr., Ch. 369, "Mobilehomes and Mobilehome Parks"; Miller & Starr, Cal. Real Estate 3rd 31:42, 31:51.

§798.75.5. Mobilehome Park Rental Agreement Disclosure Form.

(a) The management shall provide a prospective homeowner with a completed written disclosure form concerning the park described in subdivision (b) at least three days prior to execution of a rental agreement or statement signed by the park management and the prospective homeowner that the parties have agreed to the terms and conditions of the rental agreement. The management shall update the information on the disclosure form annually, or, in the event of a material change in the condition of the mobilehome park, at the time of the material change in that condition.

(b) The written disclosure form shall read as follows:

Mobilehome Park Rental Agreement Disclosure Form

THIS DISCLOSURE STATEMENT CONCERNS THE MOBILEHOME PARK KNOWN AS

_____ LOCATED AT _____
     park name   park address

IN THE CITY OF _____ COUNTY OF _____
STATE OF CALIFORNIA.
THIS STATEMENT IS A DISCLOSURE OF THE CONDITION OF THE PARK AND PARK COMMON AREAS AS OF _____ IN COMPLIANCE WITH SECTION 798.75.5 OF THE CIVIL CODE.
              date

IT IS NOT A WARRANTY OF ANY KIND BY THE MOBILEHOME PARK OWNER OR PARK MANAGEMENT AND IS NOT A SUBSTITUTE FOR ANY INSPECTION BY THE PROSPECTIVE HOMEOWNER/LESSEE OF THE SPACE TO BE RENTED OR LEASED OR OF THE PARK, INCLUDING ALL COMMON AREAS REFERENCED IN THIS STATEMENT. THIS STATEMENT DOES NOT CREATE ANY NEW DUTY OR NEW LIABILITY ON THE PART OF THE MOBILEHOME PARK OWNER OR MOBILEHOME PARK MANAGEMENT OR AFFECT ANY DUTIES THAT MAY HAVE EXISTED PRIOR TO THE ENACTMENT OF SECTION 798.75.5 OF THE CIVIL CODE, OTHER THAN THE DUTY TO DISCLOSE THE INFORMATION REQUIRED BY THE STATEMENT.

Are you (the mobilehome park owner/mobilehome park manager) aware of any of the following:

A. Park or common area facilities	B. Does the park contain this facility?		C. Is the facility in operation?		D. Does the facility have any known substantial defects?		E. Are there any uncorrected park citations or notices of abatement relating to the facilities issued by a public agency?		F. Is there any substantial, uncorrected damage to the facility from fire, flood, earthquake, or landslides?		G. Are there any pending lawsuits by or against the park affecting the facilities or alleging defects in the facilities?		H. Is there any encroachment, easement, nonconforming use, or violation of setback requirements regarding this park common area facility?	
	Yes	No	Yes	No	Yes	No	Yes	No	Yes	No	Yes	No	Yes	No
Clubhouse														
Walkways														
Streets, roads, and access														
Electric utility system														
Water utility system														
Gas utility system														
Common area lighting system														
Septic or sewer system														
Playground														
RV storage														
Parking areas														
Swimming pool														
Spa pool														
Laundry														
Other common area facilities*														

*If there are other important park or common area facilities, please specify (attach additional sheets if necessary):

_____

If any item in C is checked "no", or any item in D, E, F, G, or H is checked "yes", please explain (attach additional sheets if necessary):

The mobilehome park owner/park manager states that the information herein has been delivered to the prospective homeowner/lessee a minimum of three days prior to execution of a rental agreement and is true and correct to the best of the park owner/park manager's knowledge as of the date signed by the park owner/manager.

Park Owner/Manager: _____ By: _____ Date: _____
                         print name   signature

I/WE ACKNOWLEDGE RECEIPT OF A COMPLETED COPY OF THE PARK OWNER/MANAGER STATEMENT.

Prospective Homeowner
Lessee _____ Park Owner/Manager _____
Date: _____   Title

Prospective Homeowner
Lessee _____ Park Owner/Manager _____
Date: _____   Title

Leg.H. 1999 ch. 517.

§798.76. Age Requirements Enforceable; Condition.

The management may require that a prospective purchaser comply with any rule or regulation limiting residency based on age requirements for housing for older persons, provided that the rule or regulation complies with the federal Fair Housing Act, as amended by Public Law 104-76, and implementing regulations. **Leg.H.** 1978 ch. 1031, 1992 chs. 182, 666, 1993 ch. 1277, 1996 ch. 61, effective June 10, 1996.

Ref.: W. Cal. Sum., "Constitutional Law" §754; Miller & Starr, Cal. Real Estate 3rd 25:125, 31:24, 31:42.

§798.77. Waiver Prohibited.

No rental or sale agreement shall contain a provision by which the purchaser or homeowner waives his or her rights under this chapter. Any such waiver shall be deemed contrary to public policy and shall be void and unenforceable. **Leg.H.** 1978 chs. 1031, 1033, 1982 ch. 1397, 1983 ch. 519.

Ref.: Cal. Fms Pl. & Pr., Ch. 369, "Mobilehomes and Mobilehome Parks"; Miller & Starr, Cal. Real Estate 3rd 31:42.

§798.78. Sale of Mobilehome by Heir, Joint Tenant, or Personal Representative of Estate.

(a) An heir, joint tenant, or personal representative of the estate who gains ownership of a mobilehome in the mobilehome park through the death of the owner of the mobilehome who was a homeowner at the time of his or her death shall have the right to sell the mobilehome to a third party in accordance with the provisions of this article, but only if all the homeowner's responsibilities and liabilities to the management regarding rent, utilities, and reasonable maintenance of the mobilehome and its premises which have arisen since the death of the homeowner have been satisfied as they have accrued pursuant to the rental agreement in effect at the time of the death of the homeowner up until the date the mobilehome is resold.

(b) In the event that the heir, joint tenant, or personal representative of the estate does not satisfy the requirements of subdivision (a) with respect to the satisfaction of the homeowner's responsibilities and liabilities to the management which accrue pursuant to the rental agreement in effect at the time of the death of the homeowner, the management shall have the right to require the removal of the mobilehome from the park.

(c) Prior to the sale of a mobilehome by an heir, joint tenant, or personal representative of the estate, that individual may replace the existing mobilehome with another mobilehome, either new or used, or repair the existing mobilehome so that the mobilehome to be sold complies with health and safety standards provided in Sections 18550, 18552, and 18605 of the Health and Safety Code, and the regulations established thereunder. In the event the mobilehome is to be replaced, the replacement mobilehome shall also meet current standards of the park as contained in the park's most recent written requirements issued to prospective homeowners.

(d) In the event the heir, joint tenant, or personal representative of the estate desires to establish a tenancy in the park, that individual shall comply with those provisions of this article which identify the requirements for a prospective purchaser of a mobilehome that remains in the park. **Leg.H.** 1979 ch. 198, 1982 chs. 477, 1397, 1989 ch. 745.

Ref.: Cal. Fms Pl. & Pr., Ch. 369, "Mobilehomes and Mobilehome Parks"; Miller & Starr, Cal. Real Estate 3rd 31:42.

§798.79. Repossession and Sale of Mobilehome.

(a) Any legal owner or junior lienholder who forecloses on his or her security interest in a mobilehome located in a mobilehome park shall have the right to sell the mobilehome within the park to a third party in accordance with this article, but only if all of the homeowner's responsibilities and liabilities to the management regarding rent, utilities, and reasonable maintenance of a mobilehome and its premises are satisfied by the foreclosing creditor as they accrue through the date the mobilehome is resold.

(b) In the event the legal owner or junior lienholder has received from the management a copy of the notice of termination of tenancy for nonpayment of rent or other charges, the foreclosing creditor's right to sell the mobilehome within the park to a third party shall also be governed by Section 798.56a. **Leg.H.** 1979 ch. 1185, 1982 chs. 477, 1397 §33.5, 1983 ch. 1124, operative July 1, 1984, 1990 ch. 1357, 1991 ch. 190.

Ref.: Cal. Fms Pl. & Pr., Ch. 369, "Mobilehomes and Mobilehome Parks"; Miller & Starr, Cal. Real Estate 3rd 31:42.

§798.80. Listing Agreement Between Park Owner and Real Estate Broker—Notice to Residents' Organization.

(a) Not less than 30 days nor more than one year prior to an owner of a mobilehome park entering into a written listing agreement with a licensed real estate broker, as defined in Article 1 (commencing with Section 10130) of Chapter 3 of Part 1 of Division 4 of the Business and Professions Code, for the sale of the park, or offering to sell the park to any party, the owner shall provide written notice of his or her intention to sell the mobilehome park by first-class mail or by personal delivery to the president, secretary, and treasurer of any resident organization formed by homeowners in the mobilehome park as a nonprofit corporation, pursuant to Section 23701v of the Revenue and Taxation Code, stock cooperative corporation, or other entity for purposes of converting the mobilehome park to condominium or stock cooperative ownership interests and for purchasing the mobilehome park from the management of the mobilehome park. An offer to sell a park shall not be construed as an offer under this subdivision unless it is initiated by the park owner or agent.

(b) An owner of a mobilehome park shall not be required to comply with subdivision (a) unless the following conditions are met:

(1) The resident organization has first furnished the park owner or park manager a written notice of the name and address of the president, secretary, and treasurer of the resident organization to whom the notice of sale shall be given.

(2) The resident organization has first notified the park owner or manager in writing that the park residents are interested in purchasing the park. The initial notice by the resident organization shall be made prior to a written listing or offer to sell the park by the park owner, and the resident organization shall give subsequent notice once each year thereafter that the park residents are interested in purchasing the park.

(3) The resident organization has furnished the park owner or park manager a written notice, within five days, of any change in the name or address of the officers of the resident organization to whom the notice of sale shall be given.

(c) Nothing in this section affects the validity of title to real property transferred in violation of this section, although a violation shall subject the seller to civil action pursuant to Article 8 (commencing with Section 798.84) by homeowner residents of the park or the resident organization.

(d) Nothing in this section affects the ability of a licensed real estate broker, as defined in Article 1 (commencing with Section 10130) of Chapter 3 of Part 1 of Division 4 of the Business and Professions Code, to collect a commission pursuant to an executed contract between the broker and the mobilehome park owner.

(e) Subdivision (a) does not apply to any of the following:

(1) Any sale or other transfer by a park owner who is a natural person to any relation specified in Section 6401 or 6402 of the Probate Code.

(2) Any transfer by gift, devise, or operation of law.

(3) Any transfer by a corporation to an affiliate. As used in this paragraph, "affiliate" means any shareholder of the transferring corporation, any corporation or entity owned or controlled, directly or indirectly, by the transferring corporation, or any other corporation or entity controlled, directly or indirectly, by any shareholder of the transferring corporation.

(4) Any transfer by a partnership to any of its partners.

(5) Any conveyance resulting from the judicial or non-judicial foreclosure of a mortgage or deed of trust encumbering a mobilehome park or any deed given in lieu of such a foreclosure.

(6) Any sale or transfer between or among joint tenants or tenants in common owning a mobilehome park.

(7) The purchase of a mobilehome park by a governmental entity under its powers of eminent domain. **Leg.H.** 1986 ch. 648, 1990 ch. 421, 1994 ch. 219.

Ref.: Miller & Starr, Cal. Real Estate 3rd 31:44.

§798.81. Sale of Used Mobilehome Within Park—Prohibited Practices by Park Management.

The management (1) shall not prohibit the listing or sale of a used mobilehome within the park by the homeowner, an heir, joint tenant, or personal representative of the estate who gains ownership of a mobilehome in the mobilehome park through the death of the owner of the mobilehome who was a homeowner at the time of his or her death, or the agent of any such person other than the management, (2) nor require the selling homeowner to authorize the management to act as the agent in the sale of a mobilehome as a condition of approval of the buyer or prospective homeowner for residency in the park. **Leg.H.** 1988 ch. 1033, 1989 ch. 745.

Ref.: Miller & Starr, Cal. Real Estate 3rd 31:42.

§798.82. Park Management Disclosure—Manufactured Home or Mobilehome Subject to School Facilities Fee.

The management, at the time of an application for residency, shall disclose in writing to any person who proposes to purchase or install a manufactured home or mobilehome on a space, on which the construction of the pad or foundation system commenced after September 1, 1986, and no other manufactured home or mobilehome was previously located, installed, or occupied, that the manufactured home or mobilehome may be subject to a school facilities fee under Sections 53080 and 53080.4 of, and Chapter 4.9 (commencing with Section 65995) of Division 1 of Title 7 of, the Government Code. **Leg.H.** 1994 ch. 983.

§798.83. Sale or Transfer of Mobilehome Within Park—Limitation on Repairs or Improvements Required by Management.

In the case of a sale or transfer of a mobilehome that will remain in the park, the management of the park shall not require repairs or improvements to the park space or property owned by the management, except for damage caused by the actions or negligence of the homeowner or an agent of the homeowner. **Leg.H.** 1997 ch. 367.

Ref.: Cal. Fms Pl. & Pr., Ch. 369, "Mobilehomes and Mobilehome Parks."

ARTICLE 8
Actions, Proceedings, and Penalties

Action against management for failure to maintain park in good and working order—Notice to management. §798.84.
Attorney's fees. §798.85.
Award of $2,000 for each willful violation or punitive damages. §798.86.
Improper maintenance of physical improvements in common facilities as public nuisance. §798.87.
Injunctions against continuing or recurring violations of mobilehome park rules. §798.88.

§798.84. Action Against Management for Failure to Maintain Park in Good and Working Order—Notice to Management.

(a) No action based upon the management's alleged failure to maintain the physical improvements in the common facilities in good working order or condition or alleged reduction of service may be commenced by a homeowner unless the management has been given at least 30 days' prior notice of the intention to commence the action.

(b) The notice shall be in writing, signed by the homeowner or homeowners making the allegations, and shall notify the management of the basis of the claim, the specific allegations, and the remedies requested. A notice by one homeowner shall be deemed to be sufficient notice of the specific allegation to the management of the park by all of the homeowners in the park.

(c) The notice may be served in the manner prescribed in Chapter 5 (commencing with Section 1010) of Title 14 of Part 2 of the Code of Civil Procedure.

(d) For purposes of this section, management shall be deemed to be notified of an alleged failure to maintain the physical improvements in the common facilities in good working order or condition or of an alleged reduction of services upon substantial compliance by the homeowner or homeowners with the provisions of subdivisions (b) and (c), or when management has been notified of the alleged failure to maintain or the alleged reduction of services by a state or local agency.

(e) If the notice is served within 30 days of the expiration of the applicable statute of limitations, the time for the commencement of the action shall be extended 30 days from the service of the notice.

(f) This section does not apply to actions for personal injury or wrongful death. **Leg.H.** 1988 ch. 1592.

Ref.: Miller & Starr, Cal. Real Estate 3rd 31:6, 31:35.

§798.85. Attorney's Fees.

In any action arising out of the provisions of this chapter the prevailing party shall be entitled to reasonable attorney's fees and costs. A party shall be deemed a prevailing party for the purposes of this section if the judgment is rendered in his or her favor or where the litigation is dismissed in his or her favor prior to or during the trial, unless the parties otherwise agree in the settlement or compromise. **Leg.H.** 1978 chs. 1031, 1033, 1983 ch. 519.

Ref.: Cal. Fms Pl. & Pr., Ch. 369, "Mobilehomes and Mobilehome Parks"; Miller & Starr, Cal. Real Estate 3rd 31:35.

§798.86. Award of $2,000 for Each Willful Violation or Punitive Damages.

(a) If a homeowner or former homeowner of a park is the prevailing party in a civil action, including a small claims court action, against the management to enforce his or her rights under this chapter, the homeowner, in addition to damages afforded by law, may, in the discretion of the court, be awarded an amount not to exceed two thousand dollars ($2,000) for each willful violation of this chapter by the management.

(b) A homeowner or former homeowner of a park who is the prevailing party in a civil action against management to enforce his or her rights under this chapter may be awarded either punitive damages pursuant to Section 3294 of the Civil Code or the statutory penalty provided by subdivision (a). **Leg.H.** 1978 chs. 1031, 1033, 1982 ch. 1397, 1983 ch. 519, 1997 ch. 141, 2003 ch. 98 (AB 693).

Ref.: Cal. Fms Pl. & Pr., Ch. 369, "Mobilehomes and Mobilehome Parks"; Miller & Starr, Cal. Real Estate 3rd 31:35.

§798.87. Improper Maintenance of Physical Improvements in Common Facilities as Public Nuisance.

(a) The substantial failure of the management to provide and maintain physical improvements in the common facilities in good working order and condition shall be deemed a public nuisance. Notwithstanding Section 3491, this nuisance may only be remedied by a civil action or abatement.

(b) The substantial violation of a mobilehome park rule shall be deemed a public nuisance. Notwithstanding Section 3491, this nuisance may only be remedied by a civil action or abatement.

(c) A civil action pursuant to this section may be brought by a park resident, the park management, or in the name of the people of the State of California, by any of the following:

(1) The district attorney or the county counsel of the jurisdiction in which the park, or the greater portion of the park, is located.

(2) The city attorney or city prosecutor if the park is located within the jurisdiction of the city.

(3) The Attorney General. **Leg.H.** 1982 ch. 1392, 1983 ch. 187, 1990 ch. 1374, 2002 ch. 141 (AB 2382).

Ref.: Cal. Fms Pl. & Pr., Ch. 369, "Mobilehomes and Mobilehome Parks"; Miller & Starr, Cal. Real Estate 3rd 31:8, 31:24, 31:31.

§798.88. Injunctions Against Continuing or Recurring Violations of Mobilehome Park Rules.

(a) In addition to any right under Article 6 (commencing with Section 798.55) to terminate the tenancy of a homeowner, any person in violation of a reasonable rule or regulation of a mobilehome park may be enjoined from the violation as provided in this section.

(b) A petition for an order enjoining a continuing or recurring violation of any reasonable rule or regulation of a mobilehome park may be filed by the management thereof with the superior court for the county in which the mobilehome park is located. At the time of filing the petition, the petitioner may obtain a temporary restraining order in accordance with subdivision (a) of Section 527 of the Code of Civil Procedure. A temporary order restraining the violation may be granted, with notice, upon the petitioner's affidavit showing to the satisfaction of the court reasonable proof of a continuing or recurring violation of a rule or regulation of the mobilehome park by the named homeowner or resident and that great or irreparable harm would result to the management or other homeowners or residents of the park from continuance of recurrence of the violation.

(c) A temporary restraining order granted pursuant to this subdivision shall be personally served upon the respondent homeowner or resident with the petition for injunction and notice of hearing thereon. The restraining order shall remain in effect for a period not to exceed 15 days, except as modified or sooner terminated by the court.

(d) Within 15 days of filing the petition for an injunction, a hearing shall be held thereon. If the court, by clear and convincing evidence, finds the existence of a continuing or recurring violation of reasonable rule or regulation of the mobilehome park, the court shall issue an injunction prohibiting the violation. The duration of the injunction shall not exceed three years.

(e) However, not more than three months prior to the expiration of an injunction issued pursuant to this section, the management of the mobilehome park may petition under this section for a new injunction where there has been recurring or continuous violation of the injunction or there is a threat of future violation of the mobilehome park's rules upon termination of the injunction.

(f) Nothing shall preclude a party to an action under this section from appearing through legal counsel or in propria persona.

(g) The remedy provided by this section is nonexclusive and nothing in this section shall be construed to preclude or limit any rights the management of a mobilehome park may have to terminate a tenancy. **Leg.H.** 1991 ch. 270.

ARTICLE 9
Subdivisions, Cooperatives, and Condominiums

Definitions. §799.
Applicability of article. §799.1.
Advertising—Contents, size, and placement of sign. §799.1.5.
Mobilehome not to be listed or shown without resident's written authorization. §799.2.
Right of entry by ownership or management. §799.2.5.
When management may require removal of mobilehome from park. §799.3.
Management's right to prior approval of mobilehome purchaser who will remain. §799.4.
Age requirements enforceable. §799.5.
Waiver prohibited. §799.6.
Advance written notice of interruption in utility service. §799.7.
Park management disclosure—Manufactured home or mobilehome subject to school facilities fee. §799.8.
Senior homeowner—Right to share mobilehome with care giver or with relative who requires care. §799.9.
Displaying political campaign sign—Dimensions; duration; exceptions. §799.10.

§799. Definitions.

As used in this article:

(a) "Ownership or management" means the ownership or management of a subdivision, cooperative, or condominium for mobilehomes, or of a resident-owned mobilehome park.

(b) "Resident" means a person who maintains a residence in a subdivision, cooperative, or condominium for mobilehomes, or a resident-owned mobilehome park.

(c) "Resident-owned mobilehome park" means any entity other than a subdivision, cooperative, or condominium for mobilehomes, through which the residents have an ownership interest in the mobilehome park. **Leg.H.** 1978 ch. 1031, 1979 ch. 198, 1996 ch. 61, effective June 10, 1996, 1997 ch. 72.

§799.1. Applicability of Article.

This article shall govern the rights of a resident who has an ownership interest in the subdivision, cooperative, or condominium for mobilehomes, or a resident-owned mobilehome park in which his or her mobilehome is located or installed. In a subdivision, cooperative, or condominium for mobilehomes, or a resident-owned mobilehome park, Articles 1 (commencing with Section 798) to 8 (commencing with Section 798.84), inclusive, shall apply only to a resident who does not have an ownership interest in the subdivision, cooperative, or condominium for mobilehomes, or the resident-owned mobilehome park, in which his or her mobilehome is located or installed. **Leg.H.** 1995 ch. 103 §2, 1996 ch. 61, effective June 10, 1996, 1997 ch. 72.

§799.1.5. Advertising—Contents, Size, and Placement of Sign.

A homeowner or resident, or an heir, joint tenant, or personal representative of the estate who gains ownership of a mobilehome through the death of the resident of the mobilehome who was a resident at the time of his or her death, or the agent of any of those persons, may advertise the sale or exchange of his or her mobilehome or, if not prohibited by the terms of an agreement with the management or ownership, may advertise the rental of his or her mobilehome by displaying a sign in the window of the mobilehome, or by a sign posted on the side of the mobilehome facing the street, or by a sign in front of the mobilehome facing the street, stating that the mobilehome is for sale or exchange or, if not prohibited, for rent by the owner of the mobilehome or his or her agent. Any such person also may display a sign conforming to these requirements indicating that the mobilehome is on display for an "open house," unless the park rules prohibit the display of an open house sign. The sign shall state the name, address, and telephone number of the owner of the mobilehome or his or her agent. The sign face may not exceed 24 inches [1] in width and 36 inches in height. Signs posted in [2] **front** of a mobilehome pursuant to this section may be of an H-frame or A-frame design with the sign face perpendicular to, but not extending into, the street. A homeowner or resident, or an heir, joint tenant, or personal representative of the estate who gains ownership of a mobilehome through the death of the resident of the mobilehome who was a resident at the time of his or her death, or the agent of any of those persons, may attach to the sign or their mobilehome tubes or holders for leaflets that provide information on the mobilehome for sale, exchange, or rent. **Leg.H.** 1978 chs. 1031, 1033, 1979 ch. 198, 1983 ch. 519, 1995 ch. 103 §1 (renumbered from §799.1), 2004 ch. 302 (AB 2351), 2005 ch. 22 (SB 1108) §12.

§799.1.5. 2005 Deletes. [1] from [2] from

Ref.: Cal. Fms Pl. & Pr., Ch. 369, "Mobilehomes and Mobilehome Parks"; Miller & Starr, Cal. Real Estate 3rd 9:41.

§799.2. Mobilehome Not to Be Listed or Shown Without Resident's Written Authorization.

The ownership or management shall not show or list for sale a mobilehome owned by a resident without first obtaining the resident's written authorization. The authorization shall specify the terms and conditions regarding the showing or listing.

Nothing contained in this section shall be construed to affect the provisions of the Health and Safety Code governing the licensing of mobilehome salesmen. **Leg.H.** 1978 ch. 1031, 1979 ch. 198, 1983 ch. 519.

Ref.: Cal. Fms Pl. & Pr., Ch. 369, "Mobilehomes and Mobilehome Parks."

§799.2.5. Right of Entry by Ownership or Management.

Except as provided in subdivision (b), the ownership or management shall have no right of entry to a mobilehome without the prior written consent of the resident. The consent may be revoked in writing by the resident at any time. The ownership or management shall have a right of entry upon the land upon which a mobilehome is situated for maintenance of utilities, trees, and driveways, for maintenance of the premises in accordance with the rules and regulations of the subdivision, cooperative, or condominium for mobilehomes, or resident-owned mobilehome park when the homeowner or resident fails to so maintain the premises, and protection of the subdivision, cooperative, or condominium for mobilehomes, or resident-owned mobilehome park at any reasonable time, but not in a manner or at a time that would interfere with the resident's quiet enjoyment.

(b) The ownership or management may enter a mobilehome without the prior written consent of the resident in case of an emergency or when the resident has abandoned the mobilehome. **Leg.H.** 2004 ch. 302 (AB 2351).

2004 Note: It appears the Legislature inadvertently omitted the subdivision (a) designation.

§799.3. When Management May Require Removal of Mobilehome From Park.

The ownership or management shall not require the removal of a mobilehome from a subdivision, cooperative, or condominium for mobilehomes, or resident-owned mobilehome park in the event of its sale to a third party. **Leg.H.** 1978 chs. 1031, 1033, 1979 ch. 198, 1996 ch. 61, effective June 10, 1996, 1997 ch. 72.

Ref.: Cal. Fms Pl. & Pr., Ch. 369, "Mobilehomes and Mobilehome Parks"; Miller & Starr, Cal. Real Estate 3rd 31:31.

§799.4. Management's Right to Prior Approval of Mobilehome Purchaser Who Will Remain.

The ownership or management may require the right to prior approval of the purchaser of a mobilehome that will remain in the subdivision, cooperative, or condominium for mobilehomes, or resident-owned mobilehome park and that the selling resident, or his or her agent give notice of the sale to the ownership or management before the close of the sale. Approval cannot be withheld if the purchaser has the financial ability to pay the fees and charges of the subdivision, cooperative, or condominium for mobilehomes, or resident-owned mobilehome park unless the ownership or management reasonably determines that, based on the purchaser's prior residences, he or she will not comply with the rules and regulations of the subdivision, cooperative, or condominium for mobilehomes, or resident-owned mobilehome park. **Leg.H.** 1978 ch. 1031, 1979 ch. 198, 1983 ch. 519, 1996 ch. 61, effective June 10, 1996, 1997 ch. 72.

Ref.: Cal. Fms Pl. & Pr., Ch. 369, "Mobilehomes and Mobilehome Parks."

§799.5. Age Requirements Enforceable.

The ownership or management may require that a purchaser of a mobilehome that will remain in the subdivision, cooperative, or condominium for mobilehomes, or resident-owned mobilehome park, comply with any rule or regulation limiting residency based on age requirements for housing for older persons, provided that the rule or regulation complies with the provisions of the federal Fair Housing Act, as amended by Public Law 104-76, and implementing regulations. **Leg.H.** 1978 ch. 1031, 1993 ch. 1277, 1996 ch. 61, effective June 10, 1996, 1997 ch. 72.

Ref.: Cal. Fms Pl. & Pr., Ch. 369, "Mobilehomes and Mobilehome Parks."

§799.6. Waiver Prohibited.

No agreement shall contain any provision by which the purchaser waives his or her rights under the provisions of this article. Any such waiver shall be deemed contrary to public policy and void and unenforceable. **Leg.H.** 1978 chs. 1031, 1033, 1983 ch. 519.

Ref.: Cal. Fms Pl. & Pr., Ch. 369, "Mobilehomes and Mobilehome Parks."

§799.7. Advance Written Notice of Interruption in Utility Service.

The ownership or management shall provide, by posting notice on the mobilehomes of all affected homeowners and residents, at least 72 hours' written advance notice of an interruption in utility service of more than two hours for the maintenance, repair, or replacement of facilities of utility systems over which the management has control within the subdivision, cooperative, or condominium for mobilehomes, or resident-owned mobilehome park, if the interruption is not due to an emergency. The ownership or management shall be liable only for actual damages sustained by a homeowner or resident for violation of this section.

"Emergency," for purposes of this section, means the interruption of utility service resulting from an accident or act of nature, or cessation of service caused by other than the management's regular or planned maintenance, repair, or replacement of utility facilities. **Leg.H.** 1992 ch. 317, 1996 ch. 61, effective June 10, 1996, 1997 ch. 72.

§799.8. Park Management Disclosure—Manufactured Home or Mobilehome Subject to School Facilities Fee.

The management, at the time of an application for residency, shall disclose in writing to any person who proposes to purchase or install a manufactured home or mobilehome on a space or lot, on which the construction of the pad or foundation system commenced after September 1, 1986, and no other manufactured home or mobilehome was previously located, installed, or occupied, that the manufactured home or mobilehome may be subject to a school facilities fee under Sections 53080 and 53080.4 of, and Chapter 4.9 (commencing with Section 65995) of Division 1 of Title 7 of, the Government Code. **Leg.H.** 1994 ch. 983.

§799.9. Senior Homeowner—Right to Share Mobilehome With Care Giver or With Relative Who Requires Care.

(a) A senior homeowner may share his or her mobilehome with any person 18 years of age or older if that person is providing live-in health care, live-in supportive care, or supervision to the homeowner pursuant to a written treatment plan prepared by a physician and surgeon. A fee shall not be charged by management for that person. That person shall have no rights of tenancy in, and shall comply with the rules and regulations of, the subdivision, cooperative, or condominium for mobilehomes, or resident-owned mobilehome park. As used in this subdivision, "senior homeowner" means a homeowner or resident who is 55 years of age or older.

(b) A senior homeowner who resides in a subdivision, cooperative, or condominium for mobilehomes, or a resident-owned mobilehome park, that has implemented rules or regulations limiting residency based on age requirements for housing for older persons, pursuant to Section 799.5, may share his or her mobilehome with any person 18 years of age or older if this person is a parent, sibling, child, or grandchild of the senior homeowner and requires live-in health care, live-in supportive care, or supervision pursuant to a written treatment plan prepared by a physician and surgeon. A fee shall not be charged by management for that person. Unless otherwise agreed upon, the management shall not be required to manage, supervise, or provide for this person's care during his or her stay in the subdivision, cooperative or condominium for mobilehomes, or resident-owned mobilehome park. That person shall have no rights of tenancy in, and shall comply with the rules and regulations of, the subdivision, cooperative, or condominium for mobilehomes, or resident-owned mobilehome park. As used in this subdivision, "senior homeowner" means a homeowner or resident who is 55 years of age or older. **Leg.H.** 1997 ch. 72.

Ref.: Cal. Fms Pl. & Pr., Ch. 369, "Mobilehomes and Mobilehome Parks."

§799.10. Displaying Political Campaign Sign—Dimensions; Duration; Exceptions.

A resident may not be prohibited from displaying a political campaign sign relating to a candidate for election to public office or to the initiative, referendum, or recall process in the window or on the side of a manufactured home or mobilehome, or within the site on which the home is located or installed. The size of the face of a political sign may not exceed six square feet, and the sign may not be displayed in excess of a period of time from 90 days prior to an election to 15 days following the election, unless a local ordinance within the jurisdiction where the manufactured home or mobilehome subject to this article is located imposes a more restrictive period of time for the display of such a sign. In the event of a conflict between the provisions of this section and the provisions of Title 6 (commencing with Section 1350) of Part 4 of Division 2, relating to the size and display of political campaign signs, the provisions of this section shall prevail. **Leg.H.** 2003 ch. 249 (SB 116).

2003 Note: It is the intent of the Legislature that enactment of this bill not affect any other form of political expression by a homeowner or resident of a mobilehome park where that expression is not associated with an election or political campaign. Stats. 2003 ch. 249 (SB 116) §4.

CHAPTER 2.6
RECREATIONAL VEHICLE PARK OCCUPANCY LAW

Art. 1. Definitions. §§799.20-799.32.
Art. 2. General Provisions. §§799.40-799.46.
Art. 3. Defaulting Occupants. §§799.55-799.59.
Art. 4. Defaulting Tenants. §§799.65-799.67.
Art. 5. Defaulting Residents. §§799.70, 799.71.
Art. 6. Liens for Recreational Vehicles and Abandoned Possessions. §799.75.
Art. 7. Actions and Proceedings. §§799.78, 799.79.

ARTICLE 1
Definitions

Title. §799.20.
Definitions to govern construction. §799.21.
"Defaulting occupant" defined. §799.22.
"Defaulting resident" defined. §799.23.
"Defaulting tenant" defined. §799.24.
"Guest" defined. §799.25.
"Management" defined. §799.26.
"Occupancy" and "occupy" defined. §799.27.
"Occupant" defined. §799.28.
"Recreational vehicle" defined. §799.29.
"Recreational vehicle park" defined. §799.30.
"Resident" defined. §799.31.
"Tenant" defined. §799.32.

§799.20. Title.

This chapter shall be known and may be cited as the Recreational Vehicle Park Occupancy Law. **Leg.H.** 1992 ch. 310 §2.

§799.21. Definitions to Govern Construction.

Unless the provisions or context otherwise require, the following definitions shall govern the construction of this chapter. **Leg.H.** 1992 ch. 310 §2.

§799.22. "Defaulting Occupant" Defined.

"Defaulting occupant" means an occupant who fails to pay for his or her occupancy in a park or who fails to comply with reasonable written rules and regulations of the park given to the occupant upon registration. **Leg.H.** 1992 ch. 310 §2.

§799.23. "Defaulting Resident" Defined.

"Defaulting resident" means a resident who fails to pay for his or her occupancy in a park, fails to comply with reasonable written rules and regulations of the park given to the resident upon registration or during the term of his or her occupancy in the park, or who violates any of the provisions contained in Article 5 (commencing with Section 799.70). **Leg.H.** 1992 ch. 310 §2.

§799.24. "Defaulting Tenant" Defined.

"Defaulting tenant" means a tenant who fails to pay for his or her occupancy in a park or fails to comply with reasonable written rules and regulations of the park given to the person upon registration or during the term of his or her occupancy in the park. **Leg.H.** 1992 ch. 310 §2.

§799.25. "Guest" Defined.

"Guest" means a person who is lawfully occupying a recreational vehicle located in a park but who is not an occupant, tenant, or resident. An occupant, tenant, or resident shall be responsible for the actions of his or her guests. **Leg.H.** 1992 ch. 310 §2.

§799.26. "Management" Defined.

"Management" means the owner of a recreational vehicle park or an agent or representative authorized to act on his or her behalf in connection with matters relating to the park. **Leg.H.** 1992 ch. 310 §2.

§799.27. "Occupancy" and "Occupy" Defined.

"Occupancy" and "occupy" refer to the use of a recreational vehicle park lot by an occupant, tenant, or resident. **Leg.H.** 1992 ch. 310 §2.

§799.28. "Occupant" Defined.

"Occupant" means the owner or operator of a recreational vehicle who has occupied a lot in a park for 30 days or less. **Leg.H.** 1992 ch. 310 §2.

§799.29. "Recreational Vehicle" Defined.

"Recreational vehicle" has the same meaning as defined in Section 18010 of the Health and Safety Code. **Leg.H.** 1992 ch. 310 §2.

Ref.: Miller & Starr, Cal. Real Estate 3rd 31:34.

§799.30. "Recreational Vehicle Park" Defined.

"Recreational vehicle park" or "park" has the same meaning as defined in Section 18862.39 of the Health and Safety Code. **Leg.H.** 1992 ch. 310 §2, 2004 ch. 530 (AB 1964).

Ref.: Miller & Starr, Cal. Real Estate 3rd 31:34.

§799.31. "Resident" Defined.

"Resident" means a tenant who has occupied a lot in a park for nine months or more. **Leg.H.** 1992 ch. 310 §2.

§799.32. "Tenant" Defined.

"Tenant" means the owner or operator of a recreational vehicle who has occupied a lot in a park for more than 30 consecutive days. **Leg.H.** 1992 ch. 310 §2.

ARTICLE 2
General Provisions

Rights under chapter cumulative. §799.40.
Nonapplication to mobilehomes and manufactured homes. §799.41.
Waiver of rights prohibited. §799.42.
Registration agreement—Form and content. §799.43.
Registration—Copy of rules and regulations. §799.44.
Rental agreement for occupancy in excess of 30 days. §799.45.
Sign at entry to park indicating that recreational vehicle may be removed from premises. §799.46.

§799.40. Rights Under Chapter Cumulative.

The rights created by this chapter shall be cumulative and in addition to any other legal rights the management of a park may have against a defaulting occupant, tenant, or resident, or that an occupant, tenant, or resident may have against the management of a park. **Leg.H.** 1992 ch. 310 §2.

Ref.: Miller & Starr, Cal. Real Estate 3rd 31:34.

§799.41. Nonapplication to Mobilehomes and Manufactured Homes.

Nothing in this chapter shall apply to a mobilehome as defined in Section 18008 of the Health and Safety Code or to a manufactured home as defined in Section 18007 of the Health and Safety Code. **Leg.H.** 1992 ch. 310 §2.

§799.42. Waiver of Rights Prohibited.

No occupant registration agreement or tenant rental agreement shall contain a provision by which the occupant or tenant waives his or her rights under the provisions of this chapter, and any waiver of these rights shall be deemed contrary to public policy and void. **Leg.H.** 1992 ch. 310 §2.

Ref.: Miller & Starr, Cal. Real Estate 3rd 31:34.

§799.43. Registration Agreement—Form and Contents.

The registration agreement between a park and an occupant thereof shall be in writing and shall contain, in addition to the provisions otherwise required by law to be included, the term of the occupancy and the rent therefor, the fees, if any, to be charged for services which will be provided by the park, and a statement of the grounds for which a defaulting occupant's recreational vehicle may be removed as specified in Section 799.22 without a judicial hearing after the service of a 72-hour notice pursuant to this chapter and the telephone number of the local traffic law enforcement agency. **Leg.H.** 1992 ch. 310 §2.

Ref.: Miller & Starr, Cal. Real Estate 3rd 31:34.

§799.44. Registration—Copy of Rules and Regulations.

At the time of registration, an occupant shall be given a copy of the rules and regulations of the park. **Leg.H.** 1992 ch. 310 §2.

Ref.: Miller & Starr, Cal. Real Estate 3rd 31:34.

§799.45. Rental Agreement for Occupancy in Excess of 30 Days.

The management may offer a rental agreement to an occupant of the park who intends to remain in the park for a period in excess of 30 consecutive days. **Leg.H.** 1992 ch. 310 §2.

§799.46. Sign at Entry to Park Indicating That Recreational Vehicle May Be Removed From Premises.

At the entry to a recreational vehicle park, or within the separate designated section for recreational vehicles within a mobilehome park, there shall be displayed in plain view on the property a sign indicating that the recreational vehicle may be removed from the premises for the reasons specified in Sections 799.22 and 1866 and containing the telephone number of the local traffic law enforcement agency. Nothing in this section shall prevent management from additionally displaying the sign in other locations within the park. **Leg.H.** 1992 ch. 310 §2, 2004 ch. 530 (AB 1964).

ARTICLE 3
Defaulting Occupants

72-hour written notice prior to removal of vehicle. §799.55.
Service of notice; 7-day period for removal of vehicle of physically incapacitated occupant or nonmotorized vehicle. §799.56.
Required statement in notice. §799.57.
Removal of vehicle by police or sheriff. §799.58.
Care required in removal of vehicle. §799.59.

§799.55. 72-Hour Written Notice Prior to Removal of Vehicle.

Except as provided in subdivision (b) of Section 1866, as a prerequisite to the right of management to have a defaulting occupant's recreational vehicle removed from the lot which is the subject of the registration agreement between the park and the occupant pursuant to Section 799.57, the management shall serve a 72-hour written notice as prescribed in Section 799.56. A defaulting occupant may correct his or her payment deficiency within the 72-hour period during normal business hours. **Leg.H.** 1992 ch. 310 §2, 2004 ch. 530 (AB 1964).

Ref.: Miller & Starr, Cal. Real Estate 3rd 31:34.

§799.56. Service of Notice; 7-Day Period for Removal of Vehicle of Physically Incapacitated Occupant or Nonmotorized Vehicle.

(a) The 72-hour written notice shall be served by delivering a copy to the defaulting occupant personally or to a person of suitable age and discretion who is occupying the recreational vehicle located on the lot. In the latter event, a copy of the notice shall also be affixed in a conspicuous place on the recreational vehicle and shall be sent through the mail addressed to the occupant at the place where the property is located and, if available, any other address which the occupant has provided to management in the registration agreement. Delivery of the 72-hour notice to a defaulting occupant who is incapable of removing the occupant's recreational vehicle from the park because of a physical incapacity shall not be sufficient to satisfy the requirements of this section.

(b) In the event that the defaulting occupant is incapable of removing the occupant's recreational vehicle from the park because of a physical incapacity or because the recreational vehicle is not motorized and cannot be moved by the occupant's vehicle, the default shall be cured within 72 hours, but the date to quit shall be no less than seven days after service of the notice.

(c) The management shall also serve a copy of the notice to the city police if the park is located in a city, or, if the park is located in an unincorporated area, to the county sheriff. **Leg.H.** 1992 ch. 310 §2.

Ref.: Miller & Starr, Cal. Real Estate 3rd 31:34.

§799.57. Required Statement in Notice.

The written 72-hour notice shall state that if the defaulting occupant does not remove the recreational vehicle from the premises of the park within 72 hours after receipt of the notice, the management has authority pursuant to Section 799.58 to have the recreational vehicle removed from the lot to the nearest secured storage facility. **Leg.H.** 1992 ch. 310 §2.

Ref.: Miller & Starr, Cal. Real Estate 3rd 31:34.

§799.58. Removal of Vehicle by Police or Sheriff.

Subsequent to serving a copy of the notice specified in this article to the city police or county sheriff, whichever is appropriate, and after the expiration of 72 hours following service of the notice on the defaulting occupant, the police or sheriff, shall remove or cause to be removed any person in the recreational vehicle. The management may then remove or cause the removal of a defaulting occupant's recreational vehicle parked on the premises of the park to the nearest secured storage facility. The notice shall be void seven days after the date of service of the notice. **Leg.H.** 1992 ch. 310 §2.

Ref.: Miller & Starr, Cal. Real Estate 3rd 31:34.

§799.59. Care Required in Removal of Vehicle.

When the management removes or causes the removal of a defaulting occupant's recreational vehicle, the management and the individual or entity that removes the recreational vehicle shall exercise reasonable and ordinary care in removing the recreational vehicle to the storage area. **Leg.H.** 1992 ch. 310 §2.

Ref.: Miller & Starr, Cal. Real Estate 3rd 31:34.

ARTICLE 4
Defaulting Tenants

Termination of tenancy for nonpayment of rent or other charges. §799.65.
Termination or refusal to renew for reasons other than nonpayment of rent or other charges. §799.66.
Eviction—Governing requirements. §799.67.

§799.65. Termination of Tenancy for Nonpayment of Rent or Other Charges.

The management may terminate the tenancy of a defaulting tenant for nonpayment of rent, utilities, or reasonable incidental service charges, provided the amount due shall have been unpaid for a period of five days from its due date, and provided the tenant has been given a three-day written notice subsequent to that five-day period to pay the total amount due or to vacate the park. For purposes of this section, the five-day period does not include the date the payment is due. The three-day notice shall be given to the tenant in the manner prescribed by Section 1162 of the Code of Civil Procedure. Any payment of the total charges due, prior to the expiration of the three-day period, shall cure any default of the tenant. In the event the tenant does not pay prior to the expiration of the three-day notice period, the tenant shall remain liable for all payments due up until the time the tenancy is vacated. **Leg.H.** 1992 ch. 310 §2.

Ref.: Miller & Starr, Cal. Real Estate 3rd 31:34.

§799.66. Termination or Refusal to Renew for Reasons Other Than Nonpayment of Rent or Other Charges.

The management may terminate or refuse to renew the right of occupancy of a tenant for other than nonpayment of rent or other charges upon the giving of a written notice to the tenant in the manner prescribed by Section 1162 of the Code of Civil Procedure to remove the recreational vehicle from the park. The notice need not state the cause for termination but shall provide not less than 30 days' notice of termination of the tenancy. **Leg.H.** 1992 ch. 310 §2, 1994 ch. 167.

§799.67. Eviction—Governing Requirements.

Evictions pursuant to this article shall be subject to the requirements set forth in Chapter 4 (commencing with Section 1159) of Title 3 of Part 3 of the Code of Civil Procedure, except as otherwise provided in this article. **Leg.H.** 1992 ch. 310 §2.

ARTICLE 5
Defaulting Residents

Termination or refusal to renew right of occupancy of defaulting resident—Reasons. §799.70.
Eviction—Governing requirements. §799.71.

§799.70. Termination or Refusal to Renew Right of Occupancy of Defaulting Resident—Reasons.

The management may terminate or refuse to renew the right of occupancy of a defaulting resident upon the giving of a written notice to the defaulting resident in the manner prescribed by Section 1162 of the Code of Civil Procedure to remove the recreational vehicle from the park. This notice shall provide not less than 60 days' notice of termination of the right of occupancy and shall specify one of the following reasons for the termination of the right of occupancy:

(a) Nonpayment of rent, utilities, or reasonable incidental service charges; provided, that the amount due has been unpaid for a period of five days from its due date, and provided that the resident shall be given a three-day written notice subsequent to that five-day period to pay the total amount due or to vacate the park. For purposes of this subdivision, the five-day period does not include the date the payment is due. The three-day notice shall be given to the resident in the manner prescribed by Section 1162 of the Code of Civil Procedure. The three-day notice may be given at the same time as the 60-day notice required for termination of the right of occupancy; provided, however, that any payment of the total charges due, prior to the expiration of the three-day period, shall cure any default of the resident. In the event the resident does not pay prior to the expiration of the three-day notice period, the resident shall remain liable for all payments due up until the time the tenancy is vacated.

(b) Failure of the resident to comply with a local ordinance or state law or regulation relating to the recreational vehicle park or recreational vehicles within a reasonable time after the resident or the management receives a notice of noncompliance from the appropriate governmental agency and the resident has been provided with a copy of that notice.

(c) Conduct by the resident or guest, upon the park premises, which constitutes a substantial annoyance to other occupants, tenants, or residents.

(d) Conviction of the resident of prostitution, or a felony controlled substance offense, if the act resulting in the conviction was committed anywhere on the premises of the park, including, but not limited to, within the resident's recreational vehicle.

However, the right of occupancy may not be terminated for the reason specified in this subdivision if the person convicted of the offense has permanently vacated, and does not subsequently reoccupy, the recreational vehicle.

(e) Failure of the resident or a guest to comply with a rule or regulation of the park which is part of the rental agreement or any amendment thereto.

No act or omission of the resident or guest shall constitute a failure to comply with a rule or regulation unless the resident has been notified in writing of the violation and has failed to correct the violation within seven days of the issuance of the written notification.

(f) Condemnation of the park.

(g) Change of use of the park or any portion thereof. **Leg.H.** 1992 ch. 310 §2.

§799.71. Eviction—Governing Requirements.

Evictions pursuant to this article shall be subject to the requirements set forth in Chapter 4 (commencing with Section 1159) of Title 3 of Part 3 of the Code of Civil Procedure, except as otherwise provided in this article. **Leg.H.** 1992 ch. 310 §2.

ARTICLE 6
Liens for Recreational Vehicles and Abandoned Possessions

§799.75. Lien on Recreation Vehicle for Charges Due; Disposition of Abandoned Possessions.

The management shall have a lien upon the recreational vehicle and the contents therein for the proper charges due from a defaulting occupant, tenant, or resident. Such a lien shall be identical to that authorized by Section 1861, and shall be enforced as provided by Sections 1861 to 1861.28, inclusive. Disposition of any possessions abandoned by an occupant, tenant, or resident at a park shall be performed pursuant to Chapter 5 (commencing with Section 1980) of Title 5 of Part 4 of Division 3. **Leg.H.** 1992 ch. 310 §2.

Ref.: Miller & Starr, Cal. Real Estate 3rd 31:34.

ARTICLE 7
Actions and Proceedings

Prevailing party entitled to attorneys' fees. §799.78.
Additional award for violation of chapter by management. §799.79.

§799.78. Prevailing Party Entitled to Attorneys' Fees.

In any action arising out of the provisions of this chapter, the prevailing party shall be entitled to reasonable attorney's fees and costs. A party shall be deemed a prevailing party for the purposes of this section if the judgment is rendered in his or her favor or where the litigation is dismissed in his or her favor prior to or during the trial, unless the parties otherwise agree in the settlement or compromise. **Leg.H.** 1992 ch. 310 §2.

Ref.: Miller & Starr, Cal. Real Estate 3rd 31:34.

§799.79. Additional Award for Violation of Chapter by Management.

In the event that an occupant, tenant, or resident or a former occupant, tenant, or resident is the prevailing party in a civil action against the management to enforce his or her rights under this chapter, the occupant, tenant, or resident, in addition to damages afforded by law, may, in the discretion of the court, be awarded an amount not to exceed five hundred dollars ($500) for each willful violation of any provision of this chapter by the management. **Leg.H.** 1992 ch. 310 §2.

Ref.: Miller & Starr, Cal. Real Estate 3rd 31:34.

CHAPTER 2.7
FLOATING HOME RESIDENCY LAW

Art. 1. General Provisions. §§800-800.9.
Art. 2. Rental Agreement. §§800.20-800.26.
Art. 3. Rules and Regulations. §§800.30-800.37.
Art. 4. Fees and Charges. §§800.40-800.50.
Art. 5. Homeowner Meetings. §§800.60, 800.61.
Art. 6. Termination of Tenancy. §§800.70-800.75.
Art. 7. Transfer of a Floating Home. §§800.80-800.91.
Art. 8. Transfer of a Floating Home Marina. §800.100.
Art. 9. Actions, Proceedings, and Penalties. §§800.200, 800.201.
Art. 10. Cooperatives and Condominiums. §§800.300-800.306.

ARTICLE 1
General Provisions

Title. §800.
Governing definitions. §800.1.
"Management" defined. §800.2.
"Floating home" defined. §800.3.
"Floating home marina" defined. §800.4.
"Rental agreement" defined. §800.5.
"Homeowner" defined. §800.6.
"Change of use" defined. §800.7.
"Resident" defined. §800.8.
"Tenancy" defined. §800.9.

§800. Title.

This chapter shall be known and may be cited as the Floating Home Residency Law. **Leg.H.** 1990 ch. 1505.

§800.1. Governing Definitions.

Unless the provisions or context otherwise requires, the following definitions shall govern the construction of this chapter. **Leg.H.** 1990 ch. 1505.

§800.2. "Management" Defined.

"Management" means the owner of a floating home marina or an agent or representative authorized to act on his or her behalf in connection with matters relating to a tenancy in the floating home marina. **Leg.H.** 1990 ch. 1505.

§800.3. "Floating Home" Defined.

"Floating home" has the same meaning as defined in subdivision (d) of Section 18075.55 of the Health and Safety Code. **Leg.H.** 1990 ch. 1505.

§800.4. "Floating Home Marina" Defined.

"Floating home marina" means an area where five or more floating home berths are rented, or held out for rent, to accommodate floating homes, but does not include a marina where 10 percent or fewer of the berths are leased or held out to lease to floating homes nor a marina or harbor (a) which is managed by a nonprofit organization, the property, assets, and profits of which may not inure to any individual or group of individuals, but only to another nonprofit organization; (b) the rules and regulations of which are set by majority vote of the berthholders thereof; and (c) which contains berths for fewer than 25 floating homes. **Leg.H.** 1990 ch. 1505, 1991 ch. 942.

§800.5. "Rental Agreement" Defined.

"Rental agreement" means an agreement between the management and the homeowner establishing the terms and conditions of a tenancy. A lease is a rental agreement. **Leg.H.** 1990 ch. 1505.

§800.6. "Homeowner" Defined.

"Homeowner" means a person who owns or resides in a floating home which is in a floating home marina pursuant to a rental agreement with management. **Leg.H.** 1990 ch. 1505.

§800.7. "Change of Use" Defined.

"Change of use" means a use of the floating home marina for a purpose other than the rental, or the holding out for rent, of five or more floating home berths, and does not mean the adoption, amendment, or repeal of a floating home marina rule or regulation. A change of use may affect an entire floating home marina or any portion thereof. "Change of use" includes, but is not limited to, a change of the floating home marina or any portion thereof to a condominium, stock cooperative, or any form of ownership wherein spaces within the floating home marina are to be sold. **Leg.H.** 1990 ch. 1505.

§800.8. "Resident" Defined.

"Resident" means a homeowner or other person who lawfully occupies a floating home. **Leg.H.** 1990 ch. 1505.

§800.9. "Tenancy" Defined.

"Tenancy" means the right of a homeowner to the use of a berth within a floating home marina on which to locate, maintain, and occupy a floating home, and accessory structures or vessels, including the use of the services and facilities of the floating home marina. **Leg.H.** 1990 ch. 1505.

ARTICLE 2
Rental Agreement

Management to provide copies of required notices upon request. §800.20.
Written rental agreement to be furnished to prospective tenant—Required provisions. §800.21.
Provisions permitted by law. §800.22.
Rental agreement—Agreed upon term of tenancy. §800.23.
Waiver of chapter prohibited. §800.24.
Membership in restricted club as condition for tenancy prohibited. §800.25.
Management to make available copy of Floating Home Residency Law. §800.26.

§800.20. Management to Provide Copies of Required Notices Upon Request.

Unless otherwise provided, the management shall make available to floating homeowners, upon request, copies of all notices required by this article and Article 3 (commencing with Section 800.30). Leg.H. 1990 ch. 1505.

§800.21. Written Rental Agreement to Be Furnished to Prospective Tenant—Required Provisions.

The rental agreement shall be in writing and shall contain, in addition to the provisions otherwise required by law to be included, all of the following:

(a) The term of the tenancy and the rent therefor.

(b) The rules and regulations of the floating home marina.

(c) A reference to this chapter and a statement that a copy of it is available from the marina upon request.

(d) A provision specifying that it is the responsibility of the management to provide and maintain physical improvements in the common facilities in good working order and condition.

(e) A description of the physical improvements to be provided the homeowner during his or her tenancy.

(f) A provision listing those services which will be provided at the time the rental agreement is executed and will continue to be offered for the term of tenancy and the fees, if any, to be charged for those services.

(g) All other provisions governing the tenancy. Leg.H. 1990 ch. 1505.

§800.22. Provisions Permitted by Law.

The rental agreement may include other provisions permitted by law, but need not include specific language contained in state or local laws not a part of this chapter. Leg.H. 1990 ch. 1505.

§800.23. Rental Agreement—Agreed Upon Term of Tenancy.

(a) A homeowner shall be offered a rental agreement for (1) a term of 12 months, (2) a lesser period as mutually agreed upon by both the homeowner and the management, (3) a longer period as mutually agreed upon by both the homeowner and the management, or (4) a longer period as necessary to secure financing from a conventional lending institution.

(b) Rental agreements for a prescribed term shall not contain any terms or conditions with respect to charges for rent, utilities, or incidental reasonable service charges that would be different during the first 12 months of the agreement from the corresponding terms or conditions that would be offered to the homeowner or homeowners on a month-to-month basis. Leg.H. 1990 ch. 1505.

§800.24. Waiver of Chapter Prohibited.

No rental agreement for a floating home berth shall contain a provision by which the homeowner waives his or her rights under any of the provisions of this chapter. Any waiver of these rights shall be deemed contrary to public policy and void. Leg.H. 1990 ch. 1505.

§800.25. Membership in Restricted Club as Condition for Tenancy Prohibited.

Membership in any private club or organization which is a condition for tenancy in a floating home marina shall not be denied on the basis of race, color, religion, sex, national origin, ancestry, or marital status. Leg.H. 1990 ch. 1505.

§800.26. Management to Make Available Copy of Floating Home Residency Law.

On or before March 12, 1991, the management shall notify all floating homeowners, in writing, that a copy of the Floating Home Residency Law is available to them, upon request, from the management. Leg.H. 1990 ch. 1505.

ARTICLE 3
Rules and Regulations

Hours of common area facility. §800.30.
Amendment to rules or regulations—Notice. §800.31.
No right of entry to floating home without prior written consent of resident; exception for emergency or abandonment. §800.32.
Written notice to homeowners of floating home marina matters. §800.33.
Disclosure of floating home marina operator. §800.34.
Management's right to enter floating home—When exercisable. §800.35.
Abandonment of floating home not owned by marina; notice of belief of abandonment. §800.36.
Abandonment of floating home owned by marina. §800.37.

§800.30. Hours of Common Area Facility.

Each common area facility shall be open or available to residents at all reasonable hours, and the hours of the common area facility shall be posted at the facility. Leg.H. 1990 ch. 1505.

§800.31. Amendment to Rules or Regulations—Notice.

A rule or regulation of the floating home marina may be amended at any time with the consent of a homeowner, or without his or her consent upon written notice to him or her of not less than six months. Written notice to a new homeowner, whose tenancy commences within the required period of notice, of a proposed amendment shall constitute compliance with this section where the written notice is given to him or her before the inception of his or her tenancy. Leg.H. 1990 ch. 1505.

§800.32. No Right of Entry to Floating Home Without Prior Written Consent of Resident; Exception for Emergency or Abandonment.

(a) Except as provided in subdivision (b), and notwithstanding any other provision of law to the contrary, the ownership or management of a floating home marina,